Changing Course

**Recent Titles in
Studies in Higher Education**

Changing Course

MAKING THE HARD DECISIONS TO ELIMINATE ACADEMIC PROGRAMS

Peter D. Eckel

Studies in Higher Education
Philip G. Altbach, Series Editor

Westport, Connecticut
London

Library of Congress Cataloging-in-Publication Data

Eckel, Peter D.
   Changing course : making the hard decisions to eliminate academic programs / Peter D. Eckel.
       p. cm.—(Studies in higher education)
     Includes bibliographical references and index.
     ISBN 0–313–32225–2 (alk. paper)
     1. Education, Higher—United States—Curricula.   2. Curriculum change—United States.   3. Curriculum planning—United States.   I. Title.   II. Studies in higher education (Westport, Conn.).
LB2361.5.E34   2003
378.1′99′0973—dc21   2002033386

British Library Cataloguing in Publication Data is available.

Library of Congress Catalog Card Number: 2002033386
ISBN: 0–313–32225–2

First published in 2003

Praeger Publishers, 88 Post Road West, Westport, CT 06881
An imprint of Greenwood Publishing Group, Inc.
www.praeger.com

Printed in the United States of America

The paper used in this book complies with the Permanent Paper Standard issued by the National Information Standards Organization (Z39.48–1984).

10   9   8   7   6   5   4   3   2   1

To Erin

There is nothing more difficult to carry out, nor more doubtful of success, nor more dangerous to handle, than to initiate a new order of things. For the reformer has enemies in those who profit by the old order, and only lukewarm defenders in all those who would profit by the new order.

—Machiavelli, *The Prince*

Contents

Preface

Most American colleges and universities are facing difficult choices about how they will allocate (and reallocate) their increasingly scarce resources (both human and fiscal) and, more broadly, what they will do as an institution and how they will do it. Institutions are called upon to make, as one past university president said, choices that "are becoming painful" (Kennedy, 1994, p. 85) and that have the potential to make significant change and affect academic priorities of the institution. The new recession, fundamentally different than past financial downturns because of changes in funding patterns and increases in demand (Breneman, 2002), is pressing institutions to do new things and offer new programs while struggling to maintain costs and seek new sources of income.

The actions they may be forced to take could easily include drastic steps such as closing academic programs, as institutions have limited options through which to gain financial flexibility. The intended (but not always realized) purpose of program discontinuance is to strategically reshape an institution. Deciding to terminate programs is a difficult decision, and then deciding which to close is trying to any institutional leader because the changes can be emotionally charged, faculty can lose their jobs and have their life's work interrupted, and the cuts have the potential to threaten institutions' core values and alter institutional identities. Terminating programs creates turmoil and stress among those involved in making the decisions and those affected by the outcomes. These decisions can stir the emotions of administrators, faculty, trustees, alumni, the media, and policy makers. Rarely will they result in business as usual. Instead, they call for special processes and new insights, creating challenges for administrative and faculty leaders alike.

The purpose of this book is to investigate the processes through which universities respond to new demands and make the difficult decisions to change their courses by altering academic program offerings. Many institutions have tremendous difficulty with and fail to accomplish program discontinuance. Academic program termination processes are not well documented in the research literature, nor are they well understood by those charged with making and carrying out the discontinuance decisions. Much of what we know about how organizations function and how they change is based upon assumptions of growth, which are not applicable when cutting back. This book will help to fill those voids.

This book is written around the experiences of four research universities—the University of Maryland at College Park, Oregon State University, the University of Rochester (NY), and Kent State University (OH)—that terminated academic programs. It describes the processes each used to close programs, explores the criteria used to make these decisions, highlights the roles of leadership and shared governance in the discontinuance process, and offers suggested actions for administrative and faculty leaders.

This book is intended for those individuals, such as president and provosts, state policy makers, faculty leaders, and higher education scholars, concerned with the strategic direction, leadership, decision making and governance, and financial well being of colleges and universities. Its case studies and findings would be of interest to those seeking to better understand how colleges operate and might be used in higher education graduate programs and professional development programs or for leadership retreats. Finally, its findings contribute to the higher education and organizational behavior literature and should be of interest to higher education, non-profit, and organizational scholars.

The first chapter of the book explores the context of program elimination in American higher education. It describes the environment that may soon push more colleges and universities to close particular academic programs and introduces the strategy of program termination and its challenges. It also describes the American Association of University Professors (AAUP)'s recommended processes for program termination. This chapter finally frames the study, identifying the importance of leadership, shared governance, and external forces in program closure, and describes its methodology.

The next four chapters describe each of the processes used to eliminate academic programs at the four universities. The chapters share a common structure: listing the programs closed, setting the context each institution found itself facing, and describing the processes used in depth, including any resistance to the closures. The chapters also explore why those involved thought the process worked and describes the results and effects of the closures as perceived by those on campus, including both the anticipated as well as unanticipated results. The chapters conclude with a more nuanced explo-

ration of key elements to offer a deeper understanding of the process of program termination.

The last three chapters explore the commonalities and differences of the
cases and generate a set of insights about program elimination useful to higher
education leaders and academics. Chapter six investigates the key common
elements across the four processes with a particular focus on the similarities
in the context leading to program closure as a sought-after strategy and with
an explicit discussion of leadership, governance, and external factors in program termination. Chapter seven shifts from the processes involved to the
criteria used to identify specific programs for closure. It answers, when the
rubber hits the road, what programs are actually selected to be terminated.
Although common wisdom focuses on quality, centrality, and cost, the experiences of these four universities suggest other criteria are used. The final
chapter brings together the insights from the cases and the two previous synthesis chapters to suggest council for academic leaders. The ideas offered are
both helpful for those seeking guidance on closing programs as well as for
those seeking to prevent the closure of their program. It additionally explores
the trade offs of savings, costs, and tenure and discusses the importance of
attending to process and not focusing solely on outcomes. The study concludes with suggested modifications to AAUP policy and outlines future research helpful to further understand academic program termination.

A word of caution to those reading this book for guidance on closing programs. Although I have spent tremendous time and energy to present the
stories of program closure as linear, clean, and orderly (and thus understand-
able) processes, in actuality they are anything but. Program termination is
difficult, it is complex, and the human emotions run high, complicating the
picture. I offer here my interpretations of the events at four universities and
adhere to rigorous research practices (see the methodology appendix). That
said, some individuals involved in various parts of each process might differ
in their telling of the story, wishing to stress more the anxiety created by the
closures on their colleagues, the malevolence of the leadership, or, on the
other hand, the brilliance of those responsible for leading the way. The interviews suggest a high degree of coherence, yet, as with any difficult and
potentially contentious matter at a university, people will have their own opinions and argue over details, nuance, and emphasis. Complex processes in any
differentiated organization, particularly ones with unclear goals, weak lines of
communication, and ambiguous leadership responsibilities are much messier
in reality than on paper, which limits me to a chronological and straightforward recitation.

Finally, although this book has my name on its cover, it is by no means a
solo act. I thank the following people for their assistance, contributions, energy, and involvement.

First, I would like to acknowledge and thank those people at the University
of Maryland at College Park, Oregon State University, the University of

Rochester, and Kent State University for spending their valuable time and sharing with me their stories related to program discontinuance. I appreciate their candor and honesty as well as the assistance of key people in helping to set up the interviews.

Second, I would like to thank my dissertation advisor, Robert Birnbaum, for his guidance, persistence, and willingness to help me think through the sticky issues of institutional change and the process of conducting this study and presenting its findings. I appreciate the opportunity to work with and learn from a top-notch scholar (which is an understatement to say the least) who is able to challenge conventional wisdom and make one (especially me) think much more complexly. This study is much better because of his questioning and doggedness.

I thank Madeleine Green of the American Council on Education (ACE). She provided me the opportunity to think with her over the years about institutional change. What started out as an unpaid internship at ACE has returned innumerable dividends as my work continues at the Council. Working with her and others at ACE, including Donna Shavlik, Debra (Carter) Wilds, Colleen Allen, Barbara Hill, and Estela Lopez, on issues of higher education transformation and change has been and continues to be a tremendous experience.

Thanks also go to the members of my doctoral committee: Susan Komives, Frank Schmidtlein and Andy Wolvin, all of the University of Maryland. Their interest in my development as a scholar and student of higher education leadership and organization is much appreciated.

Thanks also to the other scholars and friends who have made the experience of collecting research for this book as well as my doctoral education unforgettable—Dick Chait, Adrianna Kezar, Kim Kelley, Jaci King, Rhonda Malone, KerryAnn O'Meara, Walt Person, Damon Riley, and Cathy Trower. Thank you for over the years reading draft upon draft of ideas (some good, some half-baked, and others pretty terrible) and for helping me think through the muddles of this and all those preliminary projects.

Finally, a special thanks goes to Erin Rooney-Eckel. This work is dedicated to her, as she is most important in my life, even though at times when I was working on this study it probably didn't feel like it.

In closing, the saying *a day late and a dollar short* appropriately captures the motivations for a book on academic program termination. Such activity typically occurs when resources fall consistently short with little signs of yielding in the near future. The intention of this book is to help university decision makers—administrators, faculty, and board members—make wise decisions in the difficult process of terminating academic programs. It seeks to prevent leaders from making ineffective decisions or developing faulty processes that will result in more problems than create solutions. How can we prevent good ideas from appearing a day late? This phase is also apt for this book because of its timing. Based upon events that occurred in the early and mid-1990s, its path to print has been slow, but hopefully arrives not too late for those seeking information on program termination. Nevertheless, the stories or these four universities' journeys of program termination remain relevant to the challenges facing university leaders a decade later. The stories, for the most part, wear well as institutions again face difficult financial times. I hope that even with the timing of this book, readers find their dollars well spent, and the ideas they glean not a day late.

CHAPTER 1

Making Hard Decisions in a Changing Environment

For most American colleges and universities, the pendulum has swung from the heyday of growth, prosperity, and public favor to a time marked by increased competition, globalization, decreased public funding, and heightened calls for accountability—all of which means that higher education can no longer follow well-worn paths of operating seeking growth and expansion with little regard to outside demands. Instead, the future for many institutions will be marked by the challenge of having to make hard decisions regarding priorities, what to support, and what not to. These demands will call on institutional leaders to implement different types of changes that have the potential to significantly affect the relatively insulated academic areas of the institution. These choices reflect the "re" words so prevalent in organizational life throughout the last ten years—reducing, reallocating, refocusing, and restructuring. These trends do not apply only to the business functions of the institution; their results increasingly will be felt in academic programs and departments.

Institutions can no longer afford to be everything to everyone. As the former president of the University of Michigan wrote:

All universities have some capacity to become more efficient or productive. Such actions may allow some institutions to retain their existing portfolio of programs and activities, while achieving desired levels of quality. For most, the dominant strategy will still need to be the painful process of focusing resources to achieve quality by shedding missions and activities. (Duderstadt, 2000, p. 166)

The purpose of this book is to investigate those "shedding" processes through which institutions respond to new environmental demands and make the difficult decisions to change their directions by altering academic program offerings. Its particular focus is on terminating academic programs, a change that has the potential to be extremely difficult and potentially volatile, because it challenges the core of the academic enterprise and must be done in an environment of shared decision making. Many institutions have tremendous difficulty with and fail to accomplish program discontinuance (Dougherty, 1979; Kennedy, 1994; Cole, 1994; Melchiori, 1982a). This book is written around the experiences of four American research universities that terminated academic programs. It describes the processes each used to close programs, explores the criteria used to make these decisions, and highlights the roles of leadership, shared governance, and external influences in the discontinuance process. It concludes with suggested actions for both administrative and faculty leaders.

CHANGING LANDSCAPES; CHANGING PRIORITIES

Higher education is facing large challenges on two fronts—one from new fiscal realities placed upon colleges and universities in an increasingly intense competitive environment and the other from increased public demands. First, financial times are continually changing for American public higher education, with little sign of improvement (Breneman, 1993, 2002; Hovey, 1999; Callan, 2002). The "economic fundamentals" have changed (Massey, 1994, p. 4), creating a new playing field with a different set of rules (Breneman, 1997). State allocations do not keep pace with expenses, federal research dollars are unreliable, the stock market is unstable, foundation support is waning, and the tuition-paying public will no longer stand for tuition increases to make up budgetary shortfalls (Hovey, 1999; Ikenberry & Hartle, 2000; Morino Institute, 2001). According to *The Chronicle of Higher Education*, in 2002–2003, 37 states faced a budget deficit which had drastic impacts on higher education funding (Selingo, 2002).

Even when economies were growing, institutions did not see proportional increases in their public allocations or returns from endowments (Hovey, 1999). Instead, colleges and universities turned to entrepreneurial activities to create new funding opportunities (Clark, 1998; Marginson & Considine, 2000), frequently with little attention to the effect these activities have on teaching and scholarship (Slaughter & Leslie, 1997). At the same time, higher education costs are increasing as a result of increased administrative costs, more outlays for student services and scholarships, and higher instructional expenditures for library books and journals, research equipment, computers, and other educational necessities. Reducing expenses by itself is difficult; however, when coupled with challenges of remaining competitive in the intensifying higher education marketplace, the difficulties grow exponentially. The current dilemma facing much of higher education is to develop institutional strategies that couple the challenges of improving academic quality with reducing academic expenses.

The fiscal and environmental challenges shaping higher education have been brought together under the label "postindustrial environment" (Cameron & Tschirhart, 1992). Observers who subscribe to the postindustrial concept suggest that the changes are not temporary; instead, they exert intense, unceasing pressure on institutions to change in fundamental ways (Dill & Sporn, 1995b; Cameron & Tschirhart, 1992). For example:

> Environmental demands have shifted from asking the university to do what it does for less money to asking the university to change what it does. The contemporary question is not whether higher education can continue business-as-usual given increased environmental turmoil; rather, the question is what sort of universities will emerge from adaptation to these inexorable demands. (Gumport & Prusser, 1997, p. 455)

Additionally, as costs spiral upward, those paying public higher education's bills—taxpayers, state legislatures, and tuition-paying students and their families—are demanding more from their investments and increasing their scrutiny (Harvey & Immerwahr, 1995b; Ikenberry & Hartle, 2000). The National Governors' Association in 2001 launched its first concerted effort to influence higher education. As its press release stated, the intention was "to elevate national and state dialogue on postsecondary education and to equip governors and their advisors with the ability to diagnose problems, conceptualize issues, identify policy options and implement new public policy."

Higher education is under the scrutiny of public officials who, unfortunately, are often disappointed with the results they see. The authors of one highly visible, national report ten years ago criticized higher education and opened by writing: "A disturbing and dangerous mismatch exists between what American society needs of higher education and what it is receiving" (The Wingspread Group, 1993, p. 1). Many public officials believe this remains true today. Respondents in a poll of community and civic leaders "voiced criticisms about the quality of graduates from all levels of postsecondary studies, including undergraduate, graduate, and professional preparation; the utility and value of university research; mishandling of issues of race, gender, and political correctness; and organization and general mismanagement" (Harvey & Immerwahr, 1995b, p. 53).

Finally, during the last few years the market worldwide has increasingly become the instigator of change as well as constraint (Marginson & Considine, 2000; Newman & Courturier, 2001; Pew Higher Education Roundtable, 1997 Slaughter & Leslie, 1997). Cutbacks in traditional funding sources, rising expenses, and demands from students and their families and from future employers of graduates are pushing institutions to become increasingly responsive to the marketplace. Colleges and universities are undertaking changes to make themselves more desirable to those who are more and more often voting with their dollars and their feet. Without revisiting and expanding traditional curricula, institutions fear being perceived as outdated and out of touch with the times as potential students (and their tuition-generated revenue) are presented with multiple options, including viable ones outside of traditional higher education, such as through IT certification programs (Adelman, 2000) and corporate universities (Newman & Scurry, 2001). To be seen as responsive to new markets and thus capitalize on new opportunities, institutions continue to explore and develop new majors and degree programs, which further tax stable or declining resources. The demands of the market to do new things and set different priorities are difficult to meet without the extra cushion of uncommitted resources that was available in the past.

Not all voices are as pessimistic about the shape of the academy or the need for drastic actions due to a transformed environment. For example, some disagree that universities have lost much public favor (Prewitt, 1994) and other factors such as increases in public giving to higher education may act as surrogates of public confidence. Chait (1998) identifies a list of healthy indicators such as record enrollments and increases in proportions of 18–24 year-old students across multiple demographic groups, increased government investment in student aid, soaring alumni contributions, the tremendous influx of international students, and "even among notoriously cynical faculty, almost 76 percent of some 34,000 respondents from 384 colleges rated 'overall job satisfaction' either satisfactory or very satisfactory in 1995–96" (p. 40). One might conclude from these that higher education cannot be that bad off. Nevertheless, even the supporters do not let higher education rest on its past laurels and challenge institutions to keep pace with the demands of change (see, for example, Levine, 2000).

THE STRATEGY OF PROGRAM TERMINATION

Colleges and universities are not islands isolated from the mainland of society. Instead, changes externally lead institutions to exploit opportunities in the transformed environments and defend against newly created threats (Marginson & Considine, 2000; Hardy, 1995; Keller, 1983). Institutions continually make internal modifications, adjustments, and even go through transformations (Eckel & Kezar, 2002). The pressures institutions are facing have led many to raise difficult and fundamental decisions about how they will allocate and reallocate their increasingly scarce resources (both human and fiscal) and, more broadly, what they will do as an institution and how they will do it. To cope with the challenges of shrinking resources, heightened market demands, and increased public scrutiny, colleges and universities have two realistic options: (1) they try to expand their pool of fiscal resources by identifying new sources of income such as raising tuition or increasing enrollments and/or (2) they go through a retrenchment process, typically attempting to cut waste and overlap, reorganize administratively, and cut back

(Breneman, 1993; El-Khawas, 1994; Massey, 1994; Slaughter & Leslie, 1997). This book focuses exclusively on cutting back; others have written about entrepreneurialism in higher education (see for example Clark, 1998; Fairweather, 1988; Marginson & Considine, 2000; Slaughter & Leslie, 1997). Institutions cannot continue to focus exclusively on expanding revenues; they will eventually cross the point of diminished returns or impede their social missions. The limits of new sources of funding and their potential mission conflicts will inevitably force institutional leaders to leave the revenue side of their ledgers to focus on reducing their expenditures (Duderstadt, 2000). As for cutting back:

No single university can cover all subjects with all approaches. . . . Universities increasingly have to make hard choices not to cover all attractive subjects or to do some only in token fashion and not to offer a range of competing perspectives in each subject. (Clark, 1995, p. 161)

Leaving a field or discipline because of program discontinuance shifts the products and services an institution uses and produces, thus changing the way it interacts with the environment and, in turn, its institutional strategy. One of the ways in which institutions cut back is by eliminating academic programs. Cutting back through program elimination may become increasingly commonplace as higher education is no longer an industry growing but has matured, and future institutional change will need to be accomplished more frequently through substitution than through addition (Levine, 1997). Decisions such as program discontinuance, consciously or unconsciously, directly affects institutional strategy (Hardy, Langley, Mintzberg, & Rose, 1983; Mintzberg, 1987). These decisions can very well change the very nature and direction of an institution.

Across-the-Board or Targeted Cutbacks

When institutions cut back, they may use across-the-board approaches, targeted approaches, or some combination of the two (Hardy, 1987; Pfeffer & Salancik, 1978; Temple, 1986; Whetten, 1981). In most cases of cutting back institutions opt for across-the-board cuts over targeted ones (Dougherty, 1979; El-Khawas, 1994; Hardy, 1987, 1987/1988; Rubin, 1979). Across-the-board cuts, as well as savings through opportunities such as hiring freezes and unplanned attrition, are viewed as "trimming the fat" (Whetten, 1981). These approaches are not concerned with intentionally changing the ways in which the organization interacts with its environment (Pfeffer & Salancik, 1978). This approach causes less stress than strategic, targeted cuts because it does not require evaluative decisions among units difficult to compare or anyone to make unpopular decisions; those responsible for managing the change are more experienced with the processes to make across-the-board cuts, and, finally, the shared nature of university decision-making makes targeted cuts difficult (Cameron, 1983; Whetten, 1981).

Although across-the-board approaches are more frequently used, some authors and researchers view this approach as a poor choice. They believe these cuts borrow against the future of the organization; weaken the organization's capacity through its reliance on hiring freezes and random attrition that ignore institutional priorities, strengths and core competencies; and do not save sufficient money (Behn, 1988; Levine, 1997; Levine, Rubin & Wolohojian, 1981; Temple, 1986). The negative results of across-the-board cuts include things such as deferred maintenance, delays in equipment replacement (Levine, Rubin & Wolohojian, 1981), and the haphazard deterioration of academic programs (Mortimer & Tierney, 1979).

On the other hand, targeted approaches, where particular units or programs face deeper reductions, or even elimination, are much more difficult for university administrators to make because they require a complex series of choices that have the potential for significant institutional repercussions. They terminate an area or unit and alter the organization's relationships with its environment (e.g. the institution no longer offers nursing). These targeted cuts consist of an evaluation of one unit against others based upon criteria to maximize the organization-environment fit as it is the hope that some of the existing programs will be curtailed or eliminated so that others might be expanded (Pfeffer & Salancik, 1978; Slaughter, 1993). Choices have to be made among competing priorities. The past president of Stanford (Kennedy, 1994) illustrated what frequently occurs at institutions attempting targeted closures:

In a recent round of harsh budget cuts at Stanford, we involved a group of distinguished faculty from all fields. They worked hard and faithfully with us on all aspects of the processes, and in almost all respects, their judgments were thoughtful and fair. In one regard, however, they demonstrated the point that I am making. They frequently worried that we were cutting too much "across-the-board," and not singling out whole programs for elimination; yet, they could not develop a consensus on which programs should go. There was private advice to us, of course, on what victim "the administration" might select—and in nearly every case the recommended deletion was a discipline far from the domain of the recommenders. (p. 95)

The Case for Cutting Back

In organizations that are constrained in the range of ways they can increase or reallocate their fiscal resources, such as universities, hospitals or government agencies, program discontinuance is one of the few viable options in which they can cut back to create flexibility to pursue new strategic directions (Behn, 1988; Hardy, 1987; Pettigrew, Ferlie, & McKee, 1992). Program discontinuance can become a "necessary adaptive mechanism" (Dougherty, 1979,

p. 1) for a university to respond to changed environments. The intended (but not always realized) purpose of program discontinuance is to strategically reshape an institution by internally reallocating limited resources so that some fields and functions receive a larger proportion than other areas and units. From this perspective, eliminating select programs helps ensure a healthy organization (Vignola, 1974) by shifting its strategic direction. Program reduction may be an "adjustment that is an appropriate response to the environment, and enhances rather than diminishes long-term viability" (Weitzel & Jonsson, 1989, p. 93), not a sign of organizational decline.

Strategic closures eventually may become more commonplace in today's changing environment. The postindustrial argument suggests that in the new, restructured environment, institutions face a significant downturn in available resources and must undergo a series of reductions. Because the fiscal environment has been restructured it will not return to past behaviors, which looking back appear to be flush times. As institutions adapt to this new reality they will most likely undergo a series of financial adjustments. In most cases, in the first generation of cutbacks, institutions have choices of strategic or non-strategic retrenchment approaches. They may choose to trim the fat or they may engage in targeted cuts. Even those that select the targeted route may not close academic programs and instead terminate other types of activities. However, the continued financial decline will lead to subsequent additional cutback decisions that will eventually target particular academic programs and become strategic (Gumport & Prusser, 1997; Slaughter, 1993, 1995). The additional reductions become compounded and force strategic approaches because institutions have spent all of their organizational slack—a cushion of spare resources and capacities (March, 1994)—to pay for the non-strategic cuts (Levine, 1978). Gumport and Prusser (1997) identified this pattern:

The emerging premise is that postsecondary institutions must now consider the redesign of core academic structures and processes. Demands for academic restructuring [which by definition is strategic] grow out of a post retrenchment context that assumes significant administrative cuts have already been made. (p. 454)

Eventually the belt can be tightened no more. The continued changes in the environment may eventually force institutions to make strategic decisions and terminate academic programs and restructure core academic functions.

The Challenges of Selective Cutbacks

Program discontinuance is a difficult type of decision to make in higher education, so much so that some observers label it the "hard decision" (see for example Cole, 1994). Its difficulty lies in the fact that the changes can be emotionally charged (Dill & Sporn, 1995b), faculty can lose their jobs and have their life's work interrupted (American Association of University Professors, 1995), and the cuts have the potential to threaten institutions' core values and alter institutional identities (Dougherty, 1979; Melchiori, 1982b). Unlike other types of decisions in higher education, such as a new curriculum or a revised endowment investment plan, program closures send "shock waves through the university community" (Hardy, 1990b, p. 317). They create inner turmoil and stress among those involved in making the decisions and those affected by the outcomes (Gumport, 1993). They draw the attention (and passions) of administrators, faculty, and trustees (Dougherty, 1979; Melchiori, 1982b). They may also lead to significant re-directions in institutional strategies (Cameron, 1983; Hardy, 1990a), creating additional upheaval. Program discontinuance is undesirable to many faculty, staff, administrators, and students in the organization. Institution leaders do not want to make evaluative choices among programs, as no one wants to be charged with terminating colleagues' programs, and typically, no such mechanisms exist through which to proceed.

In addition to the difficulty of the decision, higher education leaders, as well as scholars, do not know much about this type of retrenchment. First, much of what we know about how organizations function and how they change is based upon assumptions of growth, which are not applicable when cutting back or discontinuing programs (Boulding, 1975; Jick & Murray, 1982; Levine, 1978; Melchiori, 1982b). Most of the experiences of today's administrators and faculty are predisposed toward growth because the environment in which they came of age and learned their administrative jobs was one of expansion (Behn, 1988; Breneman, 1993; Williams, Olswant, & Hargett, 1986; Yezer, 1992). In fact, this bias is so strong that one study found that stable institutions (i.e., not growing) were perceived by their members to share many of the same characteristics as institutions in decline (Cameron, Whetten, Kim, & Chaffee, 1987). Second, program discontinuance decisions are atypical and infrequent. Thus, the responsibilities for leading the efforts fall to the inexperienced who most likely do not know how to (or even want to) initiate action, build support for a decision such as this, or work with the affected programs in the aftermath of a closure. As Duderstadt (2000) noted, "The possibility of reallocating resources away from ongoing activities to fund new endeavors has only recently been seriously considered. Strategies from the business world aimed at cutting costs and increasing productivity are relatively new to our campuses" (p. 167). Managing retrenchment requires a different mindset than managing growth (Zammuto, 1986). The actions required call for intentional strategies to mitigate the negative consequences of cutting back (Cameron, Whetten, Kim, & Chaffee, 1987). Levine's (1979) statement captures the difficulty of understanding change through cutbacks as compared to understanding growth:

Taking a living thing like an organization apart is no easy matter; a cut may reverberate throughout the whole or in a way no one could predict by just analyzing its growth and pattern of development. (p. 180)

Conceptually program discontinuance is an ambiguous type of institutional change, one that is operationally unclear in its depth and scope (Mortimer & Tierney, 1979; Strohm, 1981). Although program discontinuance is treated in the literature as a specific activity, in selecting institutions for this study I found that in actuality institutions engaged in program discontinuance may be undertaking any number of distinct, albeit related, activities. Program discontinuance includes: (a) the termination of degree offerings while the academic unit is kept intact (e.g., discontinuing a Ph.D. in English literature while keeping the English department and continuing to offer undergraduate English degrees); (b) the dismantling of the academic unit and the termination of degree offerings (e.g., closing the journalism department and stopping all degrees offered in journalism); or (c) the merging of two units to create a new one so that the previous units no longer exist. To focus this study, I investigated the first two types of program discontinuance—those that terminated degree offerings while keeping intact the academic unit, and those that dismantled the academic unit and terminated degree offerings. Merging two units was not explored because it may be more akin to administrative restructuring than to the types of program discontinuance that is the focus of this study and it may not be as traumatic as the other types of change. In some instances it may simply be renaming two programs and creating a common office staff.

Influences on the Process

The processes through which institutions terminate academic programs were anticipated to be highly complex and nuanced. To get a toehold on the ways in which institutions close programs, this study began by identifying three potential key elements identified from the literature to focus the process: leadership, shared governance, and external influences. Each area became an anchor for the inquiry and the data analysis.

Leadership

Leaders and the notion of leadership receive a significant amount of attention in the organizational change literature. Some writers discuss the roles leaders need to fulfill to make change happen (Heifetz, 1995; Schein, 1992), others mention the need for leaders to adopt new mindsets and perceptions as essential to organizational change (Nystrom & Starbuck, 1984; O'Toole, 1995; Senge, 1994), and still others suggest actions for leaders to take (Kotter, 1995) to bring about change. Even with all the differing opinions, one thing is clear—intended change involves leadership in some way, at some point, and at some level. To narrow the concept of leadership for this study, I focus on the actions and perspectives of those individuals in formal campus roles who were expected to exhibit leadership (Birnbaum, 1992). Leadership in program discontinuance processes was anticipated to come from senior administrators (particularly the president and chief academic officer), senate chairs, deans, faculty union presidents, and, possibly, trustees.

The concept of leadership is a difficult one with which to work as the research and opinions as to what comprises effective academic leadership are inconclusive (Birnbaum, 1992). For example, one camp of authors speaks of the power of the presidency as a needed element for change to occur: "stronger leadership for tougher times" says the subtitle of an AGB report (Association of Governing Boards of Colleges and Universities, 1996). Those who subscribe to this perspective believe authoritative presidents (and boards of trustees which support them) are central for institutional change to occur (see for example, Fisher, 1994). On the other hand, others write that those in top leadership positions may in most cases do more to inhibit than advance change. For example, O'Toole (1995) argues that frequently organizational leaders are the primary resistance to change as they "subscribe to and defend current attitudes and dominant ideologies" (p. 245). They do not want to lose their places of organizational privilege. Other leadership scholars suggest that although not irrelevant, the role of top administrators is not as influential as commonly thought (Birnbaum, 1992; Cohen & March 1986). From this perspective, the leadership thus needed to make difficult changes may come from within the ranks of organization and not just from the top (Green, 1988, 1996; Senge, 1992).

The process used to discontinue academic programs might be much more simple and straightforward if university leaders simply exerted strong leadership and made decisions in a top-down manner. Nevertheless, the muscle-view of administration is not readily used in times calling for difficult decisions (although some central administrations do engage in it). While presidents may be the single most influential position on a campus (Cohen & March, 1986), many realize their limits (Birnbaum, 1992; Kennedy, 1994). "If there is an issue at hand that the faculty cares deeply about and you can't persuade them, you certainly can't bulldoze them," is the advice offered by former college president Walker (1979, p. 10).

Leaders are bound by their institutional histories and cultures, and they are dependent upon faculty support to get their jobs accomplished. Institutional history and culture shape what campus leaders can do and how they function (Kuh & Whitt, 1988; Schein, 1992). Because the culture of most colleges and universities is one of participation, discussion, and reflection, leaders are bound by those cultural parameters. Leaders in mature organizations like most colleges and universities are often selected because they share many of the assumptions and values that are consistent with the organization's culture (Schein, 1992).

Additionally, institutions must adhere to organizational processes that are consistent with their institution's culture to effect desired change (Kezar & Eckel, 2002). Processes that do not adhere to cultural norms will have a short shelf-life and will not last (Schein, 1992). Change agents who have experience and success with implementing change and have reached administrative positions in which they must make these difficult decisions have learned ways to operate and gained an understanding that they must adhere to cultural norms and processes. Most people are all too familiar with the painful lessons learned from attempts to change institutions that backfired because leaders did not follow cultural and historical patterns. These mistakes had lasting negative effects because they quickly become a part of institutional memory.

The second major reason why leaders do not use their administrative prerogative is because they recognize the importance of faculty support to get things done. A vote of no-confidence by the faculty can often have the power to end presidential careers. Most presidents know that ultimately they as administrators are expendable and that the faculty no doubt can find a successor (Birnbaum, 1992; Walker, 1979). Research on presidential leadership (Birnbaum, 1992) suggests that presidential support by faculty is dependent upon the belief by faculty that they have influence in institutional direction setting and that presidents will adhere to expectations of participation determined through current governance structures. These two elements create limits for central administrators because administrators may lose the much needed faculty support if they violate norms and expectations. If success is dependent upon a willingness to be influenced and expectations of faculty participation, invoking top-down decision-making in a highly visible and potentially volatile situation, such as program discontinuance, is extremely risky. This risk usually constrains the options of leaders to participative avenues.

Thus, leadership regarding program closure may be as much of an art as a science. That said, the research questions that guided this study related to leadership were: What are the roles of leaders? Who fills the leadership positions when programs are closed? What do they do? What don't they do?

Shared Governance

The second anchor of this study is shared governance, the processes through which faculty, administrators, and trustees interact to make institutional decisions. It is through the shared governance process that most key university stakeholders conjointly answer questions such as: "How do research universities define their priorities? Who decides what to build, what to favor, what to contract, and what to eliminate? What gives the process legitimacy?" (Cole, 1994, p. 5).

Shared governance has been both criticized and applauded for its role in institutional decision making. Some writers suggest that shared governance cannot make tough decisions because of its inclusive nature (Association of Governing Boards of Universities and Colleges, 1996; Cole, 1994; Kennedy, 1994). Supporters, on the other hand, say shared governance is central to successful institutional change because it involves faculty in decision making and allows decisions to be thoroughly discussed and debated (Blau, 1994; Rosovsky, 1990; Walker, 1979). No matter one's view on its effectiveness, shared governance will play a key role (possibly facilitating, possibly inhibiting) in important and potentially controversial institutional decision making, such as program termination.

Shared governance is about participation, about the ways in which people are involved in institutional decision making and how they are organized to interact. Because shared governance is tied tightly to participation the experiences and perspectives of those involved cannot be divorced from the decision making process, which influence how participants view a decision, how they participate, and the outcomes for which they push. Considering terminating programs can have negative effects on those who may be participating in the decision making process. The experiences of those participating are compounded by the difficult financial circumstances typically accompanying program closure decisions. For example, a group of studies on retrenchment in higher education show that in a down-turned environment: (1) People develop a short-term orientation as they become focused on the immediate situation to the exclusion of any long term perspectives that may lead to better solutions (Cameron, Whetten, Kim & Chaffee, 1987; Gioia & Thomas, 1996). (2) They lose their desire to innovate and experiment (Cameron, Whetten & Kim, 1987; Cameron, Whetten, Kim & Chaffee, 1987). (3) They become wary of making mistakes because they see them as having a high cost (Cameron, Whetten, Kim & Chaffee, 1987; Zammuto, 1986). (4) Fighting among subunits increases (Cameron, Whetten, & Kim, 1987; Zammuto, 1986) and a loss of consensus among members ensues (Gumport, 1993). (5) The cutbacks additionally hurt morale (Behn, 1988; Cameron, Whetten, & Kim, 1987). Low morale occurs because the participants are under extreme pressure, frequently are doing their own job as well as the jobs of others who left, and they are working with limited (or no) rewards or incentives (Hardy, 1988; Williams, Olswant, & Hargett, 1986).

Under these circumstances, the institution does not have the needed trust, excitement, experimentation, collaboration, or any other elements most likely important to successful academic change efforts that depend upon participation and joint decision making. Administrators cannot smoothly implement cutback decisions without involving faculty (Dougherty, 1979; Rubin, 1979). Faculty who are fearful, untrusting, short-term oriented, and fighting among themselves are unlikely to become involved in a constructive fashion, or might make decisions motivated by self-preservation rather than institutional vitality. The setting in which administrators and faculty must work is oriented to the short-term, is conservative, fearful, risk-adverse, and composed of infighting. From the literature, one can speculate that a challenge of successful program termination might be associated with overcoming these harmful contextual elements and their impact on those participating in the decision process.

Given the institutional circumstances surrounding program termination, what is the role of shared governance? To what extent can shared governance be an effective arena to make potentially hard and adverse decisions? This study attempted to uncover patterns of shared governance and participation, which helped answer the following research questions: What patterns of campus governance were present in the processes through which institutions discontinued academic programs? Who was involved, who decided who decides, and what did they decide? To what extent was the decision making shared? What types of decisions were made separately by faculty, administrators, trustees, and what decisions were made collectively?

External Forces

Universities as discussed are not isolated entities, but rather they are affected by forces, people, and politics external to themselves. They receive revenue from the states, conduct research for the federal government and corporations, and provide services to local communities. They provide knowledge, new ideas, and educated graduates to the community. The boundaries between a university and its environment are becoming ever more permeable (Gumport & Sporn, 1999; Slaughter & Leslie, 1997) allowing institutions to be influenced by outside forces (Aldrich, 1979; Pfeffer & Salancik, 1978; Scott, 1987). Rothblatt (1995) cited "disappearing boundaries" (p. 30) between universities and their environments as an increasing phenomenon that is creating a host of new problems for institutions.

Changes in the external environment are one of the important factors related to initiating program termination on campuses (Falk & Miller, 1993; Gumport, 1993; Volkwein, 1984) as institutions respond to reduced external funds, competition and the market, and new societal demands. However, external influences not only press institutions to change, but they also influence the directions in which they change and the criteria by which they make their decisions (Schmidt, 1997; Slaughter, 1993).

This study additionally is concerned with the potential influence of external actors and forces that may shape the outcomes of the discontinuance process. Leadership and shared governance may be internal factors that shape program termination, but to what extent is the process shaped by outside factors? The impact of the environment on internal organizational behavior can be explained through a resource dependency model that views organizations as "inexplicably bound up in the conditions of their environments" (Pfeffer & Salancik, 1978, p. 1). An organization's environment creates a dynamic process of action and reaction through which organizations attempt to achieve a state of stability through a series of exchanges with their environments. This dynamic process leads to variations in an organization's control, direction, and position dictated by shifts in the environment. Changed environments demand responses if institutions are to survive (Cameron, 1983; Chaffee, 1984; Gioia & Thomas, 1996). Research therefore shows that when institutions become aware of salient changes in the environment that influence the products or services institutions receive or produce, they respond accordingly (see for example, Manns & March, 1978; Slaughter & Leslie, 1997).

Paying attention to factors outside of the organization and acknowledging a wider sphere of influence may lead to a more thorough understanding of how programs are discontinued. Simply focusing on internal dynamics may tell only part of the story. To what extent, if any, are different types of external influences present in program termination decisions? If they are present, who is involved, in what ways, and with what effect?

UNDERSTANDING PROGRAM TERMINATION

Changing the ways any organization conducts its business and modifying the business it conducts are not simple, easily accomplished tasks; it is something for which few models exist in any sector (Drucker, 1994). This is especially true when the organization is complicated by an expectation of shared decision making and the changes are as potentially controversial as program elimination. Academic program termination processes are not well documented in the research literature, nor are they well understood by those charged with making and carrying out the discontinuance decisions.

The literature does not elaborate on the concept of program discontinuance nor does it explain how program discontinuance decisions were made or what steps were followed, being of little use to those academic leaders seeking advice. Most of the literature that discussed program discontinuance subsumes the concept within the larger topic of retrenchment. Program discontinuance is frequently identified as one of many ways that institutions engage in retrenchment or cutback management. Thus, little research exists that specifically investigates the process of academic program discontinuance apart from the broader concept of retrenchment. Even within the retrenchment literature, little is known about the *processes* of how institutions successfully cut back. The relevant writings tend to fall into one of two categories. The first group is comprised of opinions and normative essays—"how things should be done" (see for example Dickeson, 1999 and Massey, 1994), and the second group includes research that documents the range of institutional retrenchment responses—what was done—such as managing enrollments, reducing administrative overhead, or eliminating departments (see for example El-Khawas, 1994). Thus, little empirical research documents how retrenchment was undertaken, let alone the subset of the ways in which programs were discontinued and the consequences.

Second, most academic leaders understand the challenges of program termination, but few have the know-how or the experience to discontinue academic programs (Cole, 1994; Kennedy, 1994). A void in the management literature added to the inexperience of managers cutting back makes for additional challenges during tough financial times (Behn, 1988; Boulding, 1975; Levine, 1978). The question political scientist Levine asked over 20 years ago remains unanswered by most university administrators: "Put squarely, without growth, how do we manage public organizations?" (Levine, 1978, p. 317).

Advice from the AAUP

The American Association of University Professors (AAUP) has outlined how programs should be discontinued, but with no indication that their views are guided by research. In their *Policy Documents and Reports* (2001), the AAUP suggests that institutions adhere to a set of guidelines for program discontinuation. These guidelines are important because the AAUP, the voice of the academic profession, is active on many campuses and in the courts representing faculty interests. The association works for faculty both formally through collective bargaining arrangements and informally through professional association, outreach, and representation. The suggested AAUP guidelines follow:

1. There should be early, careful, and meaningful faculty involvement in decisions relating to the reduction of instructional and research programs. . . .
2. Given a decision to reduce the overall academic program, it should then become the primary responsibility of the faculty to determine where within the program reductions should be made. Before any such determinations become final, those whose life's work stands to be adversely affected should have the right to be heard.
3. Among the various considerations, difficult and often competing, that have to be taken into account in deciding upon particular reductions, the retention of a viable academic program should necessarily come first. Particular reductions should follow considerable advice from the concerned departments, or other units of academic concentration, on the short-term and long-term viability of reduced programs.
4. As particular reductions are considered, rights under academic tenure should be protected. The services of a tenured professor should not be terminated in favor of someone without tenure who may at a particular moment seem to be more productive. Tenured faculty members should be given every opportunity . . . to readapt with a department or elsewhere with the institution; institutional resources should be made available for assistance in readaptation. (p. 193)

Depending upon the use and adoption of AAUP policies and their incorporation into faculty handbooks, on many campuses AAUP policies become part of employment contracts to which administrators must legally adhere. In such cases, institutions may need to place the faculty in the primary role of the decision-making process. The process should be highly consultative, especially with those in the targeted programs. Both short- and long-term viability should be considered, and any tenured faculty in closed departments should be moved to another department. At institutions in which these policies are not part of the contract, the guidelines still represent a professional standard, which may have a significant presence in how faculty expect the discontinuance process to proceed. These policies greatly reduce the ability of a few administrators to make decisions shifting academic priorities and resources.

SIGNIFICANCE OF THE STUDY

This study sought to understand the concept of program discontinuance and the processes through which universities closed programs. The primary intent was to gain a deeper understanding of the paths that were followed and how tough decisions were made and implemented with a specific focus on how elements of shared governance, leadership, and external forces influenced the process. The findings might be helpful to academic leaders who are attempting to discontinue programs. Discontinuing programs on most campuses is a last ditch effort (Breneman, 1993; Massey, 1994; Yezer, 1992) and one which is painful and emotional for those involved (Dill & Sporn, 1995b; Gumport, 1993; Hardy, 1993). The results should help campus change agents better understand the termination process and possibly help them make tough decisions and undertake program discontinuance more effectively and efficiently (in terms of human and fiscal resources).

The second intent was to investigate differences and similarities in the discontinuance processes of institutions engaged in different types of program discontinuance activities. This study identified two potentially distinct activities—unit closure and program closure. By studying similarities and differences between types of program discontinuance processes, a more refined understanding of the phenomenon under study was intended.

The third intent was to explore the impact of the discontinuance process on the institution from the perspectives of the participants. Although the four institutions in this study discontinued academic programs, the impact of those outcomes might have differed. For example, at one campus the process might lead to extreme distrust of the administration, while a different institution might experience renewed energy and commitment from a similar undertaking. It was instructive to learn whether the impact of the outcomes, as seen by those involved, met the intended goals of the discontinuation and what the effects, both expected and unexpected, of the process were on the campus. These findings may be informative to others considering program discontinuance as a solution to their institutional dilemmas, as it may or may not actually be a cure for their ills.

A final intent of this research was to illuminate some of the issues related to the broader topic of institutional change in academe. The higher education literature is rife with statements about the nature of change in higher education and the presence (or absence) of shared governance and leadership in this process. Many of the statements are contradictory and others, although well thought out, are not substantiated by much research. Through this study, I hoped to say something about institutional change using the research findings to add a note of clarity. Knowing more about this specific type of change may help academic leaders better judge the relevance of the statements (both criticisms and accolades) made about institutional change, shared governance, and academic leadership.

Specifically this study investigated the following questions to understand better how universities discontinue academic programs:

1. How did institutions go about the process of cutting academic programs?
   (a) What elements of leadership influenced the program discontinuance process?
   (b) What elements of shared governance influenced the program discontinuance process?
   (c) What external forces influenced the program discontinuance process?
2. What were the effects of the program discontinuance process on the institution?
3. Are there common themes that were present among the institutional processes used and the elements involved in discontinuing academic programs? What lessons can be drawn from the four cases about the program discontinuance process?

Framing the Process

Universities are complex organizations. To understand the complicated organizational processes through which institutions discontinued academic programs this study incorporated the multilens framework of Bolman and Deal (1991) as a heuristic mechanism through which to organize the data and paint a broader picture. Their framework summarized different schools of organizational thought into four perspectives or, as the authors labeled them, "frames"—the structural frame, the human resources frame, the political frame, and the symbolic frame. Each frame provides a conceptual road map for understanding organizations, offering alternative explanations to observed phenomena.

The *structural* frame views organizations as formations comprised of formal lines of authority and communication with distinct roles for different organizational actors, hierarchies, and rules (Bolman & Deal, 1991). From this perspective, how the institution is organized and structured and the policies and procedures people follow influence the processes through which its goals are set, decisions are made, and work is completed (Mintzberg, 1993). Through this frame, the researcher looked for clues related to formal organizational structures and lines of authority, references to institutional roles and rules, and decisions which followed articulated organizational goals.

The *human resources* frame views organizations from a humanistic perspective. It focuses on the organizational actors who have "needs, feelings, and prejudices" (Bolman & Deal, 1991, p. 14). It recognizes that the people within the organization shape the organization, thus making their feelings and emotions central to what occurs and how the work is accomplished (Bensimon, 1992). From the human resources frame, I looked for elements of "humanism." For example, concerns about people's feelings and emotions and how they might be personally affected by the termination of programs, discussions and language concerning people's sense of personal connection to the organization or their units, references to personal loss and recovery, and decisions which take into account a sense of caring.

The *political* frame is based upon the premise that different interest groups are constantly in conflict as they compete for power and scarce organizational resources. To obtain these resources interest groups are continually forming coalitions, which dissolve and reform into new configurations as the issues at hand shift. Within this frame, bargaining, negotiation, and compromise are daily realities, coalitions form and dissolve as organizational issues change, and problems arise because power is concentrated in the wrong coalitions or is too dispersed to accomplish any tasks (Bolman & Deal, 1991). The political frame helped to capture and organize elements such as coalition alignment, re-alignment, affiliations; power brokering; and influencing negotiation and conflict.

The *symbolic* frame views organizations as systems of shared meanings and beliefs (Bensimon, 1992). The important elements are the interpretations which organizational members assign to events and activities, thus making rituals, stories and myths, and symbols important (Bolman & Deal, 1991). From the symbolic perspective, it is argued that these have a stronger influence over what occurs within the organization than rules, policies, or managerial direction (Bolman & Deal, 1991). This final frame helped the researcher to attend to symbolic actions, discussions of beliefs, values and meanings, and the use of rituals, ceremonies, and theater.

By using multiple perspectives together, one gains "a more comprehensive understanding of organizational life because any one theoretical perspective invariable offers only a partial account of a complex phenomenon" (Van de Ven & Poole, 1995, p. 511). It is a useful mechanism to highlight different aspects of processes or events that might go unnoticed when using only one theoretical lens (Birnbaum, 1988; Neumann, Bensimon, & Birnbaum, 1989). Because the process of program discontinuance has many actors, elements, and nuances, a multiple frame perspective might be helpful in illuminating aspects that might otherwise go unnoticed by a less complex approach.

Methods

The following section briefly discusses the study's methodology. A more detailed description appears in the Appendix. This study used a multisite case study method to investigate program closure because its purpose was to explain and understand complex processes that were hard to quantify and control (Merriam, 1988; Yin, 1994). The intent was to capture and understand what happened, how, and why through the perspectives of those involved (Parkhe, 1993; Van Maanen, 1979) and to make cross-site comparisons with the hope of obtaining results to begin to build explanations (Herriott & Firestone, 1983; Yin, 1994).

To be eligible for participation in this study, institutions had to have discontinued at least one academic program that had not been reinstated and must be a Research University following the 1994 Carnegie Classification system (Carnegie Foundation for the Advancement of Teaching, 1994). This study incorporated nuts and bolts criteria for program discontinuance rather than subjective outcome-based criteria (e.g., the discontinuance process led to positive institutional results or it lead to institutional dysfunction). This approach considered the effect of the process on each institution as an element of the investigation, which is explored through the second research question. Through media reports and discussions with higher education association executives, I generated a list (which was surprisingly small) of research universities that had discontinued academic programs. From this list I identified four universities for the study. They were the University of Maryland at College Park, Oregon State University, the University of Rochester (NY), and Kent State University (OH).

With the help of campus administrators at each university, three groups of potential informants were identified: (1) individuals involved in the discontinuance process, such as key central administrators or members of involved governance committees; (2) those involved from outside the institution, such as board members or alumni; and (3) individuals from the units which were terminated who might still be on-campus. I then conducted focused interviews with between 12 and 15 people on each of the four campuses and I reviewed documents obtained from the informants, including material such as meeting minutes, speeches, white papers, memos, and institutional reports. Data was analyzed following qualitative techniques first within each case and then across cases looking for common themes and trends using a three-step process (Miles & Huberman, 1994).

To ensure rigor I adhered to the case study principles outlined by Yin (1994): (1) the use of multiple sources of evidence; (2) the construction of a database of information or case report specifically for the case study; and (3) the development of a logical chain of evidence describing the rationale and the processes used that connects the findings to the collected data. Additional safeguards to ensure trustworthiness and credibility of the findings (Lincoln & Guba. 1985) were taken. For example, I engaged in peer debriefing, a process of conversing at periodic intervals with non-involved professionals to keep the inquirer honest in drafting propositions, explore methodological next steps, and help make sense of the data by talking through it (Lincoln & Guba, 1985). Also a key informant from each of the institutions read each case and offered suggestions. In two of the cases the individual responsible for leading the process read and commented on the case. In the third instance the president at the time read the case, and in the final case, two participants from different stages of the process commented on the draft case.

CONCLUSION

Program discontinuance is a difficult decision to make because it usually takes place in austere times or when the environment dramatically shifts; its outcomes are likely to have an adverse impact on some; people might not believe it is needed or that the institution should engage in it; and leaders are inexperienced at making that type of decision (Cameron, 1983; Dougherty, 1979; Levine, 1978; Levine, Rubin, & Wolohojian, 1981). Combine these elements with the fact that the academy is highly participative and grounded in a history of collegiality, shared governance, and professional prerogative, and one can begin to understand the challenges of program closure.

The next four chapters present the stories of program termination at each of the four institutions. Each chapter presents a case following a similar format, beginning with listing the programs closed. The cases then offer the context, noting the key decision makers and governance structures, and describing the situations that led to program closures. The process is then spelled out including a discussion of any resistance to the closures. The next section presents why those involved thought the process worked. Each chapter then explores the results and effects of the closures as perceived by those on campus. They conclude with an exploration of key elements through Bolman and Deal's (1991) four frames to gain a deeper understanding of what occurred and how each institution went about terminating programs.

CHAPTER 2

The University of Maryland at College Park: Making "Hard Choices" While "Preserving Enhancement"

On April 24, 1992, the College Park Senate of the University of Maryland at College Park (UMCP), during a three-hour special meeting, approved a set of recommendations from the provost to eliminate seven academic departments and one college. The units closed and degrees terminated were the following:

- the Department of Agriculture and Extension Education, thus terminating bachelor's, master's and doctoral degrees in Agricultural and Extension Education;
- the Department of Housing and Design, thus terminating a bachelor's degree in Housing, Advertising Design and Internal Design;
- the Department of Textiles and Consumer Economics, thus terminating bachelor's degrees in Textiles, Apparel Design, Textile Marketing/Fashion Merchandising and Consumer Economics, and master's and doctoral degrees in Textiles and Consumer Economics;
- The Department of Industrial, Technological and Occupational Education, thus terminating M.A., M.Ed., Ed.D. and Ph.D. degrees in Industrial, Technological and Occupational Education and six bachelors' degrees in Industrial Technology;
- the Department of Radio, Television and Film, thus terminating bachelor's, master's and doctoral degrees in Radio, Television and Film;
- The Department of Recreation, thus terminating bachelor's, master's and doctoral degrees in Recreation;
- The Department of Urban Studies and Planning, thus terminating bachelor's and master's degrees in Urban Studies (but keeping a Master of Community Planning degree and moving it into the School of Architecture); and
- The College of Human Ecology (but keeping all its degree programs except those listed above and distributing them among the various remaining colleges).

Although legally still requiring acceptance by the president and approval by the Board of Regents, the College Park Senate vote, for all intents and purposes, concluded the discontinuance process begun at the start of the 1990–1991 academic year.

THE PLAYERS OF CAMPUS GOVERNANCE AND DECISION MAKING

The governance and academic decision-making apparatus at UMCP included the following players:

Academic Planning Advisory Committee (APAC). A joint faculty-administration committee, advisory to the provost, was created to investigate and review the financial implications of changes in academic programs. Twelve faculty members (including the chair-elect of the senate), four administrators, and an undergraduate student, selected and appointed by the provost and confirmed by the senate comprise the committee. The provost, who is a non-voting member, chairs APAC.

The College Park Senate is the primary campus governance body, which is a campus-wide senate comprised predominately of elected faculty, but includes student and staff representatives. Each year its members elect the leadership of the senate. The body's leader, the chair, comes from the senate and serves two consecutive one-year terms, the first year as chair-elect and the second as chair. One of the duties of the chair-elect is to appoint senate committee members and chairs. The senate takes action on the senate floor based upon committee recommendations on which the senate as a whole votes. *Programs, Curricular and Courses Committee (PCC)* is a standing committee of the senate that deals with curricular changes, including program discontinuance.

The president and the provost were long-time campus citizens. The president spent his career at the institution beginning as an assistant professor and moving through the administrative ranks to become a well-liked president. The provost also had many years of service to the university, first as a long-time faculty member and then as provost. The president and provost strongly believed in the value of shared decision making and viewed the senate as an essential player in institutional governance. They both believed that the faculty were able and important contributors to institutional decision making.

FROM ENHANCEMENT TO RETRENCHMENT

In 1988, the State of Maryland reorganized its public higher education system and designated UMCP as the Flagship Campus, at which time the institution adopted the *1989 Enhancement Plan*, a well-received strategic plan that set forth "goals of excellence and earmarked certain disciplinary emphasis for special attention." In 1990, the state, facing a recession, asked all state agencies, including public higher education, to undergo extreme budget recisions. In the 1990–1991 academic year, UMCP faced a total reduction of $24.5 million or 10% of its state budget. Of that $24.5 million, Academic Affairs was responsible for identifying $10 million. Said the provost, "I recall saying to someone on my staff 'this is the end of life as we know it.'"

This reduction in state funding was the second set of cutbacks the university had faced in a narrow time frame. The year previously, academic year 1989–1990, the campus faced a cut of $20.5 million in its state appropriations. To cope with the first round of state cuts, the administration engaged in a series of typical cost-saving measures, such as hiring and salary freezes, and limiting travel, but they did not discontinue any programs. However, in a two-year period, the campus had lost a drastic $45 million in public funds, an 18% reduction in state support, which called for new (and potentially drastic) measures.

In the fall of 1990 faculty and administrative leaders felt the push and pull of two forces on campus. First, they had begun efforts—and possibly more importantly, many of the faculty and deans and most of the senior administration had the widespread desire—to become a premier public research university via the *Enhancement Plan*. Second, the institution faced severe financial retrenchment. The opening of the initial report submitted by the provost to the president that outlined the retrenchment procedures and offered preliminary recommendations illustrates this point:

We are all aware of the financial difficulties that the State of Maryland is experiencing. Yet, while fiscal circumstances have precipitated a comprehensive strategic analysis of our academic programs, we are committed to the belief that this analysis must be driven by fundamental considerations of enhancement, centrality, and excellence. Reduced budgets have altered the timetable of the Enhancement Plan, but they have neither stopped the process of enhancement nor altered our mission. Nor can they be permitted to do so. (*Preserving Enhancement*, March 1, 1991)

This tension was to become the driving force for the termination process. The idea of enhancement tapped into the hopes of the campus, and its faculty and staff, and provided a palatable call to action. The campus viewed the difficult decisions that were to be done, closing academic programs, as for the good of the institution and linked to the goals of enhancement. Many faculty believed that making "judicious cuts" would lead to a better university. Program closures became a path to enhancement, counteracting the unfavorable and undesirable with the desirable.

THE PROCESS: JOINTLY IDENTIFYING PROGRAMS FOR TERMINATION

After numerous discussions, and heated and sometimes personal debates, the provost persuaded the president and other vice presidents to let the Di-

vision of Academic Affairs reduce the number of academic units and departments and, at the same time, continue across-the-board reductions such as
terminating pending contracts, halting equipment purchases, and reducing
the number of part-time faculty. From the provost's perspective, the financial
recession was a bona fide crisis, but one that could be used as a lever to move
the institution. One faculty member on APAC said:

It became pretty clear pretty quickly that if we were to give back all of that money to
the state in an across-the-board fashion, it would really wreak havoc on the campus. . . .
We could strengthen the profile of the university if we made judicious cuts and enhance
the departments that made the university a good university—maybe even make it a
better university—and remove those parts that were a drain on resources [and] that
didn't add to the mission and goals of the University of Maryland.

The provost saw his challenge as designing a process that would be viewed
by the campus as legitimate, but one that would allow programs to be identified for closure. He was convinced by the president and other vice presidents
to use current decision-making structures, which in this case was the joint
faculty-administrative group APAC, rather than develop an ad hoc body that
he might lead, which he at one time seriously considered. The provost was
cautious developing the process the institution would follow; he sought to
move intentionally, as he realized that closing programs is an extremely threatening proposition. He said, those individuals leading the efforts knew "there
would be hell to pay," if the campus did not endorse the proposed outcomes
as well as the process.

The provost and the assistant provost asked APAC to design a process to
identify academic programs for termination that would be extensively inclusive and open. It could not be "top down," said the provost, nor could it be
completely open-ended. The process had to be balanced so that it would lead
to program closures, but the provost and APAC would not predetermine
which units or how many would be discontinued. They believed that the
process of identifying programs was central to the ultimate success of the
initiative.

Working to Preserve Enhancement

The objective, as framed by campus leaders, was to work toward enhance-
ment in fiscally constraining times. To do this, the provost asked the Executive
Committee of the Senate to develop a set of principles for closing units. The
Executive Committee acted without the full senate because of the short time
frame requested by the provost. They responded through a document called
Criteria for Planning that identified six criteria for the fiscal review of programs.
The Executive Committee framed these criteria as the following questions:

1. Is the program central to the campus, viewed in terms of pertinence to and support of growth, preservation and communication of knowledge, and the campus' mission and priorities?

2. What is the quality and reputation of the program and faculty, considering national rankings, accreditation and unit review outcomes, research productivity and significance, qualifications of entering students, quality of graduate placement, and attrition of students?

3. What is the current and projected importance and demand for the program?

4. Does the program duplicate work elsewhere on campus or within the University of Maryland System?

5. Are there strategic opportunities for comparative advantage of the program because of the time, the location, or the talents of the faculty within the program?

6. What are the costs of maintaining the program vs. bringing the program to an increased level vs. savings resulting from any reductions in the program?

They additionally identified three principles that were repeatedly noted as important to the process: First, no tenured faculty members would lose their positions, although institutional policies on appointments and program reduction made it possible to terminate faculty appointments because of discontinuance. Second, all currently enrolled students would be given a reasonable time to complete their degrees. Campus leaders wanted to ensure students that they would be able to earn degrees in their chosen majors. Third, program closures would not disproportionately affect women students or students of color. The campus had a strong commitment to diversity, and those leading the discontinuance process did not want to see their process undermine university-wide efforts or have their efforts to close programs derailed by proponents of these issues.

Concurrently, the provost requested a report from the dean of each college identifying programs to close. The provost strongly suggested that each college form its own "mini-APAC" to make recommendations and draft their reports. The deans, most with input from their faculty, identified the programs they believed could be discontinued. Upon submission of the dean's reports, APAC divided itself into sub-groups to conduct their own reviews starting with the reports submitted by the deans, and including available internal or external program reviews and meetings with deans, faculty, and department chairs from all of the colleges. Each sub-group then informed the other APAC members as to its findings. From the statistical descriptive data and other information collected, the provost and APAC identified nine departments and two colleges for potential elimination, although many involved admitted it was an imperfect business. Most of the recommendations closely followed those of the deans, and deviations occurred in only three cases, two of which were the proposed elimination of two colleges by APAC and the provost, something not suggested by the deans.

One of the reasons this initial identification process went smoothly, according to those involved, was because of insider knowledge about the institution by APAC members. One person on APAC said:

People knew the campus. I don't think you could have found out these things [which programs were weak] in the time that we found them out had people not known already. . . . It required a kind of academic judgment, a judgment about academic quality that frankly [an outsider] would not have had. It was an insider's judgment and that was very important. . . . You know where the water leaks, as it were.

Based upon the work of APAC, the provost drafted a first report, *Preserving Enhancement*, and submitted it to the president in early March 1991, seven months after the Labor Day recision. The units the provost identified included the Departments of Agriculture and Extension Education; Hearing and Speech Sciences; Housing and Design; Industrial, Technical, and Occupational Education; Nuclear Engineering; Radio, Television and Film; Recreation; and Urban Studies and the Colleges of Library and Information Services and Human Ecology. The report outlined APAC's recommendations and listed the recommendations from the deans highlighting their similarities and differences.

With the release of the first report, the provost wanted to stress to the campus that these recommendations were preliminary and that they were open to debate and modification. In an article in the faculty-staff newspaper that listed the recommendations of *Preserving Enhancement*, the provost clearly reminded the campus of its retrenchment goals and of the potential for pain associated with the necessary cutbacks. He kept the key issues centrally on the table, recognizing the challenges, but, possibly more importantly, keeping people focused on the ultimate (and desirable and agreed upon) goal of enhancement. At the same time, he reassured people that the process to identify programs for closure would try to minimize harm and take care of those affected as best possible. In the faculty and staff newspaper, he wrote:

Our ultimate goal must be to keep in mind the good of the entire institution. . . . This process may be painful, but it's the price the university pays for an open system. I feel that we have a sensible process in place, and we will do our best to protect the university and all of our people to the greatest extent possible. It is extremely difficult to have to scale back the scope of some programs. The challenge is to emerge from this process with the best university that we can possibly have. If we can learn to make tough decisions and choices that are not always palatable, then I believe that the outcome will be a strong university. And that will benefit us all. (*Outlook*, 1991, February 25, p. 2)

Exploring the Implications

To keep his promise and review the initial recommendations carefully in the broader context of the entire institution, the provost, his staff and APAC set up a second series of campus-wide sub-committees. One subcommittee was assigned to each of the 18 recommendations to begin investigating the *implications* of the recommended closures. The subcommittees were not asked to address the validity of the recommendations, but to investigate how the closing of each unit might affect the campus and the state, identify alternatives to closing, and suggest options for the faculty within the units if they were dissolved. The provost said that this subcommittee strategy allowed him to do some important things to facilitate the process. First, it was a mechanism to involve a tremendous amount of people. Approximately 120 faculty became involved in the discontinuance process through these sub-committees, approximately 10% of UMCP's total full-time, tenured faculty. Second, the provost could assign people to the subcommittees who were committed to institutional enhancement and who recognized the necessity of program closure. Third, he could cross-fertilize campus thinking by intentionally structuring sub-committee assignments. Each sub-committee was comprised of faculty from various departments within and outside of the college and at least one faculty member from the targeted unit. Additionally, this process provided a second look for the units under review.

The sub-committees conducted extensive investigations, which included collecting additional hard data, meeting with department chairs and faculty, and, in some cases, holding open hearings. Sub-committees collected curricula, faculty CVs, enrollment data, graduation rates, and other descriptors of departmental vitality. As one member of an APAC sub-committee commented, "It was a fairly intensive operation, and I got to know the department better than I wanted to."

At the conclusion of the second round of sub-committee work, APAC held a series of open hearings for department supporters to make their cases to continue the program and to provide additional evidence that might influence the closure decisions. These open hearings provided departmental supporters with a public forum; they could present data and tell their stories in an attempt to sway campus thinking.

While the subcommittees were at work and APAC's open hearings were underway, the provost and associate provost spent significant amounts of time and energy meeting with the targeted units and talking with faculty. The provost said:

My role, other than being sort of coordinating leader of all of this was to take good advice and to do a lot of talking. I spent personally maybe 8 to 10 hours a day just talking about this process. I had breakfast with department chairs twice a week. We would get random groups of department chairs from all over the campus and we would explain what was going on. I would take a lot of abuse.

The personal contact and interaction did not go unnoticed with faculty. A faculty member in a targeted unit said:

The Provost . . . because of how we felt we were being treated was easy to hate. But on the other hand, he is someone who I can really admire because he was placed in a really tough, tough position. He . . . was still taking the time to come over here and listen to the faculty basically yell at him.

The amount of access to the provost and the time spent listening helped move the process along. These elements created a sense of openness where faculty in targeted units believed they had opportunities to influence outcomes. They were not ignored. At the same time, it allowed the provost opportunities to reiterate why the institution was undertaking this strategy. All of which went to make the process more legitimate.

Making "Hard Choices"

Based upon the information gathered through the summer, sub-committees, and the open hearings, the provost, with guidance from APAC, produced a second report, *Hard Choices: The Next Step in Preserving Enhancement* at the end of January, 1992. This report identified seven departments—Agriculture and Extension Education; Housing and Design; Radio, Television and Film; Urban Studies and Planning; Industrial, Technological and Occupational Education; Recreation; and Textiles and Consumer Economics—and one college—Human Ecology—for elimination. The report gave specific recommendations college by college, an explanation and rationale for each decision, details for each recommendation including faculty lines, office and lab space, enrollment numbers, other regional institutions offering the programs, and the total reallocation of moneys. The report additionally outlined the potential effects on minority and women students for each closure.

At the same time, the president reinforced the importance of what the institution was attempting to accomplish. He talked about tough decisions, about the importance of excellence, and about the difficulties created by the unfavorable economic environment. He also publicly supported the work of the provost, of APAC, and of the sub-committees. By acknowledging the points that he did, he reinforced the seriousness of the task at hand and its importance to the future of the university. The president worked to deflect criticism and attention that could derail the process. The provost said that although he was under pressure, the president took a lot more heat than he did, which allowed him to be somewhat protected and keep the process moving forward. The president also played a hands-off role in the closure process. He did not try to explicitly influence results or protect certain units, something recognized by faculty. His staying out of the way sent a strong message to faculty that the outcomes were dependent upon their leadership, not administrative strong-arming.

The report *Hard Choices* was significant because APAC not only identified programs to be terminated but also removed three units previously named from closure—the Departments of Hearing and Speech in the College of Behavioral and Social Sciences, Nuclear Engineering in the College of Engineering, and the College of Library and Information Sciences. Removing programs from the list may have helped facilitate the process by sending a strong message of fairness to the campus. The provost mentioned that removing units created a sense of fairness and proved to campus that this effort and all of the work of APAC and its subcommittees was "not a gimmick." It also helped generate support for the process from people in the once-closed programs. They could point to the fact that they were able to make a convincing case to save their unit and that the process was open and flexible. One faculty member in a targeted program that was dropped from the list of affected units referred to the process as "eminently fair" because of the ability to remove targeted programs from the list of closures. He, and others, believed that the administration was not trying to simply run roughshod over the faculty. The provost, upon reflection, said that he believed the effect of removing programs and the legitimacy it added to the process eventually helped the senate reach an almost unanimous conclusion about which programs to close.

Those interviewed gave the following reasons for having the three programs removed from consideration: Nuclear Engineering was removed because it ran a nuclear reactor on campus that APAC believed was financially unfeasible to dismantle, and because it had a unique relationship with another institution in the University of Maryland system, University College (UMUC). UMUC operated a revenue-generating distance education program for nuclear plant technicians and managers that was dependent upon the UMCP Nuclear Engineering program. A deal was worked out for UMUC to subsidize the costs of the program, thus keeping it intact. Hearing and Speech was removed because of the originally unrecognized social contributions the program made to the state and region through its hearing and speech clinic. The College of Library and Information Services was removed because its faculty and off-campus supporters were able to demonstrate the significant role the college played within the state, the contributions the college made to the campus, and the existence of a higher-than-first-estimated projected student demand.

The Senate's Turn

The recommendations in *Hard Choices* were passed on at the end of January 1992 to the College Park Senate to be acted upon by the close of the academic year. The senate decisions would then be forwarded to the president, and ultimately, to the board of trustees. The senate vote was key, because without its support, the president most likely would not agree to the closures and the process would reach an impasse.

By chance, in the year the cuts were to occur, all of the senate committee chairs became vacant as terms expired or individuals were elected to the Senate Executive Committee, making them unable to serve as committee chairs. This circumstance allowed the senate chair-elect to select new committee chairs. The chair-elect knew that the senate would be receiving the program closure recommendations and that the senate would have to act by May. Among the committees with a vacant chair was the one responsible for addressing the discontinuance recommendations, the PCC, the committee responsible for program and curricular changes. The senate chair-elect deliberately filled the PCC vacancy with a known faculty leader who had previously served three times on the senate and was a former chair of the senate. This individual had the respect of his faculty peers and was perceived by many to be, as one person noted, very levelheaded and a consensus builder. Important traits that were pointed out by many, because, as one Senate Executive Committee member said, "everybody knew it was going to be a bitch of a job."

In addition to hand-picking a chair for PCC, the Senate Executive Committee deliberately appointed senators to PCC who were well respected by faculty and could accomplish the difficult task of cutting programs. Faculty members who had won distinguished scholar-teacher awards, which recognized their talents in both research and teaching, filled three of the four vacancies on the program and curricular committee. The appointment of these award-winners gave stature to the committee and ensured little questioning by naysayers of their credentials to lead such a process. Attention to who was in key roles and what that appointment meant was an essential element of the process.

The Senate Executive Committee carefully developed a plan on how to proceed. Among the issues discussed were details of the process, such as a timetable for the PCC, how to structure the senate meetings to create orderly discussion, and how much time to allow each speaker at the meetings. PCC developed a process to collect information that included reviewing all of the materials assembled by APAC and the subcommittees, collecting additional information on its own, conducting interviews, and holding a second set of open hearings. Its members reviewed data such as enrollment and degree production numbers, and they read internal and external departmental reviews and the two provost reports on potential closures. Their goal, as described by one College Park Senate executive committee member was to create "an honest, straightforward process."

From their efforts, the members of PCC drafted a report on which the senate was to vote. All of APAC's recommendations were unanimously accepted by PCC and put forth to the College Park Senate for a final discussion and vote. Based upon one senator's suggestion, PCC intentionally structured its report so that each recommendation contained three sections. The first section outlined the points in favor of termination, the second section articulated arguments against termination, and the third section presented PCC's recommendations, which in each case was to close the unit. This format laid out arguments for and against termination, which senators noted very importantly showed the campus that PCC was aware of and had considered all sides of the argument. Critics could not argue that PCC members did not understand the whole story.

Senate leaders purposefully crafted the voting process. For example, the senate considered a proposal to vote on all of the recommendations as a total package. After some discussion, the senate decided that each recommendation must be attended to separately. Each recommendation was to eliminate a specific program or unit and by taking them as a whole, the process would have been open to criticism. They thought that this segmented process avoided one department saying that its unit was closed simply because it was part of a termination package and that if considered on its own, individual merits, it would not have been closed. The process of voting separately on each decision foreclosed a potential point of attack to those unhappy with its outcomes.

Another example of attending to process details was a discussion among the Senate Executive Committee members about the order in which the programs were to be presented, discussed, and voted on. They debated whether to start by taking up the easy or the hard votes first, or by some different order. They eventually decided to present the units alphabetically because they were worried that any other way might be interpreted as them trying to manipulate the results. Again, detailed attention to process helped keep the process on track. It avoided procedural arguments that might have been distracting to the tasks at hand.

For the final vote, the Senate Executive Committee scheduled three meetings to consider PCC's recommendations—two regular Senate meetings and one emergency meeting. However, not all the meetings were needed. Once the process began, many were surprised at how quickly the voting proceeded. Originally, one hour was allocated to each decision for discussion and the vote. Only one recommendation, Recreation, needed its full hour.

The votes for each of the eight recommendations were reported in a series of separate memorandums to the university president from the faculty senate chair (dated April 27, 1992). The overwhelming votes of the College Park Senate to close programs were the following:

- 75 to 12 to close programs in Agricultural and Extension Education;

- 100 to 2 to close programs in Housing, Advertising Design and Interior Design;

- 86 to 4 to close degree programs in Textiles, Apparel Design, Textile Marketing/ Fashion Merchandising, and Consumer Economics and close the College of Human Ecology;

- 75 to 12 to close degree programs in Industrial, Technological, and Occupational Education.

- 77 to 10 to close degree programs in Radio, Television and Film;
- 53 to 20 to close degree programs in Recreation; and
- 73 to 2 to close degree programs in Urban Studies.

After the vote to accept the PCC recommendations, faculty leaders felt a sense of accomplishment. According to one senate executive member:

The senate debate was a debate that was open; it was done with fairness and a sense of dignity; it was done in such a way that no one wanted to slam individual faculty members. These are our colleagues for 25 or 30 years. You are not happy saying to your colleagues we have to get rid of your program. . . . I think the members of the Senate would say we did something that very few schools have done and we did it with class. We did it with some bruised feelings along the way, but we did not blow the campus apart. . . . We had the courage to do it ourselves. I think it left a feeling that while we regret what had to be done—but we lost that huge sum of money—there was a belief that we had done it openly, honestly, and with dignity and with class. And that served the university very well.

The Resistance

Although academic departments and a college were closed through a process that had a high degree of consensus, campus leaders still faced resistance. Faculty, students, alumni, and friends of the units closed engaged in various protest tactics. For example, students in Radio, Television and Film held rallies on the steps of the administration building, one of which included an unfolding of a 150 foot long petition in the form of a four-foot wide wooden film reel, and a faculty member from Recreation wrote an editorial in the student newspaper. Most of the critics argued that the process was faulty and inconclusive, specifically because not all departments were reviewed. Faculty in one of the targeted programs raised the point that terminations should not proceed until all programs were reviewed and ranked from top to bottom. UMCP did not review all departments. It did not review Math, History, Economics, Electrical Engineering, Physics, or Government and Politics, to name a few. Rather the process started with the initial recommendations provided by the deans of potential closures.

Some protesters additionally moved their efforts off campus, which were equally unsuccessful. Said one faculty member on APAC:

One way the protesters tried to clog the system was through the [state] legislature. . . . And it failed. In the end, the legislature was loath to both remove $20 million [from the institution's budget] and then tell you that you couldn't do anything about it. . . . What is extremely interesting is that the departments didn't try to do this on campus or that there was no hint of success of this on campus. I mean they had to go off the campus to mount a clogging process. And again the reason I think this was true was that it was not a controversial decision to close them down. . . . They did not have an argument that they could win [on campus]. . . . So the only thing they could try to do was go off campus, and that did fail in this particular case.

WHY THEY BELIEVED THE PROCESS WORKED

The campus was able to close programs and adhere to its enhancement plan without the university, as one academic administrator said, "being ripped asunder." The following themes reflect the observations made by those involved explaining the process' results and success.

The External Pressure Created by the Recision

The very visible and painful recision of the state budget provided an important motivation for action. Most everyone on campus was well aware of the down-turned fiscal environment and the challenges that it created for the university. This pressure created a scenario of self-preservation as units not targeted realized that they might benefit or at least not be hit for cutbacks. The tight budget times may have helped prevent coalitions from forming among affected and unaffected units on campus over certain programs that were terminated. A faculty member on the College Park Senate said:

The very real, self-centered realization that if these [targeted] programs were to be maintained and the quality improved, I might lose some money in my program to support them. There was no new money coming in and money was going out, and if you are going to get additional resources . . . then it might have to come from me.

Buy-in to Enhancement

At the same time, extensive support for the enhancement goals may have helped keep the campus focused on the benefits of program elimination. Enhancement created a visible objective that reflected the institution's desires of improvement and academic excellence, something with which few academics at the research university would argue against. Campus leaders could readily invoke these values during the retrenchment process. Enhancement goals were widely shared by deans, administrators, chairs, and faculty as important. The institution was strongly committed to not losing ground regarding its enhancement progress, and closing select programs was one way to keep striving toward enhancement during difficult financial times. One academic administrator said:

The campus really does want to become one of the premier research universities. I mean everywhere you go there is sort of the feeling that especially among chairs and the deans, and the provost and the president that we have an ideal location, you know we have very strong programs in the sciences and engineering, and we can grow complementary strong programs in public affairs. We have all these potential sort of good things going for us. . . . Many of us had worked for a long time at the university and had seen a lot of progress since when we were essentially an open enrollment institution. We are now to the point where we are a pretty selective one. We were determined not to lose ground and the only way we could see that we wouldn't lose ground would be to close some lesser departments. It was also the feeling on our part that we had too many programs anyway.

The provost explicitly capitalized on the institution's desire of enhancement. He framed program discontinuance as the only viable option to continue enhancement. By stating discontinuance as *the* approach, the provost made the choice to close programs look unavoidable, which deflated potential opposition. According to one faculty member who sat on APAC:

It is funny when [the closures] look inevitable no one fights it. That I think was something the provost did. He didn't make it look mean, but he did make it look inevitable. Once it was clear to everyone that APAC was going to go down this road and the provost was going to support APAC and that the decision that got made would be implemented and the Senate would be pressed to vote; once all this was clear, I think it was basically over. . . . It was clear what was going to happen.

Protecting Tenure

Another point mentioned as key was stating up front that tenure would be protected. By guaranteeing that all tenured faculty would be found academic homes, campus leaders made the decision to close programs more palatable to faculty. The option of releasing tenured faculty members was not even a topic considered publicly, although the institution's policies and procedures could have allowed that to happen. The argument that carried the day among those leading the process was that if tenure remained a question, people will "dig in their heels," as articulated by one faculty member, and the conversation to close programs will stop in its tracks. To discuss tenure as a part of program termination is to open the process to other issues that, at a minimum, would complicate the process, and at worse, derail it completely.

Extensive and Drawn-out Involvement

Throughout this process, the provost involved faculty in key decision-making positions, including on APAC, the Senate Executive Committee, the 120 faculty in the summer sub-committees, faculty in PCC, and the senators who made the final vote. The provost provided opportunities for faculty not involved in those structures to contribute in the open hearings and encouraged deans to include college faculty in the original "mini-APAC" committees within each college that made initial recommendations. The provost said his goal was to "involve everyone in sight."

Because of the extensive involvement, people across campus recognized opportunities to be involved, to state their positions, and to influence outcomes at multiple points along the way. People on campus saw that their comments were heard and, often, acted upon. If something in the original APAC report was naïve or a sub-committee did not have all of the needed information, people could sway outcomes and change results. This ability to potentially affect results visibly sent an important message to the campus that the process, as one person said, "was not a steamroller and that it wasn't out of control." Those designing the process additionally created opportunities for involvement outside the formal discontinuance process. The provost by spending a lot of time meeting and talking with people formally and informally created additional avenues for people to state their case and be involved in the process.

These plentiful opportunities for involvement, in the end, may have helped facilitate the process as many suggested that all arguments against the closings already had been aired by the time it came to make the decisions. An APAC member noted:

[One] thing that was really important was . . . the amount of time the provost spent talking to every single unit on the campus. [For] anyone who wanted any sort of an appeal, there was always time for another discussion. I think in retrospect, that by the time it came to the Senate there was nothing worth discussing. It had been all talked out. And I think that was a brilliant strategy. They may have not liked the decision, they may have thought that it was a dumb decision, but no one could say that they didn't have their say. In fact, I think they were all too tired to complain . . . I think that was the provost's personality, but I think that was a strategy [as well]. I think it was brilliant.

Another academic administrator suggested that the long and drawn out involvement simply tired out the opposition. The process was so detailed and people had so many opportunities to participate that the process just outlasted people. He said, decisions "became *a fait accompli* before it was accomplished."

The many opportunities of involvement meant that the soon-realized outcomes were not a surprise. People knew programs were going to be terminated. One faculty member said, "No one can say that they woke up one morning to learn they were about to be terminated." The process was such that there were no surprises. Everyone on campus knew closures were imminent and people knew which programs were on the closure list.

Tapping the Best People

Those involved noted that the campus leadership was able to recruit, as one person called them, "quality people" to play major roles in the process. These individuals were said to intimately know the institution, would put institutional goals above personal goals, and could make levelheaded decisions. Possibly more importantly, they shared the same goals of enhancement and knew the realities in which the university found itself. The provost admitted that without faculty leaders willing to make hard choices, the process would not have worked. He believed a declaration by the president or the provost simply would not have been sufficient to bring about the sought after changes.

One of the important characteristics of the people involved in the process was that they were "academic insiders," as called by one person. These individuals knew the institution and how it works, and they shared common institutional goals. One of the faculty on APAC said:

You needed academics to do it. This could not have been done [alone] by administrators. . . . Academics, they are not smarter and they are not tougher and they are not braver than anybody else [is], but boy do they know how to clog up the works. That is one thing we have been taught really well. . . . We can throw crap into any drainage system and just clog it up fast. And consequently you need someone up there who is not seen as 'them'. . . . There would have been rancor of the highest order and nothing would have taken place. And the reason was there was no trust. [But here] everyone trusted the provost. They may not have liked him, but no one ever doubted that what he was doing was in good faith. . . . It probably helped that he was one of us [the faculty]. Not only was he an academic and well respected on campus as an academic, but he really was from the University of Maryland.

The provost was viewed by many as a key academic insider. One person called him a "citizen of the campus," someone who would act in the best interests of the university. Because people saw him as a member of the academic community and not representing a specific discipline, or as simply an administrator, he was given a certain amount of respect, trust, and, probably more important, leeway. One faculty member of APAC said, "He just was a well-traveled member of the academic community."

Characteristics of the Targeted Units Themselves

Those interviewed also pointed to certain characteristics of the targeted programs as factors that contributed to their closing. For example, the units closed were not central to the mission of their colleges or strongly interdependent with other units. Most of the targeted programs were professional programs, and some of them were located in non-professional colleges.

In addition, many of them were characterized as having a lack of strong leadership. One unit was so badly divided that the faculty wouldn't even speak to each other. According to many, the programs not considered for closing had stronger leadership; there was a certain coherence among the faculty; and they seemed to know what they wanted to do as a unit. Of the seven departments closed, two had acting or newly appointed chairs. Another department was in such shambles that it "shot itself in the foot," when according to its dean, its leaders demanded an external review, which was extremely critical of the department and recommended that the dean reconfigure it and bring in new people, which according to the dean, was "the equivalent of saying shut it down." The absence of strong leadership had made the units vulnerable because they were not able to secure needed resources prior to the retrenchment. They also did not have the leadership skills to defend themselves throughout the process.

RESULTS AND EFFECTS OF PROGRAM CLOSURES

Since UMCP had met its objectives and closed programs, what were the effects of the process on the campus? This section explores the results and effects of the closure process at UMCP. Interestingly enough, institutional leaders and individuals from closed units shared similar perspectives on the benefits and consequences of program closure. The provost at UMCP looking back on the process remarked, "In the end, I think I felt very good about what we had done." He laughingly continued, "I could walk across the campus without fear of annihilation."

Anticipated Results and Effects

UMCP had two primary goals for undertaking academic program discontinuance, saving money and making progress on its enhancement goals. The provost and members of APAC were able to generate a high sense of agreement across campus around these two purposes.

The first goal was to save money recalled by the state. According to some administrators and faculty, the institution had some degree of financial success. A report from the assistant provost noted that from its efforts the institution obtained $6.3 million for reallocation or reversal to the state and an additional $770,000 in cost avoidance (moneys that would have been spent to improve the quality of closed programs to acceptable levels). Of the $6.3 million saved, $2.8 million became near-term discretionary funds, money that would be immediately available. According to a report on UMCP's budget retrenchment (Florijin, 1996), the institution participated in a parallel savings process to make up for its financial shortcomings not realized through reduction. For example, the institution increased its revenue through tuition hikes and increased fees for auxiliary services; it saved through reductions in operating moneys (such as postponing facilities renewal projects and limiting travel); and it engaged in a series of across-the-board cuts.

Some interviewed said that although the institution saved money, it did not save a substantial amount. They acknowledged that certain decisions, such as keeping all tenured faculty, compromised saving. Reallocating resources from closed programs to ones targeted for enhancement could not always be controlled. One administrator pointed out that much of the money was not saved immediately, nor was the saved money easy to track. For example, said one dean, "if a faculty member decides to go to a department that is not slated for enhancement and three years later retires or moves on, that department has the line and the dollars, and they become enhanced even though it is not in the overall university plan."

The second goal of the discontinuance process was to enhance the campus. Most of the faculty, administrators, and the provost believed the process led to an improved campus. Even some of the faculty in the targeted units believed that the decisions were in the best interest of enhancing the campus. One faculty member from a closed department remarked, "breaking up was not necessarily bad since we had a home. I think the other senior faculty felt the same. . . . I think in the end, most of us are happy where we are [now]." The process of closing programs reinforced the belief that the institution was on the move. The message said UMCP was willing to make sacrifices to improve its quality—a message heartily welcomed by many.

Positive Unintended Consequences

However, saving money and working toward enhancement were not the only outcomes of the discontinuance process. According to some senior academic administrators and faculty leaders, campus morale became *stronger* as a result of the discontinuance process. This up-swing was due to the closures being viewed as a visible step toward enhancement. Others, especially the faculty involved, were pleased that shared governance had worked, enabling administrators and faculty to jointly make extremely painful and difficult choices. One faculty member who sat on APAC thought this was the faculty's "finest self-governing moment."

Negative Unintended Consequences

UMCP also felt the sting of negative unintended consequences. One frequently mentioned was the public's negative view of the institution. The external perception that the university was in a state of crisis led to other negative effects. Poor public relations, in the eyes of some, in turn, hurt student enrollment. The institution saw a drop-off in both the number and quality of student applications. Both of these factors increased the financial difficulty. For example, poorer quality students demanded more academic support resources and it also hurt retention. The closures also created a sense of panic and anxiety on the campus about what units would be cut. The process of closing programs frightened many people as they wondered if the cuts were going to continue and if they would be next. Crisis and uncertainty become distractions from the work at hand. When people worry about their futures, they are not thinking long term nor are they focusing their energy on getting their jobs done.

EXPLORING THE CASE THROUGH FRAMES

This chapter presented the story of how UMCP went about program closure. It also explored the results and effects of the process on the institution. To understand the process in more detail and to highlight points for cross-case comparison this section views key elements of the process through Bolman and Deal's (1991) four frames—political, symbolic, human resources, and structural. For this and the other cases described in the next three chapters, the explanation within each frame is presented in order of magnitude, with the frames that illuminate the most presented first.

Political Frame

The political frame views organizations as having limited resources in which interest groups form coalitions to influence decisions over those resources; it focuses on conflict, negotiation, bargaining and persuasion, attention to interest group affiliation, and coalition building (Bolman & Deal, 1991).

Those faculty and administrators who coordinated the process, the members of APAC, and specifically the provost, recognized that to be successful they had to obtain buy-in into the process and widespread consensus by various interest groups. Preventing a possible "civil war," as one faculty member said, was an important consideration to the process. Campus leaders recognized that creating political upheavals would impede meeting their objectives. Because of the nature of the problem, the process had the potential to be explosive, setting faculty against administrators and faculty against faculty. Campus leaders acknowledged the importance of coalition building and of keeping strong opposition groups from forming because bullying the faculty was not a realistic option. Leaders at UMCP engaged in three types of tactics: (1) They built supportive coalitions; (2) they foreclosed potential rallying points around which opposition might coalesce; and (3) they made politically defensible decisions.

First, to build supportive coalitions, leaders developed relationships with key interest groups, such as the senate and informal faculty leaders, by involving them in meaningful ways and asking them to shape the process and the outcomes. For example, the provost asked the Senate Executive Committee to develop the criteria and principles to guide closure decisions. Leaders intentionally selected specific people to become involved at various stages of the process. They chose people based upon their affiliation with specific groups or because they were influential leaders. For example, when APAC summer sub-committees were formed, one person from the targeted program was included as a member, and the individuals who sat on PCC as well as the person who chaired that senate sub-committee were selected wisely.

In addition to building supportive coalitions, leaders kept opposing groups from gaining enough strength to derail the process by foreclosing potential rallying points around which an opposition might coalesce. For example, the leaders designed a process that was viewed as legitimate by most on campus. Even though many on APAC had hunches about which programs would eventually be closed, they needed a legitimate process to draw these conclusions. The provost said:

I think everyone understood that this was not a process that could be a top down process. . . . Everybody immediately knew once we knew we weren't going to go the equal distribution route . . . that decisions had to be made through a [legitimate] process, even if with a little bit of thought you might have guessed how the decisions were going to turn out to be. You just couldn't say that out loud.

To create an agreeable process, the provost involved faculty and the Campus Senate at multiple points in the process in key decisions and processes: the Senate Executive Committee developed the criteria and principles for the process to adhere; faculty were involved in collecting and providing information used by APAC and the PCC; approximately 120 faculty participated as members and leaders of the APAC summer sub-committees; faculty had opportunities to present information at two sets of open hearings; and faculty had the final vote in the College Park Senate. Potential opposing interest groups included those outside the institution. For instance, administrative leaders removed Hearing and Speech, and Library Sciences from the list of potential targets because of the potential backlash from outside groups they might have faced had they discontinued those programs.

Leaders also intentionally foreclosed other possible opposition rallying points. For example, (1) they asked faculty from the affected units to sit on the APAC committee investigating the potential implications of closing their unit; (2) they made the firing of tenured faculty a non-issue by relocating affected tenured faculty to other departments; (3) the process included not one but two sets of open hearings; (4) the provost continually met with campus leaders and targeted units; and (5) the process concluded with a vote of a campus elected governance body. The process was crafted in such a way as to make it difficult for anyone to find flaws in it, even if they did not agree with the final outcomes.

In addition to what leaders did, the difficult financial times may have curtailed coalition building because people readily acknowledged the point that if the needed money did not come from the identified units it had to come from others. This financial fact of life may have prevented some unaffected units from joining forces with those targeted in order to protect themselves.

Third, in order to ensure that the process would not become a political casualty, the leadership identified programs for closure that did not have the political strength to derail the process. Most of the targeted programs shared some combination of the following characteristics: (1) they were not central to the missions of their colleges (such as professional programs in a liberal arts college); (2) they did not have the championing support of their deans or other senior administrators; (3) they lacked strong unit leadership or had novice leaders; and (4) they had low numbers of faculty and/or low numbers of students and alumni, thus they did not have the numbers to create a sizable opposition.

Symbolic Frame

The symbolic frame concerns itself with meaning, belief, and faith in organizations, and using symbols to provide direction and clarity (Bolman & Deal, 1991). In this case, the symbolic frame helps illuminate the actions taken to generate a commitment from the campus to terminate programs and to focus campus attention on the cuts as a step toward institutional enhancement. The leaders found ways to help people create important meaning in troubling and difficult times.

Framing the challenges in terms of both economic difficulties and as an important step for institutional enhancement were key symbols used by leaders to generate the needed desire of the campus community to engage in program discontinuance. The names of the two APAC reports—*Preserving Enhancement* and *Hard Choices*—are illustrative of the use of symbols. Symbols were used by campus leaders to generate commitment, to signal that times were tough, and that the continued climb toward academic excellence remained important. The symbols invoked helped to overcome the despair and difficulty of closing certain programs. They used the momentum of the *Enhancement Plan* as a vehicle to propel their discontinuance procedures forward.

Campus leaders also evoked symbols over the course of the process to keep it on track. For example, the first APAC recommendations were modified, allowing the leaders to capitalize on the belief that the process was "not a gimmick," as one person said. The president wrote articles that were symbolically significant in the student newspaper—titled "Be Tough During Trying Times" and "Maintain Excellence"—to keep people focused on the challenges at hand. The provost used his status as a "citizen of the campus" to show that closing programs was in the best interest of the campus. He was not seen to represent one faction or another, nor was he seen as out to get particular programs to the benefit of others, thus lending him credibility to get the task done. The provost also spent significant time talking and meeting with affected faculty. Those conversations helped to send a strong, clear message that the process was open, which contributed to its legitimacy.

Human Resources Frame

The human resources frame, which attends to the needs and feelings of people within the organization (Bolman & Deal, 1991), does not explain as much of what occurred at UMCP as the political and symbolic frames. It was most visible in the decision allowing students in the affected units to complete their programs, demonstrating that the leaders cared about the students in the identified programs. In addition to students, the faculty in the targeted units were also given some institutional support and assistance in moving to new academic homes. However, based upon the interpretations provided by those involved, this activity may have been done more for political reasons than for humanistic ones. An academic administrator said:

In my view, we probably could never have eliminated any departments if we had done this at the same time as we were voting to get rid of jobs. Any money we saved would just go to the lawyers, as we would be in court for the next ten years.

Additionally some of the faculty from those units wished that the administration had provided more assistance with the transition from one unit to another. They believed the move was not as "simple as just moving your stuff," according to one faculty member. There were cross-disciplinary differences between the transferred scholars and their new departments, as well as politics over staffing and budget lines that might have more been handled more effectively, which would have smoothed the process.

Structural Frame

The structural frame helps explain the use of APAC and PCC as the chosen decision-making structures. The structural frame concerns itself with organizational roles, responsibilities, goals, and functions; it attends to policies and procedures that specify who are responsible for what (Bolman & Deal, 1991). Both of those groups were already established key decision-making bodies and were responsible for the types of decisions that the campus had to make. APAC dealt with campus-wide academic programmatic and financial matters, and PCC was the senate sub-committee responsible for curricular decisions. Having these two bodies make the key sets of recommendations adhere to the expected roles and rules present on campus helped facilitate the process, as there were no procedural surprises.

The next chapter explores the process of program discontinuance at the Oregon State University, which stands in contrast in many ways to the process described here, particularly in the types of frames that dominate the institution's culture and shape the focus, attention, and priorities of campus leaders. That said, OSU and UMCP also share some striking similarities.

CHAPTER 3

Oregon State University: Coping with Ballot Measure Five

On Thursday, February 7, 1991, the president of Oregon State University informed faculty gathered in the LeSells-Stewart Center on campus and at institutional extension sites via television of the recommended closures he would be making to the Chancellor, who, in turn, would make his recommendations to the Board of Higher Education. The president's recommended closures were:

- Eliminating the College of Education; and within the college, closing the departments of postsecondary and technological education; mathematical, science and computer science education; counselor education and college student services administration; and curriculum and instruction. These closures would eliminate degree programs in industrial arts education, marketing education, reading, social science education, technology education, trade and industrial education, and training and development, and merge the remaining programs into a reorganized and consolidated College of Human Ecology and Education;

- Closing the Department of Religious Studies and the Journalism Department, terminating all degrees offered through those units, and eliminating an undergraduate degree program in broadcast media, all in the College of Liberal Arts;

- Closing the Department of General Sciences in the College of Science;

- Eliminating the hotel, restaurant and tourism management program; and closing the Management Science Department in the College of Business;

- Closing undergraduate degree programs in poultry science and soil science, and merging 17 departments into 11 in the College of Agricultural Sciences.

All of the recommendations were accepted by the trustees and acted upon by the legislature effectively closing or merging 13 departments and one college, and discontinuing 14 undergraduate degrees.

THE PLAYERS OF CAMPUS GOVERNANCE AND DECISION MAKING

Strong deans, an advisory faculty governance system, and a president and provost who made decisions through conversations with various people, such as individual deans or key faculty leaders describe OSU's decision-making history. The strong dean model allowed deans the freedom and autonomy to make their own decisions and run their colleges as they saw fit, creating a system that, as one academic administrator said, had been "talked about it in medieval terms, [where] each dean runs a dukedom or a fiefdom." This model arose from an administrative structure that, prior to 1985, did not have a provost but rather an academic administrator who acted like a personnel officer for the faculty and did not have broad institutional oversight of academic issues.

Faculty involvement in governance took place at the college and institutional levels. Reflecting college autonomy, faculty involvement varied from one college to another. In some colleges it was limited whereas the dean and associate deans made most college-level decisions. Other colleges operated through a council of department chairs or similar structure, and still others took a much more democratic approach and filled college committees through faculty elections.

At the institutional level, the *Faculty Senate* was advisory to the president and provost. It historically only provided advice and insight, and raised questions of the senior administration, but rarely challenged or opposed administrative views or decisions. The Faculty Senate has approximately 120 members. Senators are elected representatives of their college. The senate accomplishes most of its work through the actions of the executive committee and a series of standing committees, although many items were brought to the full Senate for vote. Executive committee members are chosen from the body of the senate for two-year terms. Senators who volunteered and are then confirmed by the Senate Executive Committee filled the standing committees.

The *Faculty Consultative Group (FCG)*, an ad hoc group of the Faculty Senate, is created when program cuts are imminent as required by the institution's policy document for discontinuing programs, *Guidelines for Program Redirection*. The purpose of the FCG is to "describe and discuss fully the magnitude of financial distress and to analyze options available for resolution of the problem." The 12-person committee is composed of members of the Faculty Senate executive committee and the chairs of three senate subcommittees— budgets and fiscal planning, curriculum, and faculty status. According to the procedural document, this group should *"confidentially* [emphasis added] offer constructive suggestions and comment" to the president and the provost.

The third important element in institutional decision making is the *president* and the *provost.* The president, a long-time faculty member, joined the campus as a faculty member in the early 1960s and became president in 1984, returning to campus after a stint as a senior administrator in the Reagan White House. The president saw his long-term relationship with the campus as beneficial to the process. He believed he had "a certain credibility that . . . others moving into a university anew might not have had." The other primary administrative actor was the provost, a newcomer to OSU who was hired in 1985 as the first provost of the campus following the administrative restructuring that had created the position. Many faculty and a few administrators came to view him as a professional administrator with ambitions beyond the provost-ship at OSU. Shortly after the cuts he assumed the presidency of a Midwestern research university.

Much of the institutional decision making occurred through personal communications between the president and/or the provost and college administrators, mid-level university administrators, or key faculty members. For example, the president typically engaged deans individually to solve problems, getting their feedback or input one at a time rather than collectively, meeting one-on-one with the provost to make decisions or determine the best way to respond. This style respected the strong-dean model, engaging only those individuals into whose domain the issue fell. The president also believed that speaking with people personally was the best way to keep communication open and honest.

The president spent much time working to keep a high level of personal, open communication between him and the faculty. For example, he held weekly breakfast meetings with quasi-randomly selected faculty to engage in an open dialogue about campus issues. It was also an opportunity for the president, as he said, to "float outrageous ideas and see how quickly they would be communicated on campus." He also engaged the campus community in numerous other efforts such as a strategic planning and campus visioning process and an administrative restructuring effort.

The final actors in the governance process resided off campus: the Chancellor of the State System, the Board of Higher Education, and the State Legislative Assembly. In the structure of the higher education system in Oregon, these bodies make decisions on major institutional changes following campus recommendations. In this situation, the Chancellor included the proposed OSU program closures in his larger set of system recommendations for reductions, which were then passed on to the board. The board, in turn, took its recommendations to the state assembly for action. Decisions are not final until acted upon by the state legislature.

THE CONTEXT: IN RESPONSE TO BALLOT MEASURE FIVE

Voters in the State of Oregon approved Ballot Measure Five in November 1990. This ballot measure, a citizen-led rebellion against state property tax, led to a drastic reduction in state funding for higher education. This measure shifted a larger proportion of the state's budget to public K-12 education, which in turn, reduced the amount of funds available to the state's other agencies, including public colleges and universities.

The state budgets for Oregon public higher education are on two-year cycles, and the implementation of Ballot Measure Five was to occur over a five-year period. Thus, campus administrators and faculty were able to predict their bleak financial future. One faculty member said:

I remember remarking to a group of us in the department that we felt that if Ballot Measure Five is fully implemented [that] we really wouldn't exist. There really was a feeling of futility. Of how could we possibly take these cuts over and over and over again for the next 5 or 6 years?

At the time of the president's announcement of the proposed closures, the university expected a mandated reduction of $13.4 million each year in its 1991–1993 biennium budget. The portion reduced in academic programs was approximately $3.25 million per year. To off-set the loss in state funds, in addition to cutting programs and reducing expenditures through across-the-board approaches, the institution increased its tuition by 6.75% and added a $200 per term surcharge on tuition.

The chancellor gave all institutions in the state system three months to make their recommendations so he could forward a system-wide plan to the board for action. As one academic administrator noted:

This hit us so hard so fast . . . There was certainly [going to be] campus-wide partic-ipation, but Ballot Measure Five occurred in November of '90 and decisions were being made for '91–93 fiscal year in early February. That is only a three-month period. The president did what he could to get campus input.

The president explained in the campus faculty-staff newspaper the implica-tions for the short time frame. He said: "The Chancellor's . . . deadline means we have far less time than we would prefer to have for consultation and de-liberation on campus." (*OSU This Week*, Jan 24, 1991)

At a State Board of Higher Education meeting held in December 1990, the chancellor offered a set of principles that institutions should use to guide their decisions. The principles included (1) maintaining a capacity for sustain-ability for the long term; (2) not to "consider across-the-board reductions"; (3) that "there are no unthinkable actions, reorganization and restructure of the system will require creative actions;" and (4) the system "must protect the future and maintain a capacity to expand" (Board Minutes, December 22, 1990).

Ballot Measure Five was not the first time OSU faced budget reductions. In 1988 the state faced a shortfall in revenue when the state's timber market fell on hard times, and passed on the cuts to all state agencies including public colleges and universities. The campus responded to the 1988 challenge by closing the Department of Geography and merging its faculty and many of its courses with the Department of Geology to create a new unit, the Department of Geo-Sciences.

Many on campus saw the 1988 program cuts and budget reallocation as an indicator of things to come. "There was a lot of grumbling in the legislature and that sort of thing," said one faculty member. As a result of the 1988 reductions, the president and the provost charged a committee of three deans "to develop guidelines to help us when it came time to identify those programs that would be eliminated," according to the president. This committee drafted two documents outlining both the process and the criteria for program reductions, merges and terminations. The initial drafts were reviewed by the other deans and forwarded to the Faculty Senate for review and approval. The full senate, and ultimately the president, accepted the documents with only slight modification. The first document, titled *Guidelines for Program Redirection*, laid out the process and its guiding philosophies. The companion document, *Criteria for Program Reduction, Termination and Reorganization*, spelled out the criteria to guide the decision making.

The cuts in public funding in 1988 and again in 1990 were two recent and visible examples of a history of financial tension between the state and its public higher education institutions. One faculty member said:

I have been at OSU for a little over 25 years now, and I can only remember about 3 of those years being years when we were talking about increasing anything or building anything. It has just been one round [of cuts] after another.

Being in financial distress was a way of life for the institution. What made this situation created by Measure Five different from any cuts in the past were that this time the cuts were larger, they were going to last multiple budget cycles, and system leaders encouraged institutions to discontinue programs. One academic administrator said:

For a period of years we had had very tight budgets and we were chronically dealing with how do you cut back? How do you downsize? So I was already somewhat in that mentality, although this [new ballot measure] was a quantum leap in terms of the scale, [but] it was not something new in having to deal with reductions. I always joked that I could never take a job at a university in a building mode because I had never had the experience.

THE PROCESS: TARGETING PROGRAMS FOR TERMINATION IN CONFIDENCE

According to one academic administrator:

The magnitude of the impact, I think, left no doubt in anyone's mind that if indeed the state system of higher education was going to absorb the level of impact. . . . We could not continue to support everything that we were doing up to that point. . . . There was the sense that this is of a significant magnitude that we need to make some tough choices.

Many of the faculty and administrators believed that the budget reductions were extremely serious because the directive to reduce budgets came from the outside and the size of the cutbacks was significant. The collective feeling articulated by one faculty member was that the campus was "sick and tired of just gradually bleeding . . . year after year after year." The campus consensus, which was reached through informal conversations among the cabinet, with the deans and in the faculty senate, and without having any official campuswide forums to discuss the issues, was that Measure Five was drastic and after years of continual belt tightening OSU had to discontinue select academic programs to maintain any satisfactory level of programmatic quality. "The budget cut was so severe something had to give. There was no choice," said one academic administrator.

The targeted cuts at OSU were intended to meet two goals: The primary purpose of discontinuing programs was for the institution to live within its newly reduced budgets; the second purpose was to show state legislators and voters that serious reductions to the institution would generate negative consequences for the state. For instance, the provost publicly pronounced to the local business community that:

OSU will emerge as a weaker institution as a result of the cuts. . . . It is not possible to have a recurring budget cut [and] . . . pretend to our faculty, our students, the people of the Corvallis community, legislators, and people in the state . . . that somehow we can be a better university as a result of cutting approximately 10 percent of our budget. (*The Barometer*, p. 3, February 13, 1991).

The intent of "showing bodies," as one faculty member described the purpose, was to demonstrate how these drastic measures undercut the value and contributions of the institution to the state. An academic administrator said:

There was some sense of awareness that politically there had to be some very, very visible, traumatic kinds of impacts. . . . If we were seen to continue to be able to reduce and reduce and reduce and yet everything is OK . . . we were doing ourselves in. There was a sense that we were at the point where we had really show some serious blood on the floor. Show it to the legislature and the citizenry.

The elimination of academic programs was one step among many to reduce expenses. For example, OSU restructured and streamlined its administrative structures, reduced funding to non-academic programs such as the marching band and the museum, and deferred building maintenance.

Following the Procedures

To terminate programs, the campus followed its three-step procedure outlined in *Guidelines for Program Redirection*. First, the president will present, in confidence, a proposal to the Faculty Senate Executive Committee. Second, the Executive Committee shall convene a special Ad Hoc Faculty Consultative Group (FCG), chaired by the senate president. Third, the FCG will assess the impact of the proposed program reorganization and report back to the administration.

The proposed plan "will include discussion of and will seek provisions for reassigning, re-employing and/or retraining faculty and staff whose positions are eliminated or altered by reorganizations" (p. 6). The procedures also set forth that the discussions will be held in high confidence. Both faculty and administrators believed, for the most part, confidentiality was important to the process. One faculty senate member said: "I think the bigger the audience, the more people start playing games. I don't think people would have been as candid if it was an open discussion saying that department should be eliminated." Others believed by making the process open they might create a sense of panic and frustration if people thought that their units were being considered for closure before a final decision was announced.

On the other hand, the air of secrecy limited the amount of broad campus involvement because FCG members could not talk with others to test ideas and assumptions, gather information or investigate potential secondary effects. It also had a negative effect on faculty morale because in addition to insulating faculty from painful discussions, it left them feeling in the dark. According to one member of the FCG:

What it really did was hurt morale because everyone thought they were on the cutting block then and no one really knew who was and who wasn't. So the rumors were just rampant. I mean you would hear rumors that were just horrific on campus. . . . We never could convince the provost that keeping this open would be better. I don't know which is worse: to wonder and not know, or to know and wait.

The *Criteria for Program Reduction, Termination and Reorganization* began with a paragraph that noted the complexity of using criteria and the naturally inherent ambiguity in their application. It said:

Because of its complexity and diversity a single set of specific criteria will not be applicable to all of its programs and functions. However, common to all of its activities is a commitment to its institutional goals and missions. Also inherent in its diversity is a common commitment to quality. The general principles herein stated are thus fundamental criteria and applicable to all elements of the University. (p. 1)

The document suggested that a range of criteria be weighed in making decisions to close programs but did not indicate relative weight for each. Rather than be prescriptive, it intentionally left open a range of possibilities. The document outlined three sets of criteria, two of which focused on reducing programs and one on eliminating them. The elimination criteria were framed to gave justifications for not closing departments, and included the following:

1. an objective evaluation that indicates the program has achieved a national or international reputation for exceptional quality;
2. a program that supplies significant instruction, research or service that OSU is better equipped to supply than other organizations;
3. a program that exists because of legislative statute;
4. a program that is the only one of its kind within the state;
5. a program that is essential for every university;
6. a program whose elimination would have a substantial negative impact on education and societal concerns in the state;
7. a program whose elimination would result in substantial loss of revenue;
8. a program whose cost is minimal relative to the tuition or income it generated;
9. a program that represents a substantial capital investment; and
10. a program that is characteristically staffed by members of groups protected by affirmative action.

Creating a Mosaic of Recommendations

The president and provost charged the dean of each college to independently develop a plan to reduce his budget specifying which programs would be discontinued. They then would draft a campus-wide proposal for consideration by the FCG.

Because deans have considerable autonomy to operate their colleges, the processes each dean used to respond to their charge varied by the type of decision-making structure already in place in each college. These processes ranged from, in some colleges, a department chair council to, in others, an elected faculty or joint faculty-chair advisory board, and in still others an administrative task force comprised of the dean and the associate deans, with little to no involvement from faculty or department chairs. One commonality across processes within each college was secrecy. One academic administrator said:

An interesting dimension of this was that we had to keep, and did keep, everything very quiet. . . . I am not sure it was a smart thing in retrospect. As we were in fact putting them together, people knew these discussions were going on. Department unit leaders knew these were going on, but they weren't getting [any information from] leaks. They didn't know if this involved them or not.

Once the deans drafted their scenarios, each one had a budget hearing before the provost. No decisions were made at the hearings, the provost simply heard out each dean.

Although deans were the first step in crafting institution-wide recommendations, some believed their roles and responsibilities extended beyond making the initial recommendations. As one dean said:

Probably the most important thing for a dean to do . . . [was] to help the internal community . . . understand why there was a need for change, to understand a little bit about the process about how these recommendations were developed, and to explain the rationale for how specific recommendations were developed; to try to take away some of the mystery, [and show] that there wasn't a dart board, that somebody just began saying OK let's do that one instead of this one.

Once the provost solicited the scenarios from each dean, the president's cabinet (which included the president, the provost, the vice president for finance and administration, the vice president for university relations, the vice president for student affairs, the vice president for research and graduate studies, and the university legal council) began crafting its recommendations for the FCG to review.

The Faculty Senate convened the FCG to respond to the recommendations being considered by the cabinet and to help the president and provost understand the potential implications of the recommendations. At this point confidentiality created problems as the members of the FCG had difficulty obtaining information to help their decision-making process. They could not go to deans, department heads or faculty in the targeted units to collect information or to explore hunches because they had to treat the procedures and the decisions with a high level of confidentiality.

The process between the FCG and the cabinet became iterative as a number of departments put forth by the president and provost were taken off the list because the FCG pointed out the potential, harmful spill-over. The FCG shared convincing scenarios with senior administrators and raised a set of questions that challenged the cabinet's original assumptions. Additionally, other programs were considered as potential closures because of FCG's involvement.

After discussions with the FCG, the president and the provost, with some assistance from other cabinet members, put the final recommendations together. Many faculty on campus believed that the administrators should make the final decisions. One faculty member from a non-targeted group said:

It is very difficult to basically get together and say, which of you wants to go. I was fine with [what happened]. These are decisions to me that the faculty can't make because you are basically saying to your colleagues, I think you are the one who needs to go. I think that would break down the collegiality within the university tremendously. . . . I also think it is impossible to do it from a purely faculty governance perspective. Because these are decisions that are essentially firing people and I guess I view that as an administrative function. That is what they get paid the big bucks for I think.

In order to make these final recommendations, the senior administrators believed they had to balance a number of competing priorities. First, they made sure that any one recommendation did not create significant harm to a unit either outside of a particular college or at another university. Second, the president and the provost coordinated their efforts with the Chancellor's office and other public institutions to prevent the system from eliminating similar programs across the state.

Senior administrators had to do both again all under a veil of secrecy. To many on campus, these elements created a feeling that important campus decisions were being made in a black box. Many faculty and administrators, even some of those people deeply involved at some phase of the process, believed they did not know how the final decisions actually came about. An academic administrator said:

We have some documents which describe how we go about authorizing program reduction. That is how you engage the faculty senate and how you get approval to do this. That process really begs the question . . . regarding how do you pick the targets out there. And I am not sure I have the answer. . . . They really didn't identify the question of how do you go about saying what is going to be on the table.

However, from his perspective, the president worked at keeping channels of communication open. For example, he initiated envisioning activities to help the campus chart its future. These activities provided opportunities for much of the whole campus to become involved. As the president said: "The whole environment was one of communication that we consciously tried to enhance and keep alive." He additionally provided significant access to him for faculty, the media and alumni of the university. He even went as far, according to one academic administrator, as publishing his e-mail address and his home phone number in the local newspaper. He also sponsored a series of breakfasts during which he focused on the institution's financial problems and its potential response. One faculty member commented on the breakfast series the president had started. He said:

My sense was that [the president] made sure that every faculty member from every affected unit on campus was scheduled at one of those breakfasts. It was kind of like telling you it really wasn't good to smoke, but not telling you [that] you have cancer. He was trying to prepare people but was not yet in a position to tell them what was going to happen. I would guess that at that point he wasn't really sure what was to happen. He really did try to get to the people in the units he considered really vulnerable. Of course we thought it was pretty special just to be asked to breakfast by the president.

Making the Announcement

On Thursday, November 7, 1991, the president planned to make the announcement of which programs were going to be sent as recommended closures to the Chancellor. The deans of the affected units learned that morning of the specific recommendations. Many immediately informed the soon-to-be-named units of their fate. One dean said:

We went personally. We had everyone standing by in their offices literally. Every manager in the college, standing by in their offices. We went to each of the chairs . . . and visited with them personally to tell them. It was a painful process, but it went decently well. It was done one-on-one, and it wasn't done on a Friday afternoon.

For the official announcement, the president invited faculty and the campus community to a large auditorium and had his announcement broadcast across the state to OSU faculty and staff working at off-campus sites, mostly at extension and research centers. In his announcement, the president reviewed the impact Measure Five had on the campus, calling the situation "difficult for all of us" and the "most serious challenge this institution has faced in several decades." He described the guiding philosophy used during the campus decision-making process, including "protecting the core of the university from the burden of these cuts," but also noting that "every unit will be affected, either directly or indirectly." He also added that the university must avoid across-the-board-cuts and intentionally eliminate specific areas instead. He also speculated on the implications of the cuts for the university and their impact on the campus community. About the impact on the campus, he said:

While our goal will be to reassign as many faculty and staff as possible, some administrators, staff and faculty will face termination because of program elimination and reduction. To those affected, we pledge our assistance and support. We have asked each dean or unit leader to visit with each employee, faculty or staff affected by these recommendations and to describe the processes and services available to affected individuals from this time forward. We will be outlining the options available for those displaced in a series of news articles and letters to employees. We will do our utmost to be of assistance to our colleagues and friends.

He then explained the budget cuts and announced the recommended targeted programs to meet the cuts. The president, near the end of his speech, said:

The reductions and eliminations that I have just described are serious. There was no fat; muscle will be removed. However, I ask you to remember that the programs that place Oregon State University among the nation's leading universities remain. More important, we retain the values that make us strong. The quality of our students' education remains our top priority. We continue to believe that ALL our people are important and, in the days ahead, we will treat each other with respect and humanity.

And he closed with a call to action:

Now is the time to express our strong feelings about the damage being done to Oregon by Ballot Measure Five. It is time for action . . . not rhetoric. Oregon's economy has been growing and expanding. Oregon is not an impoverished state. This state can afford to do much better in support of all levels of education. We owe that support to each other and to the future generations of Oregonians. We must have additional resources sooner rather than later. . . . Legislative action to create such additional revenue must come **NOW!!** (emphasis in original). . . . All of the reductions we will recommend to the Chancellor might not be necessary if that were to happen. Contact your legislator. We need your help **NOW!!** (emphasis in original).

After the Announcement

Shortly after the proposed cuts were announced, all of the faculty in the College of Education received letters of timely notice, or pink slips, informing them that as of July 1, their services were no longer needed. Faculty at OSU hold tenure in their departments, and the elimination of a unit can result in the termination of tenure for the faculty in that unit.

Although the college was initially dismantled and its faculty given notice, the university did not abandon the teacher preparation arena, nor in the end follow through with the lay-offs. The acting dean of education (the only person not laid-off) was given a mandate by the provost to recreate a departmentless school to meet some of the state's education needs. So even though all of the college's faculty were told they were laid off, in the end, none were actually dismissed. Some teacher preparation programs and their corresponding faculty were transferred to other colleges within the university, 22 of the laid-off faculty were rehired into the newly reconfigured School of Education based upon seniority and rank. A few faculty opted for early retirement and others resigned for positions at other institutions. This process took two years and it took a heavy psychic toll on faculty across the institution.

Handing tenured faculty in Education pink slips may have quashed some potential backlash in other units. For example, a faculty member said:

Everyone was too scared. . . . thinking they were going to be cut. Especially when they heard that Oregon State broke that sacred honor of honoring tenure and was going to fire tenured faculty. . . . People were just thankful they weren't fired. And that is a very self-serving type of feeling, but that is the way it was. . . . I think people were just relieved that they were not on the chopping block.

The administration realized that the process was painful and stressful for everyone on the campus. Senior administrators developed measures to alleviate that pain and stress accompanying closures. A faculty member said: "people did not necessarily try to stop the cuts, nor did they feel that the cuts were stoppable. But they tried to make sure that the people were taken care of in the process." One academic administrator said:

The outcomes that were most difficult [to deal with] were . . . the human impacts of these processes on the faculty who were directly affected, on students in programs, on alumni or other constituents whose link to OSU was that particular program . . . In many cases, . . . individuals had essentially devoted their career to the development of this program . . . and to see a program that they have invested in be eliminated is just like a death in the family. . . . So there was a very high emotional cost associated with it. . . . We made arrangements for anyone who wanted to access external support, some counseling and advising of any kind whether it be related to careers or simply related to trying to cope personally with the changes that were being made. To provide access to that kind of professional support for people and a few people took advantage of that.

The administration and the various affected units provided assistance to students in the affected programs. They helped students complete their programs in a reasonable time. For example, some units developed specific plans in conjunction with the provost's office that changed the sequencing of courses to help move students through their required in-major coursework more quickly.

Although the institution had charted its course in response to the cuts of 1991–1993, Measure Five was a three biennium reduction in state funding. In the first phase described here, the institution engaged in targeted and across-the-board cuts. During the next phase, the state system encouraged the campus to recommend only one program for termination—the College of Veterinary Medicine, a very costly program that produced a small number of graduates. However, efforts to close this program were half-hearted because campus administrators recognized that it was a politically unfeasible decision in the state. At one point, supporters for the college mobilized animal lovers and owners across Oregon, such as the state's eastern ranchers. They even held a rally on the steps of the capital with their llamas. In the end, the state legislature succumbed to the pressure, and not only voted to keep the program but they provided new sources of funding (state lottery proceeds) so the college would not be a drain on OSU's shrinking budget.

OSU did not cut any additional programs in the next two budget cycles. By this point, all parties realized that the cost of cutting programs was tremendous. According to one academic administrator:

It was only in the first cycle of Measure Five that the State Board allowed or encouraged a review of programs and program elimination. . . . For many parents and students . . . the question was, if I come to Oregon State University will the program that I want to major in still be there when I am ready to graduate? It created an image of program instability that lasted, and institutions in the system had to work very hard to overcome that in succeeding years. It caused people to say, let's try to protect or try to sustain programs as we encounter future reductions as a result of Measure Five.

Thus, OSU, as well as other public colleges and universities in Oregon, met their budgetary goals through tactics such as administrative review and restructuring and across-the-board cuts, steps which left programs intact. The reversal of the Chancellor's Office on its encouragement of program termination, one administrator believed, was "part of trying to reassure the public that we did have stable programs."

WHY THEY BELIEVED THE PROCESS WORKED

Overall many believed that the process worked well. The institution was able to cut programs, live within slimmer means, make a strong political statement, and avoid serious attempts to discontinue programs in the future. The following themes were mentioned as reasons those interviewed believed that the process worked.

No Choice but to Act

The institution was faced with a situation in which many faculty and administrators believed they had no choice but to act; doing nothing was not an option. This sense of urgency was created both by the size of the Measure Five cuts and because they came upon the heals of ongoing economic woes. The president said:

Ballot Measure Five was such a significant trauma for the whole state system of higher education that everyone recognized that we had to take some very hard steps. The faculty, who felt this particularly, had already stripped things down so much that the only way to [make the cuts and meet our budget] was to eliminate programs. . . . So the awareness was campus-wide that we had a serious situation to address. . . . Measure Five was such a strong and public pressure, everyone knew something must be done.

Adhering to an Accepted Process

Many faculty and administrators believed that already having an agreed upon procedure that was perceived as sound and acceptable facilitated the closures. One faculty member said:

I think people bought in because they were up-front about the process. I think it is important to have consensus on how it going to be done and the criteria that is going to be used . . . It is important to have a process that is fairly well articulated and people understand so that it doesn't seem to be arbitrary and capricious, and an unfair process.

A Window of Opportunity: The Units Themselves

The characteristics of the targeted units, as one academic administrator said, "created a window of opportunity." Their deans did not see some of the departments as central to the mission of the college. For example, Journalism was a professional program in the College of Liberal Arts. A faculty member called it "a fish out of water" because it was too professionally oriented for a College of Liberal Arts. Many of the units also had small numbers of faculty, and possibly more importantly, small numbers of tenured faculty that made the process of reassignment simpler. Other programs had small undergraduate populations, thus the negative effect was contained.

Finally, many of the affected units had just undergone a turnover in leadership. For example, when Geography was closed in 1988, its new department chair had been in the position less than a week. Journalism had hired a new chair the year before from outside academe to replace a chair of 30 years. The College of Education was in a leadership transition as the old dean had stepped down in October after a faculty vote of no confidence and was replaced by an acting dean.

In addition to a new leader, the College of Education was also in the midst of moving to a fifth-year model of teacher preparation, itself a window of opportunity that occurred because one by-product of this change was an intentional effort to reduce student enrollments and offer fewer courses, which required less faculty.

RESULTS AND EFFECTS

What results were accomplished through this process? What was the impact on the institution? What were the effects? The following quotation from a faculty member on FCG provides a pithy example:

I think overall it was as good as could be as expected. . . . We held the university together and worked through some pretty tough times. You know people who were hurt; there was no doubt when their programs were eliminated. In general, they may not have been all the best decisions, but they were justifiable decisions. . . . I think that we survived.

The situation and the closures were difficult for OSU. It made the necessary decisions, but they were not easy and they exerted a high price on the institution and its personnel. One academic administrator said: "There were no lawsuits, [so] the [results] were satisfactory, or at least acceptable." Although, lack of legal actions is not exactly a constructive standard.

Anticipated Results and Effects

The primary purpose of cutting programs was to function within a reduced budget. Everyone interviewed said the institution was able to meet its budget goals, because it had no choice; the following year's budget was simply smaller. However, no one interviewed provided a figure for how much the institution actually saved from the closures. They also did not start the process with a specific dollar goal in mind. One administrator replied: "The budget we got was the budget we got. So sure we met our [goals]." Another academic administrator said:

We didn't have a choice . . . we didn't have the money and we were not going to get the same level of budgetary support. . . . There were clearly savings . . . not big dollar amounts, but there are savings.

The second objective was to make a statement politically that continued drastic cuts would seriously hurt public higher education in the state. One faculty member said:

We had to give up programs politically because of the legislature, which is my impression. . . . My sense is that this was the board and Chancellor's office saying that this is the strategy to address the budget shortfall, and in a sense make the voters and the legislators know the impact of the cuts on the university. So the strategy was let's put scalps on the wall.

The hope was that by showing the legislature that they were cutting programs, the campus might be looked upon more favorably in the next state budget cycle. This goal was reached because, beyond pressure to drop Veterinary Medicine, OSU did not face additional pressure to continue discontinuing programs. Although successful as a strategy to persuade the chancellor to stop pushing discontinuance and to convince the state to give higher education needed resources, the termination strategy had high costs and was painful for these involved. Campus leaders spoke publicly about the pain and difficulty of the cutbacks and their language and metaphors were adopted by many on campus, including cutting muscle and bone, putting scalps on the wall, and bloody.

Positive Unintended Consequences

In addition to the primary goals, the processes of terminating programs led to a series of secondary impacts. The discontinuance process forced many of OSU's colleges, departments and programs to engage in self-examination. Many faculty thought the introspection and examination made their units stronger in the long run with a clearer sense of purpose and a more thorough understanding of the context in which the institution operated.

Probably the most dramatic effort at self-examination occurred in the College of Agricultural Sciences where the dean brought together faculty and industry leaders to explore the present needs of agriculture as a field and to re-organize the college. The result was a consolidation in undergraduate majors from 17 to 11, the creation of a new major—bio-resources research—which incorporated a pedagogy different from traditional majors, and a set of new interdisciplinary undergraduate degree programs. Shortly after implementing these changes, the college saw its enrollment rise 30% over two years, at a time when university enrollment was dropping. A college administrator said:

This [impetus] allowed us to refocus some resources. . . . If [the reductions] would not have happened we would still have these low enrollment majors. We never would have experienced the growth we have in the present. I don't think we could have developed the relevance of the curriculum in the absence of this. So overall it was a good process, but I just as soon wouldn't want to go through this again.

An additional unexpected consequence was the rise of interdisciplinary programs. Faculty and administrators noted that faculty dropped their disciplinary walls and began working together across units because they realized new initiatives would not be funded, and by joining forces they could do more with less resources. One faculty member said: "No one has the illusion that they are going to get the money to build an empire here from state resources. If you are going to do anything you are going to do it by working with other units." The results were new, creative academic initiatives, more collaborations between faculty members across traditional disciplines and a stronger sense of academic community for those choosing to participate.

Finally, this was the first time the campus put its discontinuance procedure to the test which many believed it passed, albeit not with flying colors. Senior administrators realized that the lack of communication and coordination across the deans made the process difficult to execute. The confidential element also made it extremely difficult to obtain needed information. An outcome of the 1990–1991 process was to add a Council of Academic Administrators as a parallel group to the Faculty Consultative Group in the university's procedure.

Negative Unintended Consequences

Not all of the unanticipated outcomes were positive. One cost was that the process became all consuming for those involved. It took time away from important tasks for some administrators and from the scholarship, teaching, and service for faculty. The process impeded productivity as people were either involved in the decision making or were distracted by what was going on.

This process was also extremely stressful. The stress was particularly intense in the College of Education, where tenured faculty were let go. According to one academic administrator:

There was a lot of stress and strain associated with this . . . both for the individuals who were not retained and also for the ones who were because they had a deep sense of loss of programs and loss of colleagues, almost a sense of guilt in some cases that although I survived, my colleague across the hall didn't.

The institution felt the stress and strain caused by people feeling demoralized and devalued. This consequence was especially true for people in the affected units who believed the institution was saying that their academic discipline was unimportant. An administrator in a unit that was eliminated said, he felt "the university does not value who I am or what I do. . . . I had people calling me for two years [afterwards] saying . . . Do you have any spare chairs over there that we can have? It was like dissecting the body while it was still alive." Everyone interviewed noted the negative, painful impact the cuts had on individuals across the institution.

Terminating academic programs created a negative public perception of the institution. Friends of the university, students, and the public in general interpreted the cuts to mean that the institution was in a period of decline and unstable. The negative perceptions were not just of OSU but of the entire state system of higher education.

Enrollment also dropped by approximately 1,000 students during the years of program closure. Many speculated that public perception that OSU was in a state of instability, and coupled with the fact that the board raised tuition, kept students away. Students and their parents were unsure if the budget cuts would continue and what effects continued cuts would have on the range and the quality of academic programs, as well as on their costs. At the same time, many students could not afford the accompanying tuition increases and they left OSU for the community colleges. Only six years later did enrollments equal pre-Measure Five levels.

A related unintended effect was the lost opportunities for enrollment growth. According to one administrator, teacher preparation needs in the state grew and OSU was unable to take advantage of the demand. The state's private institutions benefited instead and OSU could not gear up to fill that need and benefit from that trend because it dismantled its College of Education.

The institution also faced a backlash from alumni whose main connection to the university was through a program that was closed, which in turn hurt fund raising. One of the other noted effects of the closures was a lack of an OSU presence over time in the state's media because of closing the Journalism program, something noted by both faculty and administrators. By closing the OSU journalism program, the institution no longer had graduates working in the state's media, which resulted in less press coverage and media recognition for the university. The state's reporters instead looked to their own alma maters for expert sources.

A final noted effect of the closures was that many thought faculty curtailed much of their risk-taking, and the institution lost its ability to flexibly respond to new demands. The faculty became skeptical of trying new things or drawing attention to themselves. According to one member of FCG: "The atmosphere is one of people really scrambling to stay in place," which created apprehension about trying to effect some needed change.

EXPLORING THE CASE THROUGH FRAMES

Each of Bolman and Deal's (1991) four frames—structural, political, human resources, and symbolic—illuminates different aspects of the OSU process. These different dimensions together provide a more thorough understanding of how the process at OSU transpired.

Structural Frame

The structural frame suggests that organizations have sets of operating policies and procedures and that individuals are expected to play certain roles and fulfill certain functions because of their positions (Bolman & Deal, 1991). Through this perspective, two key aspects of OSU's discontinuance process can be understood. First, actors followed institutional policies and procedures; second, they behaved in ways that reflected their positions within the organization.

First, when I asked people at OSU to describe the discontinuance process, most of them immediately referred to the already in-place campus procedures. The campus strictly followed the policies set forth in its document, *Guidelines for Program Redirection*, which dictated how the process would unfold. The administration was to present a proposal to the Faculty Senate Executive Committee, which it did. The Senate Executive Committee was to convene the Faculty Consultative Group (FCG), which it did. Finally, the FCG was to review the proposal and advise the administration, which it did. The policy also set forth procedural guidelines to follow, such as confidentiality, which the campus strictly adhered to.

Following the pre-determined and agreed upon process helped to facilitate OSU's termination efforts. The policy expressed recognized agreements for identifying programs for discontinuance, and it may have quickened the process allowing the campus to identify programs in only three months. By having a policy in place, at an institution with a predisposition toward adhering to written protocols and following organized rules, the leaders may have avoided a time-consuming negotiation over process, criteria, and the roles various groups (i.e., faculty, deans and senior administrators) should play.

Second, from a structural perspective, organizational actors accomplish organizational goals in ways consistent with responsibilities prescribed by their positions (Bolman & Deal, 1991). For example, the deans at OSU started the process because, according to those interviewed, people in those positions were responsible for overseeing college budgets and making decisions regarding costs and expenditures. Many on campus also viewed the central administration having its own set of responsibilities that were dictated by position. Faculty and administrators noted that top administrators had the ultimate responsibility to make the final decisions because that was their job. One faculty member said, "that is what they get paid the big bucks for."

The structural framework may additionally explain the frustration of many that they did not know how decisions were made. However, when viewed from a structural perspective, the process becomes less disjointed even though the typical faculty member perceived the process to have many gaps. Because the structural frame suggests different positions fulfill different roles (for example, the role of the faculty in this process was to provide advice and the role of the president and provost was to make the final decision) and that policies dictate events, those individuals who were suppose to make the decisions did so; however, they did so in the administrative suite, as specified by the policy and roles of the institution. Thus people across campus were not witness to the logic that led to the ultimate decisions. They only saw the preliminary dean's report, then they knew the FCG was meeting with the president and provost, and finally in February, only three months later, they were invited to hear the president announce the recommendations.

Human Resources Frame

The human resources frame concerns itself with the needs of the people within the organization and focuses on issues such as emotional welfare and caring, the needs and feelings of individuals, and their personal experience (Bolman & Deal, 1991). The elements of this frame apparent at OSU include (1) leaders showing a genuine concern for those affected by the closures, and (2) the fact that they developed activities that attended to the needs of faculty and students in the closed departments.

First, the administration demonstrated a genuine concern for the people involved. For example, the president made numerous references to the human elements in his announcement, pledging assistance to affected people and using phrases like "respect and humanity." He worked with his administrative staff to provide counseling services. Other examples of a people-centered approach included when the College of Education chose to use seniority and faculty rank as the criteria for re-hiring laid-off tenured faculty rather than criteria such as quality, productivity or specialization, and the fact that the president made his announcement to everyone in a campus-wide meeting in a large auditorium and broadcasting live to all of the faculty and staff working at extension sites across the state. The high importance of confidentiality also illustrated a care for people, as many interviewed said that the secrecy built intentionally into the institution's policies and procedures was to prevent preliminary decisions, which may later be overturned, from further creating "sense of being defeated or panic or frustration," as one person said, and from creating undue stress among people who prematurely might think that their units were to be eliminated.

Leaders did not just acknowledge the difficult experiences for those in the closed units, but they developed mechanisms to attend to their needs. The president and many of the deans saw one of their primary responsibilities as helping people make sense of and prepare for what was happening. For example, the president did this through his breakfast meetings where "he basically gave faculty background on how serious the cuts were and what OSU in general terms would have to do to contend with them," according to one faculty member. One dean said he personally spoke with the faculty and staff within his college, helping them to understand what was occurring, why it was happening, and the processes through which decisions were made.

The faculty, central administrators, and college leaders took action to attend to the needs of faculty, staff, and students in the affected units. For example, administrators and faculty took extensive measures to help students through the closure process, such as rearranging course sequences and hiring additional affiliate faculty to ensure that students got through the required courses quickly. The administration also developed a series of initiatives to help faculty and staff through the transition, including personal counseling and job placement services, and travel money for junior faculty to build their curricula vitae and give them visibility to enhance their competitiveness for positions elsewhere.

Political Frame

The political frame focuses on interest groups, organizational politics, negotiation, and coalition building (Bolman & Deal, 1991). Although not as strongly evoked as the other two frames, leaders at OSU, nonetheless, worked (1) to prevent opposing coalitions from forming and (2) to make decisions that would not be derailed by politics.

To prevent opposing coalitions from forming, those leading the process engaged in a number of tactics. They did not want, as one administrator said, "everybody working against everybody else." One explanation for shrouding the process in confidentiality was political. For example, one faculty senator said: "the bigger the audience, the more people start playing games." The leaders worked at foreclosing potential rallying points around which opposition might organize. They adhered to a process that was previously agreed upon by faculty and administrators, and they involved the elected Faculty Senate through the FCG in legitimate and expected ways.

Campus leaders also made decisions that were politically savvy and could not be easily derailed. They identified programs that were, as one person said, "windows of opportunity." The units discontinued tended to have some combination of the following characteristics making them politically vulnerable: (1) They lacked strong leadership or were in a leadership transition (e.g., the

College of Education's vote of no confidence in the dean). (2) The units were not perceived as central to the mission of their colleges (e.g., Journalism was a professional program in a College of Liberal Arts). (3) The units neither had champions on or off campus, nor did they have a support base (such as large numbers of alumni, faculty or students) strong enough to prevent the decisions from being implemented. The lack of support for these programs stands in stark contrast to the support generated for Veterinary Medicine when it was threatened with closure. Off-campus supporters of the program generated strong opposition at the state level to prevent closure.

In comparison to UMCP, the political frame did not play as central a role at OSU. For example, leaders at OSU did not work to intentionally create supporting coalitions beyond adhering to their guidelines and involving the FCG of the senate. The severity of Measure Five, the extremely short time-frame of only three months, and a campus culture characterized by the structural and human resources elements may all help to explain why forming supportive coalitions was not important and did not occur.

Symbolic Frame

Those leading the closure efforts at OSU intentionally used symbolism to stress the difficulty of the challenge ahead, cutting programs in only three months. Leaders used graphic metaphors that conveyed human suffering, such as "cutting muscle and bone." The campus readily adopted these beliefs as many of those interviewed evoked phrases such as "gradually bleeding" and "devastation," and made analogies to death and grief. The use of these terms may have helped prepare the campus for the pain associated with what would eventually come to be a reduction in programs, a loss of positions, and a public ordering of institutional priorities where someone inevitably would come out at the bottom.

However, compared to the process at UMCP, OSU leaders did not work to focus the attention of the campus and work to get a commitment to close programs (a key element of the symbolic frame). The leaders believed that the environment, because of the state's history of under-funding higher education and the new threat of Ballot Measure Five, provided a powerful, externally-generated message that that extreme action was required.

CHAPTER 4

The University of Rochester: Toward a "Renaissance"

On November 16, 1995, the dean of the College,[1] with the president and provost present, announced to the department chairs gathered at an emergency meeting of the Council of Department Chairs (CDC) that four Ph.D. programs would be suspended[2] as part of a larger effort called the Renaissance Plan to return the institution to more solid financial ground. The four programs, Chemical Engineering, Mathematics, Linguistics, and Comparative Literature, would be prevented from recruiting graduate students, thus in effect terminating those programs. Four additional doctoral programs were to be refocused (History, Mechanical Engineering, Philosophy, and Earth and Environmental Science) meaning a reduction in the number of graduate students and a narrowing of each department's focus. A year prior, the graduate program in Anthropology was closed when the dean informed the department that it could not fill faculty vacancies open from retirement nor would it be allowed to admit new doctoral students.

The hope of the dean, the president, and the provost was that by discontinuing selected graduate programs and refocusing others, the institution would reduce faculty size and at the same time "reduce departmental expenditures by an estimated $3 million," according to a memo written by the dean and disseminated at the announcement to the chairs present and later that day to the campus. In addition to discontinuing four Ph.D. programs and refocusing others, the Renaissance Plan called for a decrease in undergraduate enrollment with an accompanying increase in the quality of the undergraduate students. The president, the provost, and the dean hoped that that these efforts would restore institutional financial health.

THE PLAYERS OF CAMPUS GOVERNANCE AND DECISION MAKING

The primary body for faculty governance in the College is the *Council of Department Chairs (CDC)*, a formal group that meets at least once a month and includes all of the department chairs and directors within the College, approximately 40 people. The CDC is chaired by the dean and serves as a vehicle for information exchange, as a way for the dean to collect campus opinions, and as a college-wide decision-making body.

The institution's culture is one of strong chairs, where the primary unit is the department. Departments are where appointments are made, resources allocated, curricula developed, and tenure held. Faculty select their own chairs, who tend to be consensus candidates for their positions. An important footnote is that the chairs are viewed as faculty members by the faculty and the central administration.

Two other campus governance bodies exist, the *Faculty Council* and *Faculty Senate*. The Faculty Council is the primary vehicle for faculty involvement within the College, and the Faculty Senate is a faculty vehicle for the campus as a whole. Neither is influential, nor did they play substantive roles in the discontinuance process.

Decisions not made in the CDC are usually made through extensive consultation among the president, the provost, and the dean who formed a leadership triumvirate. The *president* was newly hired in July of 1994 and charged with solving the financial problem. Coming from outside the institution he believed quickly gave him some clout in campus decision making. He said:

I wasn't identified as being an advocate of English or Political Science or Physics or some other department. . . . The [faculty] felt I was somebody who shared their academic values. So I came with a reservoir of good will and very few battle scars from the past.

The president recruited the *provost* from an appointment in the university's medical school. The president intentionally selected an institutional insider as provost because the president wanted someone "who was familiar with the landscape." The *dean of the college*, a long time faculty member and chief academic officer for the College, was the third player of the leadership triumvirate. The dean had been appointed to his position at the end of the previous administration's tenure. Under the old administration he had resigned the post in a high-profile protest over some decisions made by the past administration. When approached by the new president, he reluctantly agreed to remain in the position and help the institution through this transition. The president said:

I think that resignation [of the dean] was a mark of protest against a prior administration and the obvious pain he felt through this process gave him enormous integrity with the faculty. If you wanted an administration stooge, this guy was not it. . . . He had a lot of credibility from being in [his position] during a rough time and resigning on the prior administration, and in many ways wearing this pain on his face during the process.

To make decisions and move ahead, the three administrative actors tended to collectively explore options and think through problems and dilemmas. Sometimes their proposed solutions were then tested in the CDC, but the three administrative leaders made many institutional decisions through one-on-one conversations with campus opinion leaders, faculty and chairs, and/or members of the board.

THE CONTEXT: FINANCIALLY RESTRUCTURING THE INSTITUTION

The University of Rochester (UR) is one of the smallest (in terms of enrollment) Carnegie Research universities. Its undergraduate population at the time the discontinuance process began was approximately 4,600 students and the size of its faculty was approximately 345, down from a high a few years prior of approximately 360 faculty. Prior to the 1960s UR had been primarily a residential liberal arts college emphasizing undergraduate education. Throughout the 1960s and the 1970s its mission, as common among many of America's higher education institutions, evolved into one of research and graduate studies, and eventually became that of a Carnegie Research I University. Most faculty were "recruited not because they were good under-graduate teachers; they were recruited because they believed there was a good potential for them to do first-rate research," said one academic administrator. As part of the emphasis on graduate education and research, the institution, which is private and heavily tuition-dependent, began investing in costly graduate programs that generated little tuition income.

In addition to coping with the effects of an expanded emphasis on graduate education and research, the current administration inherited a costly history of poor endowment management. This situation created a financial solvency problem by which the institution first addressed by increasing its class size. Many of the campus decision makers believed that a larger class size simply equaled more tuition dollars. Over a 20-year period, the institution had gradually increased its enrollment by about 50 students per year, from 3,700 in 1975 to approximately 4,600 in the early 1990s. With the creep in class size, the quality of students enrolling in the institution declined, which in turn lead to a lower reputation and created a downward spiral as better students enrolled elsewhere. Accompanying enrollment growth and drop in quality was an increase in the institution's tuition discount, which is a higher percentage of student aid, and the institution's discount rate rose from 35% to over 50% in ten years. To make matters worse, the institution continuously had raised tuition faster than inflationary rates, a pattern that perpetuated the number of students who could not pay sticker price.

These problems forced the College to dip into the principal of its endowment such that endowment spending quickly rose to dangerous levels. In the years prior to the closures its draw rate was close to an unsustainable 12%. The board and campus leaders realized that something had to be done. As the dean said, the College could not "spend itself into oblivion."

Learning from Past Attempts

Previous administrators engaged in a series of traditional approaches for coping with the financial problems, such as hiring freezes and savings through random attrition, salary freezes and mid-year budget adjustments. One chair described these strategies as "knee-jerk kinds of things."

At one time, past administrators attempted to close six doctoral programs. The decisions about which programs were going to be cut were made behind closed doors by the then-dean and then-associate dean. The chairs of the targeted programs received a letter from the associate dean informing them that they were not allowed to admit any more graduate students. The fact that there was no consultation and that the process lacked a shared and open process raised a strong and vocal objection from the College's faculty. After the "eruption," as one department chair called it, over the lack of involvement in the process and the outcomes, the then-president disavowed knowledge of what was happening (which many believed was not true) and did not publicly support the dean. After that incident, the president fired the dean. Soon afterward, the old president resigned and the new president was hired. One administrator called the episode "extremely ugly and horrible." The current dean and provost said that they learned key lessons about the importance of paying attention to process, consultation, and keeping people informed.

The year before the new administration began the process to discontinue programs they announced the closure of the doctoral program in Anthropology. The department had a small number of doctoral students and had three vacant faculty lines that it had not been allowed by the dean to fill because of financial difficulties. The dean closed the Ph.D. program with little fanfare. He merely informed the chair that the institution was suspending the unit's doctoral admissions and not replacing positions. As the dean said: "It was a shot across the bow and an indicator that the administration was serious about doing something." The dean wanted to see how cuts would be received and he noticed little response to the cuts both inside and outside the unit. One faculty member in the department said, if given the chance, he most likely would have closed it himself because of a lack of interest and demand.

THE PROCESS: TOWARD A "RENAISSANCE"

The leadership realized that the college had to be structurally different to resolve its long-term and re-occurring problems. Over the past five years, the

College had relied upon measures such as salary and hiring freezes, mid-year budget adjustments, deferred maintenance, and administrative restructuring. One academic administrator called it "lurching from year to year." After a careful analysis, the president, provost and dean associated the problems that placed UR on thin financial ice with (1) a faculty that was too large and (2) a declining student quality and the ability of those students to pay tuition.

Articulating Potential Solutions

The dean, the provost, and the president believed that graduate education absorbed approximately half of a unit's faculty time, so without graduate students, a department could get by with fewer faculty. They also thought that by closing and refocusing selected Ph.D. programs, some faculty in those units would choose to leave the college to be able to work elsewhere with graduate students. Reducing programs became a method to reduce the size of the faculty through a pattern of attrition without laying off tenured academics. The dean said:

The expectations of the faculty was that they were going to both teach and do research of very high quality. As soon as you announce that you are not going to have a Ph.D. program any more, many of those faculty don't want to be here. So our expectation was . . . that we would be able to see the targeted reductions . . . simply by attrition because faculty would be motivated to leave those departments. It sounds rather impersonal and cruel, but in terms of numbers, ignoring for the moment the individuals [affected], we certainly expected in a five year period that those faculty would migrate away from those programs that had had their Ph.D. programs cut. That is voluntarily.

The goal was to reduce the size of the faculty within the College from over 340 faculty to approximately 310.

The dean, the president, and the provost thought it imprudent to eliminate entire departments because UR did not have any departments that were expendable, such as might be the case at a large research institution. They chose instead to discontinue only doctoral programs while keeping the undergraduate programs intact. The president said, "there were not many theoretically plausible scenarios that would not encroach on our undergraduate educational programs. For example, closing biology, closing English, closing physics, closing history weren't particularly viable options." They believed they could not close more than a few graduate programs without fundamentally altering the institution, making it a "very different place" and an "outlier as a research institution," said the dean. Other graduate programs were to be refocused, but not closed. The administration hoped that faculty would leave the institution voluntarily as well if they reduced a department's number of graduate students and narrowed its focus to a particular sub-specialty. Through a combination of refocusing and discontinuing certain programs they could meet their faculty reduction goals.

The College also had to reduce its large tuition discount. After an analysis by the provost, charting trends over 20 years through comparisons to aspirational peer institutions, administrators decided that their revenue problem was tightly linked to student quality and that "unless we fixed the quality problem, we would never fix the revenue problem," said the president. Their solution was to attract more talented students who were able to pay more of their tuition bill. To increase student quality, the president and the provost believed UR had to become more selective. They hypothesized that by becoming more selective (and reducing class size) the types of students they sought would be more attracted to the institution.

The administration realized that neither approach by itself—reducing the size of the faculty or closing the tuition discount rate—would yield the needed results. For example, if the institution only reduced faculty, the provost estimated the institution would have to shrink its faculty from 340 to less than 260, which the three leaders decided could not be done. The provost said: "if you take this university down to 260, you have ripped the heart out of it. It is no longer a research university." If they only reduced the tuition discount, the drain of faculty salaries would not be alleviated. They strongly believed the college had to do both.

The first step taken by the administrative leadership was to publicly identify and name the problems. The president wrote to all faculty in January of 1995, in one of his first campus-wide communiqués, articulating his view of the financial problem and these two solutions, including targeted closures. The letter sent "a very important signal to the faculty" about the problem and "set the stage for the subsequent detailed process," said the dean. "That was a kind of softening up letter. It was not news," he continued. "Most of the faculty who were semi-conscious already knew about this."

The president, the provost, and the dean learned from the institution's prior failed attempt to close graduate programs that they had to develop a process that would be seen as legitimate, one that involved the right people in the right way. The dean and provost also proposed the strategy to the CDC, the Faculty Council, and the Faculty Senate to get their feedback and more importantly involve them early on. The dean said, "it was an exercise in discussion; it didn't change my mind about what had to be done. We had thought through all these options and it was pretty clear that we were going to do targeted cuts. But it was pretty important to have that [approach] discussed."

The chairs and the faculty received the idea of targeted reductions favorably. People believed the institution would solve its long-term financial difficulties through targeted reductions, which became the solution. A department chair said:

The faculty was pretty euphoric. They were excited about a new president. They were excited about the concept that we weren't going to just cut uniformly. We had years with no pay raises . . . or very low percentages. The new president was going to look to our strengths and make cuts in our weaknesses—"prune and feed" . . . was the concept. During the spring everyone was enthusiastic about this because it was going to be somebody else's department that was going to be cut. How could they possibly cut my department? So everybody was rah, rah, rah.

Making the Process Inclusive

Although the course had been charted by the president, the provost, and the dean, the specifics of which departments' doctoral programs were to be refocused and terminated and the process to identify those programs was unspecified. In addition to the CDC, the dean and the provost also spoke about the institution's financial problems and the challenge of developing a legitimate process to the Faculty Council and the Faculty Senate. They sought to include as many faculty as possible in the dialogue and wanted to continually reinforce their earlier messages that something had to be done and program closure was the best, if not only, option.

Beyond the formal governance bodies on campus, the president, the provost, and the dean talked about the problems constantly. They also convened informal groups of faculty and held individual meetings with key faculty opinion leaders. About 20 faculty leaders were brought into the process on agreements of confidentiality, and they collectively formed "a kind of 'rump cabinet' that we could just kind of bounce ideas off of," said the provost. All of these individuals were from departments with traditionally strong doctoral programs that were in no danger of being cut. The president and provost also sought informal involvement and feedback through means that went beyond the public meetings such as e-mail. One chair said, "I know that I personally sent the president e-mails on those issues and he was very responsive."

Identifying Criteria and Collecting Data

Both faculty and administrators believed that data was needed to drive the decision-making process, and through the CDC, the dean and faculty leaders identified metrics that both believed were sound. They identified two types of information to be collected: productivity and quality. For productivity, the dean relied on a framework that already had widespread acceptance. The Parker-LeBlanc Committee developed the framework during the merger that created the College. Productivity data assembled by the dean was then shared with each chair, who he asked for comments. Some of the chairs challenged the numbers for their units, and the dean made some appropriate adjustments. The dean said:

The point was that we didn't want this to become a big issue. . . . If they don't have faith that you can do a legitimate, unbiased evaluation of [productivity], any targeted faculty cuts are going to be viewed as merely political.

To address quality, a concept that the dean believed to be much more difficult to measure, he broached the subject with the CDC. The dean wanted the chairs' input in determining the criteria to assess program quality because as he said, "if you could not convince the faculty that you had a pretty good way of evaluating quality, then they simply weren't going to trust your judgment. They were going to believe that what you did was simply political." The first suggestion was to use external rankings such as the *Gorman Report* and *US News & World Report*, but the dean quickly discovered that the rankings were not valid, and thus would not suffice. Instead, the dean decided to seek information about program quality from faculty themselves as perceived within their own units and others. One chair said:

The dean said in effect, you tell me how I can tell how good your program is. I think department chairs responded to that with varying degrees of preciseness, varying degrees of believability.

The dean and provost decided to hold a series of individual meetings over the summer with faculty and chairs from each department to collect quality data and to supplement their productivity data. These meetings allowed the dean and provost to hear first-hand faculty opinions about the termination and refocusing process and about their own departments. The dean and provost held two-on-one meetings with individual faculty members over two and a half months. The provost explained the rationale behind their approach. He said:

Nobody will stand up in a public meeting and say, such and such a program stinks [and] you ought to get rid of it. . . . I have come to the conclusion that you just can't get a meaningful discussion of these kinds of issues in public because it violates senses of academic decency. You simply don't talk about your colleagues in these kinds of public forums.

The dean and provost believed they could not hold these individual meetings with each of the approximately 340 faculty members so they chose to meet with three from each department: the chair, a department representative identified by the chair, and a representative selected by the department as a whole. A few departments refused to identify individuals for the interviews, so the provost and the dean met with the unit as a whole. The individual interviews totaled 75 in all.

Prior to the interviews, the dean sent a memo in May 1995 to all of the College's faculty providing them with the list of interview questions, referred to by one chair as "the infamous 12 questions," and asking for their comments either in writing or via e-mail. Of the 340 letters the dean sent out, he received less than a dozen written responses, at which he was surprised and "found to be actually disappointing."

In the individual interviews, the dean and provost asked faculty about unit quality, cohort departments, who they competed with for graduate students, and the placements of their graduate students. They sought information about program linkages to explore interdependencies and the potential implications of closures on other units. They also asked those with whom they met about the department's contributions to undergraduate and graduate education, its national prestige, their speculation on future job markets for graduates, what a cut of 15% would do to their department, and where they would suggest making a 15% cut in the College. Of the interviews, the dean said:

Basically we were hoping to flag any errors that we might have in our already pre-conceived notion of what we were going to do. I can say this after the fact. We pretty much knew a group of let's say 10 departments within which we were likely to make some cuts. We weren't completely convinced about which subset of those 10 we were going to make targeted cuts in. . . . We wanted to make sure we were not making some stupid mistake. Without asking them directly or handing them my blueprint, we were trying to get information that would confirm or deny the first stab that I had taken for coming up with the ultimate goal configuration for the faculty size. . . . Based upon my three years of experience analyzing the departments, looking at the quality of faculty each year for salary raises, dealing with outside offers, dealing with their teaching effectiveness, all of the things that deans do when they evaluate departments internally, . . . you don't have to be dean for more than a few years to . . . have a pretty good sense of the quality. The problem is you cannot specify precisely to a department chair how you know that. In other words, I can't give a department chair a piece of paper that says you are an A+ department for the following reasons, because the following reasons consist of things that are rather subjective.

Finally, as part of each interview, the dean and the provost asked for advice on the process. They did use the interviews only to seek input on how they would proceed, but they also used this time to convince individual faculty that a faculty committee would not be completely unbiased and representative, nor could it easily make decisions regarding closures.

Upon the conclusion of the 75 interviews, the dean, the provost, and the president sent a second letter to all college faculty reviewing the process and saying that through the interviews they had gathered significant amounts of information. In the letter, they also reiterated what was going to happen: reducing faculty size, making targeted cuts, and closing and refocusing Ph.D. programs.

Making the Hard Decisions

After collecting substantial amounts of information and meeting with faculty and the CDC, the senior administrators believed that they were the ones who would have to make the ultimate decisions on which programs were cut and refocused. The provost said:

After looking at [Yale's process which led to no cuts] very carefully, we decided we were not going to put out a trial balloon list. If we were going to do this, we were going to do this very specifically, this is the list and these programs are suspended, bang. . . . Because once they are locked in like that, the efforts to reverse the decision [are more difficult], and also when you do them all at once, it is better than picking them off one at a time. We wanted to make the decision look as irreversible as possible.

If they didn't make the decision, the dean believed there might be too much "wriggle room" and the cuts might be "undone before it is actually completed."

This decision-making strategy was a hard sell to the faculty, especially those who wanted either open hearings or a committee to decide. The dean, the provost, and the president sent a memo in mid-September to the College's faculty outlining how they were planning to proceed and asking for comments on the process. The memo included two documents: (1) a discussion document, titled "Fashioning a College Restructuring Plan" that presented the "conceptual framework that is currently guiding our formulation of a restructuring plan," and (2) a statement, titled "A Vision for the College in the 21st Century at the University of Rochester," outlining a vision for the institution that would shape the decision-making process. The dean met with the Faculty Council to review the process to date and discuss how the decisions were ultimately going to be made. At this meeting he received similar feedback as from other college academics. Many on the Faculty Council believed that the best way to identify programs for closure was to form a committee or put the recommendations to a vote in the Faculty Council. The dean said:

I think I disabused people of the notion that this [idea of faculty deciding] was a good idea, and the way I did that was by saying all right, lets imagine that we have a vote. Are we going to have a vote of the whole faculty? And people said, yeah, we think it ought to be a vote by the whole faculty, that would be fair, it is a big decision. So, I said what you mean by a vote of the whole faculty is that each faculty member gets one vote. I said, OK and the departments vary in size. We have some departments which have 30 faculty and we have some which have eight. And what do you think it might mean when it comes to vote time for which Ph.D. programs are going to be eliminated. . . . You could see the light go on, where all the faculty members from small departments said, maybe this isn't such a good idea. Maybe each person voting is not a good idea because the big departments would vote out all the little departments' Ph.D. programs. . . . I eventually got them around to thinking that taking a vote is probably not so fair. I think begrudgingly, the discussion just kind of ended with a realization that the administration . . . has the most information. And hopefully we can trust them and they will do the right thing. And there was no vote taken or anything. The conversation just kind of petered out with people realizing that this is probably the best we could do in terms of process. I think they all left that meeting thinking that this was going to happen. That it was just going to come down. They just didn't know when. And of course it did come down on November 16.

The three administrators had not yet finalized their decisions because they did not believe they had convincing evidence about program quality. They still sought a legitimate outside evaluation of program quality. In September, the National Research Council (NRC) released its rankings of graduate programs. The administrators believed the NRC rankings had a satisfactory level of validity (as compared to *US News & World Report* or the *Gorman Report*) and were the final piece of evidence they needed. The dean sent the rankings to the chairs and shared them with the College's Faculty Council, asking both groups to comment prior to their adoption.

To identify the specific programs closed and refocused and how to save $3 million, the dean, the provost, and the president together discussed different scenarios. The dean said:

This was heavily driven by budget issues . . . We had a target number for savings. Given the dollar amount, we felt we could sustain the number of cuts we did . . . [but] we could have packaged the cuts in a degree of different ways.

Putting Together the "Renaissance"

With the assistance of the dean and the provost, the president drafted a plan outlining the actions the institution would take to attend to its financial problems. The plan, named the Renaissance Plan (a name chosen because it was a "phrase about the rebirth of the institution" according to one administrator), reduced the number of faculty by closing and refocusing Ph.D. programs and by implementing an early retirement program. It identified doctoral programs in Mathematics, Chemical Engineering, Linguistics and Comparative Literature for closure, and programs in History, Mechanical Engineering, Philosophy, and Earth and Environmental Sciences to be refocused. The aggressive early retirement plan consisted of a series of incentives and a limited time window to encourage rapid participation. With tenure, the institution chose not to fire faculty in the units in which they closed programs, although they probably could have if they chose to do so, according to the dean. The intent of these strategies was that by closing programs and refocusing others, faculty who wanted to work with graduate students would voluntarily leave.

The second component of the Renaissance Plan was to increase the quality of the student body through decreasing its size and attracting students who could pay more of their tuition. But decreasing student headcount would also decrease the amount of tuition-generated revenue. The institution had opted for a strategy that had short-term costs, and to many who were aware of the institution's tuition dependency, seemed counter-intuitive. The administration had to convince the faculty and the board that not only was cutting programs and shrinking the size of the faculty a good thing, but that in the short-term, they would generate additional costs. To save money in significant ways, they believed the institution had to spend some first.

In the final stages of the plan's development, the president, the provost, and the dean convened a group of informal campus leaders to get their feedback on the soon to be public plan. They discussed the proposed cuts and refocused programs, and they presented their logic to reduce the undergraduate student population to enhance quality. This discussion, held in complete confidence, allowed the drafters of the plan to test initial reactions, an opportunity to articulate their rationale and their intended outcomes, and a chance to prepare for expected naysayers. Although accepted by most, the plan was not unanimously accepted by the gathered faculty leaders. The plan's three architects listened to and considered the concerns of those present but chose not to make any substantive changes.

Gaining Trustee Support

The administrators believed it imperative to get full board support before going any further with the plan. The provost, the dean, and the president thought that the trustees would provide the needed funds, but more importantly that they would support the administration's ideas through implementation. The dean said:

Having that board of trustees meeting was absolutely critical because they all went away with instructions for when they get the phone call from professor X or when you get the phone call from some corporation who hears what Rochester is doing as an institution, your response is, I am fully informed. I know what they are doing, [and] I know they are doing the right thing. Thank you very much for calling. It was none of this: Gee I didn't know they were going to do that, that is stupid. The trustees were 100% behind it.

To help secure the backing of the board and their agreement to spend endowment capital, the president orchestrated a special weekend retreat for the board in mid-November. The trustees took the retreat seriously, with 95% in attendance. At the retreat, the president, provost and dean unveiled the Renaissance Plan. The dean said:

It was really a remarkable experience. It wasn't just a pep talk it was a really serious discussion of the options and how we came to those conclusions. I think we all came away from that meeting feeling that we had got it mostly right.

The chair of the Board agreed and showed his personal support by donating $10 million to support the execution of the plan. Board support was important both instrumentally and symbolically. One department chair said:

Board support in many ways was fundamental to faculty support. If the Board says, we believe in this plan. We believe in this administration. We are going to put this huge pile of money on the table to support this plan. This buys a lot of credibility with the faculty.

Making the Announcement

The dean struggled with the best way to inform the department chairs about the decisions. He preferred to tell them face-to-face, but logistically he could not do so because as soon as one chair knew the word would be out. Instead, he called an emergency meeting of the CDC and gave 24-hours notice for the meeting. He believed it "very inappropriate" to make a general announcement to all the chairs at a meeting. He thought the affected units should have prior knowledge and the "courtesy of informing them ahead of time." The morning of the emergency meeting he called each of the affected chairs and told them about the decisions that were going to be unveiled at the afternoon's CDC meeting.

The dean chaired the emergency CDC meeting, with the president and the provost present, and announced their decisions to close four Ph.D. programs and refocus four others. After announcing the decisions, he discussed the general principles of why and how they came to their decisions. He handed out copies of the Renaissance Plan and a document that gave the rationale for the specific closures. In that document he wrote:

As outlined in the September memo from the president, the provost and myself, we concluded that suspending enrollments in several graduate programs was the only sensible way to selectively downsize the faculty. The conclusion is based on three premises: (1) retaining a number of outstanding Ph.D. programs is essential to our overall reputation as a first-rate research university, (2) across-the-board reductions in faculty size will likely render our strongest Ph.D. programs second-rate, and (3) given the considerable amount of faculty time spent on graduate education in the depart-ments with Ph.D. programs, and the constraints (in budget and in faculty size) already placed on these departments, any further reductions in faculty size are often incom-patible with the presence of a Ph.D. program. Given the necessity of further reducing overall faculty size within the College, we cannot afford to jeopardize the quality of our undergraduate programs by diverting limited resources to weakened Ph.D. pro-grams. In sum, we must protect our most important income stream—undergraduate tuition—not only to deliver a quality education to undergraduates, but also to maintain the quality of our best Ph.D. programs.

The rationale document also outlined the global factors, which, although not specifically weighted, guided the decisions. The document said, "the im-portance of these factors must be combined with an overall sense of what is best, and most feasible given limited resources for the College as a whole." The factors included:

- the quality of faculty and graduate students (as evidenced by awards and honors, external grant funding relative to similar disciplines, publications, hiring markets, graduate admission test scores, placements, and external rankings);
- the costs (both relative and absolute) of supporting the research/scholarly mission of the program;
- the centrality of the discipline and its current or projected importance to the undergraduate population;
- the role of graduate students in the delivery of undergraduate instruction and in the conduct of faculty research scholarship;
- critical linkages that exist (or should exist) between scholarly or instructional programs across departments;
- a consideration of which disciplines are distinctive to Rochester or could be with a modest investment. (p. 4)

The document also gave the rationale, program by program, for discontinuing or refocusing it. It reiterated the point that tenure-track appointments would not be terminated.

After the meeting the president distributed a "Dear Faculty Colleague" letter to the campus summarizing the Renaissance Plan. That letter, signed by the president, the provost and the dean, presented the plan and its underlying rationale, outlined cost controlling measures, reviewed the process used to formulate the plan, presented a series of alternatives that were considered and rejected, and set out a framework for future actions. It closed with the following paragraph:

Together we can succeed with the plan, if all faculty and staff work to achieve it. It will require change and adaptation from many, but the potential rewards are great— a highly focused and coherent undergraduate educational program, a significantly stronger student body, smaller classes, excellence in our graduate programs, and per- haps best of all, a stable and positive financial future for the College that we can all look forward to and depend upon. The alternatives, as outlined earlier, present a bleak future for the College. Thus, we set forth the Rochester Renaissance Plan as the path along which we move together. We look forward with the strongest possible enthu- siasm to proceeding together with you towards these new goals. (p. 12)

The same day as the emergency meeting announcing the actions and the campus-wide distribution of the plan, the dean mailed letters to the alumni of all the affected graduate programs informing them of the decisions. He also mailed letters to the graduate students in those departments guaranteeing them continued financial support and the opportunity to complete their de- grees. The dean also offered to help current graduate students transfer to other institutions if they desired and even offered to pay the application fees to the other programs. The dean subsequently held an open meeting for all graduate students to talk about the process and the decisions, ensure them of security, and offer them transfer assistance. The president, provost and the dean offered to collectively meet with each of the affected departments upon their request. Within the week, they met with faculty in the Departments of History, Chemical Engineering, Mathematics, and Comparative Literature. As a final part of the follow-up process, the institution set up a fund for the affected units to recruit and support post-docs. This strategy was to encourage the targeted units to continue active research agendas because the research expectations remained unchanged. The administration thought this effort might help faculty in the affected areas continue their scholarship without graduate students.

AFTER THE ANNOUNCEMENT: THE RETURN OF MATHEMATICS

Not all of the elements in the Renaissance Plan were implemented. Five months later the dean announced that the administration and the Department of Mathematics had reached an agreement to reinstate its Ph.D. program and create a smaller, more focused department, in which the number of faculty were to be reduced from 21 to 14, and not from the originally proposed 21 to 10. Additionally, the department appointed a new department chair. A large part of this negotiation centered around the department's commitment to develop a range of mathematics courses to better meet the needs of the under-graduates from other programs, such as engineering, and life and physical sciences, and a 30% reduction in the number of its Ph.D. students.

Upon the announcement of the discontinuance of the mathematics Ph.D., the Mathematics faculty raised a call to arms to their colleagues across the nation that the administration was terminating their doctoral program and that mathematics at a quality research university was under attack. One faculty member said:

It was felt that if we didn't have a Ph.D. program, that eventually the research life of the department would die. It wouldn't die immediately as the people here would still be doing research. . . . In the future, I don't believe that any serious research mathematician would choose to work in a department that didn't have a graduate program.

The Mathematics Department was able to get an article in the Sunday edition of the *New York Times* as well as numerous articles and editorials in *The Chronicle of Higher Education* describing its plight and the impact of the decision. The argument the faculty put forth was one of survival. The American Mathematical Society (AMS) joined the department's fight because they believed that if this research university could do away with its math Ph.D. program then others would follow. The AMS along with the UR Mathematics faculty organized an extensive publicity campaign, primarily letter writing, to pressure the administration to reverse its decision. In turn, the UR president received over 200 letters, including several from Nobel laureates, criticizing the proposed action and suggesting (and sometimes demanding) a reversal. The AMS and the Mathematics faculty set up and maintained Web pages. AMS also sent a delegation, called the Rochester Task Force, to investigate the issue and draft a report.

One component of the Renaissance Plan regarding mathematics was to replace the tenured faculty who chose to leave the institution with up to five non-tenure track teaching instructors. This proposed substitution became an issue around which external support coalesced. Said one academic administrator:

When it came down to adjuncts [this resonated] very, very deeply into the math community. The math community has an awful lot of these non-tenure track professors around the country teaching math courses and not having a real career. It is a very real and deep sore point. And so they just tapped into that raw wound, and threw salt in it and caused this wild cry.

Over a series of meetings, the Mathematics department was able to negotiate an agreement with the dean and the provost to retain the doctoral program. The dean said:

We continued to get pressure from outside people, and we stood firm to that pressure. And then we got a phone call from the Math department and they said we would like to get together and talk about this. . . . We had some private meetings . . . They were very fruitful meetings. They, I think, realized there were some problems and before they had been in denial about those problems. And I think they also realized that we were willing on some dimensions to bargain with them, but we couldn't bargain on the financial end of things. . . . These private discussions led to some ideas about how we might be able to maintain the bottom line and still restore a small Ph.D. program to the department.

As part of the deal, Mathematics agreed to improve their teaching and re-design course offerings by developing specific sections for undergraduate students who were not mathematics majors. They also formed new linkages with the Physics department and eventually appointed a joint faculty member. Mathematics was in turn able to increase the number of faculty lines. The new chair demonstrated that more than 11 faculty were needed to meet the undergraduate mathematics needs of the College and that they could do this with current faculty by using the money set aside for the proposed teaching faculty.

Although the designers of the Renaissance Plan eventually deviated from it, they believed the compromise met most of their intended goals. The provost said:

Math has had a turn-around in teaching that is just fabulous. They completely re-vamped the math curriculum. . . . Now, we have calculus for biologists, calculus for economists, calculus for engineers, and calculus for serious mathematicians. They went around to every department—the new chair I give great credit—that had a math requirement and [asked] what do you want your students to learn. And then they tailored sections to fulfill that and had examples in mathematics that were discipline specific, and they have got a great turnaround on how they are interacting with the rest of the university now.

Mathematics was the only department able to negotiate with the administration to save its Ph.D. program. The other decisions were not overturned. Chemical Engineering tried to follow a similar argument but was unable to reverse the decision. Because the Mathematics recision took five months before it was announced, for the most part, people said that other units had already given up any hopes for reversal.

WHY THEY BELIEVED THE PROCESS WORKED

Those involved with the closures at UR believed the process worked because the administration made a convincing case to act, paid attention to the process, made a definitive decision, and spread the impact among disciplines. They also said that the characteristics of the departments, such as absence of strong leadership and a small number of faculty and alumni, allowed the cuts to occur.

Action Was Necessary

Many across campus believed that the institution needed to take some significant action. The president, the provost, and the dean worked hard to make the case for drastic closures, which was reinforced by long-term budget problems. The president wrote his first letter to the campus framing the problem, and the provost and the dean repeatedly talked about the financial problems. Said one chair:

I would speculate that there were too many people who were too certain that we had a problem to avoid addressing it. Too much of the leadership—when I say leadership I don't just mean president, provost, dean, [but] I mean the chairs, senior scholars, faculty, influential faculty—too many people knew we had a real problem, and avoidance wasn't an option. . . . People were ready for the change because—of what I refer to the "dark years,"—had gotten bad enough that we knew this place would not be the kind of place that we wanted to continue our careers in the long-term if things didn't change. Once you agree on change, you have won 95% of the battle, because once you all agree on change you can lay out a framework in which you can get to where you need to go.

The president said:

Everything that worked here worked only because the faculty had begun to own the problem and see that there were no easy outs. Had you tried to do this and impose it because you, the administration believes it is true, and the faculty haven't bought into it being the solution, it won't work, . . . unless the faculty sees this as a salvation for the institution. And they won't see it as a salvation for the institution as a first line, but only after a lot of stress. . . . I think the institution was ready, and I don't think you can rush that one. . . . Without faculty support it is going to unravel.

Leaders also had periodically pointed to experiences of peer institutions facing similar problems. According to one academic administrator:

When Yale suddenly woke up and realized they had $100 million in deferred maintenance—that happened at a time just after our faculty understood our local situation—and our faculty went wow. I guess Yale can have financial problems too and then UCLA and the whole California system started buying out faculty and cutting salaries by 10%, which is pretty extraordinary. . . . So that sort of legitimized what we were telling them about our local financial problems. Because they saw other institutions of higher reputation having similar problems . . . we had confirming evidence . . . that this wasn't just something that we had made up.

Attention to the Process

The administration paid careful attention to how they were going to identify programs for closure. They had learned an important lesson from the previous failed attempt. They developed a process that, according to one chair, "was defensible" and "designed not to get derailed." The dean sought to create a process that was convincing, legitimate and accepted by the faculty. One way the three leaders added legitimacy was by providing multiple avenues for faculty involvement and input. Said one academic administrator, "What was done right was bringing a lot of faculty members into the tent for the discussion." The dean said that the 75 individual meetings reassured faculty that they were taking their involvement and ideas seriously. The administration took additional steps to ensure faculty involvement and to keep them informed. They spoke to the CDC, the Faculty Council, and with individual faculty, wrote memorandum, and conducted individual interviews. Many on campus had been involved in the process; they knew there was a fundamental problem and that doctoral programs were going to be closed to cope with this long-term problem.

A Definitive Administrative Decision

Many said the process worked because the administration did not publicly propose a tentative solution and offer the decisions for debate. They worked to get campus agreement on the problem, on the parameters of the solution, and on the process. Once they accomplished these elements, the only remaining task was to identify programs for termination, something the administration believed only it could make, otherwise the process would get derailed. The administrators believed that the faculty could not make the hard decisions because they didn't have the structures to do so. The president said:

We didn't put out any trial balloons. For example, . . . we didn't go to people and say, this is what we are thinking of doing, what do you think about it? Our view was that asking that question in the tentative invited the collapse of the process. The people who didn't like the outcome would mobilize all their forces in a way that would have critically undermined the ability to finally execute the plan that you tentatively announced. So . . . people knew that we would be making the decision as the administration. . . . In some respects it is a little bit hard-ball, but our sense was that this was the only way we were going to get this through and make it stick.

Balancing the Impact

Many people noted that the decision makers seemed to take into account the diversity of disciplines which they would close. A chair in an affected unit said, the decision makers "maintained a balance among the disciplines—natural science, social science and the humanities; they did not ditch any one area so it would completely disappear off the face of the map."

Board Support

Without the backing of the Board, many thought those people opposing the decisions would have had an outlet through which they could appeal. The administration intentionally sought board approval to prevent, what one person called, "an end-run." The Board also helped fund the initial costs by allowing the institution to spend its endowment capital, and the board chair gave the campus a $10 million dollar gift to implement the plan.

Characteristics of the Departments

Some characteristics of the departments closed may have contributed to the closing or refocusing of their doctoral programs. One chair said, "I think in the end they did the ones that they thought they could get away with [suspending]." Two of the four departments that had their doctoral programs cut had novice leadership. Other departments, whether lead by a new chair or not, were noted for not having strong leadership. A chair of a non-targeted program said:

They were departments that were rather poorly led and they were basically very vulnerable because they hadn't made a very good case for continuing. They all had problems, absolutely no doubt about that.

One department was likened to a dysfunctional family in which the current chair was unable to help create a common scholarly direction or even get faculty to work together. Some of the units had multiple faculty vacancies, thus they did not have many faculty to resist the decision. For example, the Comparative Literature Department had two openings and the Department of Anthropology, at the time it was closed, had numerous vacancies.

Some of the programs were relatively isolated from other units on campus and did not, or could not, form supportive coalitions. In addition to their inability to form coalitions inside the institution, most (except for Mathematics) did not have strong, active alliances outside the campus. For example, when Anthropology was closed the year previously, the faculty contacted their professional association and the response was, according to one faculty member from the department, "isn't it lovely that no one lost their jobs." Many of the programs were also small or relatively new and had not produced a substantial number of alumni who might become organized. This situation was different in Mathematics where they had produced numerous graduates, many of whom were connected to the scholarly mathematics and physics community that became quickly agitated.

EFFECTS AND RESULTS

This section explores the results, impact, and effects of the process at UR. It highlights the anticipated as well as the unintended consequences that led to both positive and negative influences.

Anticipated Results and Effects

The intended goal of the Renaissance Plan was to put the institution on solid financial ground through a reduction in faculty and a reduction in the number of students to increase student body quality and lower the tuition discount rate. A year and a half after the Renaissance Plan was unveiled the college met its target goal of 310 faculty from a starting point of over 340 and a high of approximately 360 faculty. Much of the attrition came from faculty in the targeted programs. For example, Anthropology, a department whose graduate program was cut the year prior to the Renaissance Plan then had five faculty members down from eight, Linguistics went from eight to three faculty after five left following the closure of its Ph.D. program for "credible university jobs," according to one faculty member. The Department of Modern Languages, where comparative literature was housed, lost three faculty members. Most of the faculty who left did so as a direct result of the cuts because they "decided this isn't the place for me," according to a faculty member. Non-targeted units also lost faculty through normal, expected attrition.

To reduce tuition discounting, the administration hoped to recruit more talented students who would be more willing and able to pay a larger proportion of their own tuition. Two indicators, student quality and the tuition discounting numbers, told administrators that they were making progress.

Student quality went up the first two years of the plan. SAT scores (not re-centered) of admitted students, a campus consensus indicator of quality, jumped by 100 points the first year of the plan and the SAT scores of all applicants rose 35 points. That latter point suggested to many that lower quality students no longer saw UR as a viable option and self-selected themselves out of the applicant pool. The tuition-discounting index moved down, but only by a few percentage points. Although the current administration believed this indicator suggested early progress, they expect changes to the tuition-discount ratio to occur over a five to ten year period.

Overall, most of the faculty and the administrators are pleased with the results of the Renaissance Plan. One chair said:

The Renaissance Plan enjoys widespread faculty support. They don't stand up and vote on this on a regular basis, but if you talk to people almost all the people in the strongest departments will tell you we absolutely had to do something and this was the right thing to do.

Positive Unintended Consequences

In addition to the primary goal of reducing the number of faculty and increasing student quality, the institution saw a series of secondary positive results. Administrators, department chairs, and faculty leaders noted that the process revitalized the Mathematics department ("if you can get re-energized by getting hit over the head with a two by four," said one administrator wryly). The department now has more linkages with other departments and revamped its undergraduate courses to better meet the needs of the students from other programs.

Part of the plan was to recruit higher quality students. The effect of more talented students on campus many believed has created a renewed excitement in undergraduate teaching. For instance, they noted that faculty are more enthusiastic about teaching undergraduates because the undergraduates are interested, curious, and invested in their own learning.

For the units that lost doctoral programs, interdisciplinary graduate programs have become increasingly important. Both faculty and administrators said that because interdisciplinary programs are the only outlets for some faculty to continue to work with graduate students, they have prospered.

Negative Unintended Consequences

An expected negative consequences was that good faculty would leave. Many agreed that often the faculty who are the highest quality have the strongest desires to work with graduate students. By closing doctoral programs, the institution was enticing those top faculty to look elsewhere. In some cases the top scholars in their departments left. Mathematics lost some of its bright, young professors before its program was reinstated, according to faculty in that department.

Faculty in the affected departments became demoralized. They had come to Rochester under the assumption that they were going to conduct research and mentor graduate students, and, by cutting their Ph.D. programs, the institution was taking, what one administrator called, "their lifeblood." The dean said:

It was the second class status suddenly that is associated with not having a Ph.D. program. It was a slap in the face. It is a vote of no confidence in the department. That is tough to swallow for a faculty [in those departments] . . . That was what we were shooting for.

To compound the problem, many faculty and department chairs, especially in the affected units, said the administration did not offer adequate support to the faculty in the targeted programs. For example, they did not work to smooth the transition to an undergraduate only program. One of the reasons for the lack of support may have been because the administrators wanted faculty to voluntarily leave the institution as a central step in faculty reduction. Nevertheless, the inaction of the administration left many feeling isolated and dejected.

Both faculty and administrators noted that the institution faced severe negative publicity. Said the dean: "we knew it would happen, [but] we probably underestimated the severity of the public relations. We were prepared for it but didn't realize how long-lasting it would be." Part of the negative publicity was the result of the fallout around mathematics. The institution also faced continuing negative publicity from scholars connected to the mathematics community even after the program was reinstated. Because of the negative publicity, a few graduate programs had an enrollment decline.

There were no discernible difference among the effects and results noted by various sub-groups on campus. The only difference, already touched upon, was that faculty and chairs in the affected units felt downtrodden because the administration did not help them with the transition to an undergraduate-only department.

EXPLORING THE CASE THROUGH FRAMES

The political, symbolic, human resources, and structural frames, in that order, shed light on the process at UR and differentiate it from the processes at Maryland and at Oregon State.

Political Frame

The political frame explains most of what occurred at UR. It was a campus where resources were scarce, that was comprised of varying interest groups, that had leaders who were concerned about coalitions, and tried to make decisions that would be implemented in a politically contentious environment. Rochester had past attempts at program discontinuance undone for political reasons as administrators at the time could not develop the needed support and opposing coalitions were able to derail the decisions. The leaders of the current change initiative approached their task very much from a political perspective, with a particular understanding that they would have to form supportive coalitions. Their charge was to develop, what one chair called, a "defensible" process. Three political elements were especially important to success at Rochester: forming supportive coalitions, keeping opposing coalitions from derailing the process, and making politically safe decisions.

The dean, the provost, and the president worked to develop a supportive relationship specifically with four groups: the Council of Department Chairs (CDC), the Faculty Senate, the Faculty Council, and the Board of Trustees. The president, dean, and provost involved the chairs in crafting the process and identifying criteria and measures of program quality and productivity, as well as keeping its members informed of progress along the way. The president, the dean, and the provost also believed that board support was key because the trustees had the power and authority to overturn any decisions related to program termination, and the board was needed to provide the new funds necessary to launch the Renaissance Plan. The other two formal campus governance groups, the Faculty Senate and the Faculty Council, were not active players in the process. Nevertheless, the dean, provost, and president kept them abreast of the process, asked for their input, and requested information that facilitated the process. The leadership also spent a significant amount of time talking with and working to build supportive relationships with informal campus leaders. They involved about 20 faculty leaders, outside of the department chair structure, in what the provost called a "rump cabinet" to advise the process.

The leadership also crafted the process to ensure that decisions were not viewed as merely political. They foreclosed potential rallying points by using already accepted productivity and quality criteria; confirmed the data collected with chairs and accepted suggested modifications; developed opportunities for individual faculty members to contribute through e-mail, the 12 interview questions and the individual interviews; and involved equal numbers of faculty from all departments (three faculty from each department). Finally, the administrative leaders took away opportunities for appeal by getting the trustees on board. Said one department chair:

They did not propose a solution and put it up for debate. They got everybody to agree on what the problem was. They got everybody to agree on the parameters of a solution, and then they developed a solution and said this is it. I don't think you can put a proposed solution up for debate . . . because the debate is entirely predictable [that no decision will be rendered].

One potential stumbling block in the process centered on who was to make the decisions that identified programs for closure. The dean, the provost, and the president invested significant time and energy ironing out this potentially rancorous decision. They worked to convince faculty in the individual interviews, in meetings with the CDC and with the Faculty Council that they, as administrators, were in the best position to decide, and that voting or a faculty committee would not result in the needed decisions.

Third, the three leaders made decisions that were politically low risk. One chair commented that they selected programs "that they thought they could get away with." The programs identified for discontinuance were those that were lacking strong unit leadership or had novice leaders, were equally distributed across the four areas of the college, had faculty vacancies or low numbers of faculty, and had small numbers of students and alumni, all of which made it difficult for those upset about the decisions to form influential coalitions.

The political lens helps explain why campus leaders were unable to follow through on their decision to close the Ph.D. program in Mathematics. First, campus leaders did not foreclose potential rallying points. For example, part of their plan included replacing tenure-track faculty with untenured instructors teaching service courses. An element that one person described as "tapping into a raw wound." Second, departmental leaders in mathematics were able to form potent coalitions both on and off campus. Mathematics was a large department with faculty who were well connected in academic circles and had many alumni working in the discipline. Department leaders also obtained the support of their professional society, secured letters from Nobel laureates, and generated highly visible coverage in the national press, which was especially was powerful at a time when the university that was working to recruit more academically talented undergraduates.

Symbolic Frame

The symbolic frame focuses on leaders providing meaning to set direction, and creating beliefs and faith (Bolman & Deal, 1991), perspectives that illuminate the UR process.

To generate commitment for closures the president used much of the good will accorded to a newly appointed CEO, and the dean benefited from his rift with the past administration, which was viewed as "a mark of protest against the prior administration" and gave him "integrity with the faculty."

The leaders framed the challenge facing the institution in ways that gained an institutional commitment and set the future direction. They defined and named the problem. Although many on campus were aware of some of the issues, the actions of leaders sent "a very important signal to the faculty that the president could come in [and] analyze the problem. . . . That set the stage." They articulated the problem in a way that was congruent with faculty values, enhancing academic standards by focusing on the decline in the quality of students. At the same time, they focused the campus' attention on the stress associated with long-term budget difficulties, such as the continuous belt-tightening, the mid-year budget adjustments, and the hiring and salary freezes. The leaders articulated the problems frequently and consistently. The dean said that he spent much of his time "trying to convince the department chairs that this was not something made up," and one of the first communiqués from the new president focused on the problems at hand. Campus leaders also generated energy by focusing on the similar struggles Yale, UCLA, and other top-tier institutions were having. One academic administrator said that "legitimized what we were telling them."

The leadership then broadly determined a solution and framed it in a way that was acceptable to the faculty and department chairs and that would generate excitement. The problems and the potential solutions were articulated in a way consistent with the values of a research faculty. The leaders spoke generally about determining steps to reduce the financial press departments were feeling, which included both bringing in more academically talented students who could pay more of their own tuition and building on campus strengths, which meant reducing a number of weaker Ph.D. programs, but they did not give specifics as to how many programs or which ones.

In addition to gaining a commitment to close programs, symbols also helped move the process along. The $10 million donation by the board chair, as one department chair said, "buys a lot of credibility with the faculty." The leaders also intentionally titled their strategies the Renaissance Plan, a label that signifies rebirth and renewal. Finally, the dean and provost spent a significant amount of energy collecting valid and reliable data. However, the data was not used so much to compare departments as the dean already had a hunch as which ones would be named, but collected this data so the process would not be viewed as simply political. Collecting objective data may have been more important symbolically than instrumentally in identifying programs for elimination.

Human Resources Frame

The human resources frame helps to understand the reasons behind leaders accommodating students from the affected programs. Leaders held an open meeting for graduate students in the affected programs to explain the Renaissance Plan, assured them support until graduating, and offered transfer assistance, including paying for application fees.

Structural Frame

The structural frame illuminates the processes used at UR to develop a system of checks and balances to catch any mistakes that might derail the process. Leaders periodically took their findings to the three decision-making groups on campus: the CDC, the Faculty Council and the Faculty Senate. Here they tested their hypotheses and sought confirmation for their findings.

Beyond this element, the structural frame contributes little to understanding the nuances of the UR process. Although similar to OSU in that the president, the dean, and the provost argued that they should make the final decisions, the structural frame does not illuminate their rationale. Administrators did not make the decisions because their roles dictated what they do (structural frame), but because they were the ones politically able to make and implement the hard decisions.

The final case, Kent State University, is presented in the next chapter. Already strong themes are emerging across the UMCP, OSU, and UR processes. The situation at Kent State varies somewhat, raising additional questions but also reinforcing insights appearing across the sites.

NOTES

1. The College was the largest of six colleges at the University of Rochester and the only one dealing with program closures. It was created in a 1994 merger between the College of Arts and Sciences and the School of Engineering and Applied Sciences and is responsible for the bulk of undergraduate education and much of the non-professional graduate education. It holds a separate endowment.

2. Programs were not officially terminated but rather suspended, a technical term in the State of New York that does not require state permission and leaves open the door for reinstatement.

CHAPTER 5

Kent State University: A Matter of Circumstances

In the early spring of 1996, following a series of conversations, the Dean of the College of Education, the program coordinator of the Counseling Psychology program, and the chair of the department housing that program announced the college's decision to discontinue the Ph.D. program in Counseling Psychology. This decision effectively terminated the Counseling Psychology program because the doctoral degree was the only one offered by the program. However, this decision did not lead to the closure of the Department of Adult, Counseling, Health and Vocational Education (ACHVE) that housed the program. This decision eventually was formally supported by the department's faculty, the campus' Education Policies Council, the Faculty Senate, and the institution's board of trustees, where it passed with little discussion. On September 19, 1996, the Ohio Board of Regents voted unanimously to discontinue the Ph.D. program in Counseling Psychology at Kent State University (KSU).

THE PLAYERS OF CAMPUS GOVERNANCE AND DECISION MAKING

KSU is a unionized institution with a strong history of faculty governance. Within the College of Education, most decisions are made collectively by faculty and the dean. At the time of the closure, *the dean* had been a college administrator for 16 years and had developed a strong working relationship with the faculty through constant attention to process and extremely open discussion. For example, each month she produced a communiqué that informed the faculty of the major college issues, news, and events and included a 10 to 15 page cover-article written by her. College-wide decisions typically began with small conversations among her, some faculty, program coordinators, and department chairs most closely affected by the decision. The dean then brought all interested faculty into the conversation. Sometimes decisions were made informally; other times, they became part of a formal decision-making process in the *College Advisory Council (CAC)*.

The college is organized into three large departments, each with a chair. Each department, in turn, is comprised of academic programs that number, on average, three per department. Departmental leadership includes the *department chair* and the *program coordinators*, who are the faculty leaders responsible for the management of their programs, with particular responsibility for staffing, scheduling, and collecting accreditation documentation.

The Education CAC is composed of three faculty elected from each of the three academic departments. Decisions made in the CAC relate to college academic and curricular matters, including creating or discontinuing academic programs or making substantial changes in academic offerings. CAC decisions are then passed to the *Educational Policies Council (EPC)*, the primary institution decision-making body concerned with academic policy issues. Created by the Faculty Senate charter and by-laws, this body is composed half of administrators and half of faculty, some of whom are elected senators and others whom are appointed. The EPC is the key campus-wide decision-making body on academic issues. A Faculty Senate leader noted that rarely does the Faculty Senate overturn decisions made by the EPC.

KSU's *faculty union* is affiliated with the AAUP and concerns itself primarily with issues of process and violations of the faculty contract, including requests for faculty consultation and involvement in decisions that directly affect faculty work and compensation.

THE CONTEXT: ELEMENTS THAT CONVERGE

To begin to understand the process of program discontinuance at KSU, one must be familiar with three elements that converged upon the institution approximate to one another. First, at the time of the closure, state support for higher education was cut. In 1992–93, the university faced an $8 million reduction in its $100 million state budget, and then, two years later, in 1995–96, the university faced a 3% drop in state appropriations. These reductions placed the institution under financial duress, requiring faculty hiring freezes, increasing class size, postponing renovations, and reducing the number of staff positions. A faculty member noted a few years later: "We are still digging out of some of the cuts we dealt with. There was a period we couldn't pay our phone bill; it was ridiculous."

Second, at the same time, the college had to cope with a centrally devised early retirement program to encourage senior faculty members to retire and be replaced with new, younger (and cheaper) faculty. The budget problems, coupled with the early retirement program, meant that the institution could not replace all of the retiring faculty, because in many cases, the vacated lines were held to save money.

Finally, the Ohio Board of Regents, the statewide governing body, was actively discouraging growth in Ph.D. programs and pressuring institutions to examine graduate programs and related expenditures. They wanted to encourage public universities only to support select Ph.D. programs. The Regents in 1996 initiated a formal, statewide review of nine Ph.D. programs. Two programs at KSU, English and History, were identified through the review process to no longer receive state money, thus placing the burden on the institution to either fully fund the programs or discontinue them.

Closing a Ph.D. Program in Theatre

Although the focus of this case is on closing Counseling Psychology, KSU, in an earlier process, discontinued its Theatre doctoral program. Although not explored in the same depth, this process is illustrative of the discontinuance process.

Theatre closed its doctoral program in 1992. Accompanying the departmental vote to no longer offer the Ph.D. in Theatre was a decision to introduce an MFA, a strategic shift from a terminal degree program emphasizing scholarship (Ph.D.) to one emphasizing performance and production (MFA). This recommendation passed with little fanfare in the institution's Education Policy Council, the Faculty Senate, the institution's Board of Trustees and the Ohio Board of Regents, where it was unanimously approved in September 1993.

Prior to the closure, the number of Theatre doctoral students had dropped to eight; the program had a low student completion rate, and there were only two faculty running the Ph.D. program. Students had difficulty finding enough faculty to sit on their dissertation committees and if an individual professor took leave or went on sabbatical, the program was "basically put on hold," as noted by one departmental faculty member.

The provost, because of the $8 million cut from the institution's 1992–1993 state budget and increasing pressure from the regents, pushed Theatre to consider dropping its Ph.D. and developing the MFA. Some of the faculty believed their Ph.D. program might not survive an external Regents' review and that by trading it for an MFA, they might still get a positive outcome. Their rationale was that only one MFA program in Theatre, which was at a very expensive private institution, existed in the region; most jobs for theater graduates required an MFA not a Ph.D.; and a majority of its faculty were performance and production oriented. Most of the department's faculty strongly supported the move to an MFA. Once the department had made its decision (eight in favor to two against), its recommendations passed smoothly through the CAC, the Education Policies Council, the Faculty Senate, the university's Board of Trustees, and the Regents.

The primary goal of discontinuing the Ph.D. program in Theatre was to create what the faculty thought of as a more appropriate terminal degree program for their field, the MFA. The intent was not to save money, although if additional funds were available the unit might have not acted or it might have tried to develop both programs. The department accrued several benefits from closing its doctoral program and offering the MFA. First, many faculty within the department believed that this change allowed the department to consolidate and focus its attention and resources (fiscal and human). Second, by the second year of the MFA program, the number of graduate students was nearly double those of the combined final two years of the Ph.D. program. Third, the renewed, narrow focus and the influx of production- and performance-oriented MFA students allowed the school to develop new initiatives, including higher quality productions and increased involvement in regional theater and community outreach. Finally, the program developed stronger ties with other programs within the College of Fine and Professional Arts. Theatre no longer had an outlier graduate program focusing on scholarship in a college with a professional and performance focus.

The results of the closure were not all positive, the process took a personal and demoralizing toll on the doctoral faculty. Additionally, the chair of Theatre was asked to resign by faculty in her department.

THE PROCESS IN COUNSELING PSYCHOLOGY: THE SERENDIPITY OF EVENTS

In 1995–1996, the College of Education was trying to cope with the harsh effects of the institution's early retirement initiative at the same time that the institution struggled with its second budget reduction in four years. Of the college's approximately 90 faculty, 40 took part in the early retirement program over its five years, and the college lost 15 additional faculty through normal attrition during those same years. In total, more than half of the college's faculty left between 1991 and 1996. This situation was called by many a "crisis" for the college.

The effect was that the college could not replace departing faculty on a one-to-one basis. One small program, Evaluation and Measurement, lost all four of its faculty. The School Psychology program went from five faculty to one. The Counseling Psychology program by 1995 had one faculty member, down from five. That program simultaneously had to cope with the deaths of two faculty members as well as losses of a third faculty member through the early retirement program and a fourth who was denied tenure.

The low number of faculty threatened the two counseling programs' accreditation. The American Psychological Association (APA) wrote the follow-

ing about Counseling Psychology in an accreditation review letter to the
university president:

The site visit team assessed the program's principle criterion deficiency to be that of
insufficient faculty for a doctoral program in counseling psychology. Though the program's current director is distinguished by his national leadership . . . he cannot maintain a program of this nature alone.

The college's options were limited. The tight fiscal circumstances forced
the college to make some hard decisions about which programs to rebuild
and which ones to discontinue. The faculty buy-out program had gutted numerous programs and the college had to restore select ones. One of the constraints college administrators faced in rebuilding programs was that a high
percentage of the college's programs were doctoral programs that required
senior scholars who would be qualified to become immediate members of the
graduate faculty. Thus, it had to hire associate rather than assistant professors.

The decision to discontinue programs faced by the college was not intentional or strategic, rather caused by the circumstances and limitations at that
time. One college administrator called it "serendipity." A university administrator said, the program was "closed more for unfortunate or convenient
vacancies in faculty positions as much as anything, [that] and a need to shore
up [other programs]."

A Choice between Two

The choice for the college came down to two programs facing similar situations. Both School Psychology and Counseling Psychology had gone from
five faculty to one, and both needed to replace at least three faculty to run
and sustain a viable and accredited program. Any program with less than four
faculty members would have trouble teaching the needed courses and advising
dissertations, and risked losing its professional accreditation. The loss of accreditation in these fields was extremely threatening because it is necessary
for graduates to be competitive and eligible for employment.

To decide in which program to invest their scarce resources and which to
close, college administrators held many discussions, both formal and informal,
with the faculty remaining in the two programs, the department chair, and
faculty on the CAC. A college administrator said:

[We] challenged people to come up with alternative ways of dealing with the crisis.
We didn't want to have to close anything. We put all the ways of going about this out
on the table before we started to move with some. But in the end, the buck stops with
the dean and that is what happened, when the decision had to be made.

College decision makers recognized the following factors would drive and
shape their decision-making process:

- Counseling Psychology enrolled approximately 60 Ph.D. students; had nearly a 100% placement rate for its graduates and two applications for each admissions opening. The focus of its program was on clinical adult cases (making it less central to the college's child-centered mission) and only offered doctoral degrees, requiring senior faculty. Most of its graduates left the immediate area, and similar programs existed on campus in Clinical Psychology and off-campus at another near-by university.
- School Psychology had approximately 30 doctoral students and 30 educational specialist students, allowing the newly hired to be a mix of senior and junior faculty. It focused on children and was central to the children-centered mission of the college. Most of its graduates took posts in local school districts.
- Counselor Education, another program within the department, was moved into ACHVE in 1992 in order for it and Counseling Psychology to share resources to offset the effects of budget reductions. The close proximity and the competitive relationship created tension between the two programs. In the words of one college administrator Counselor Education "wanted to see Counseling Psychology go." Some faculty described the source of the rivalry as not only related to fiscal constraints but also because counseling psychologists in many ways viewed themselves as superior to counselor educators. The tension lead to what one administrator called "irreconcilable differences" between the two programs. When the college proposed to discontinue Counseling Psychology, the Counselor Education faculty offered little support for the program or for the remaining individual Counseling Psychology faculty member.

Over the course of the many conversations the dean initiated in the college, it became clear that Counseling Psychology was not going to receive the needed resources or an infusion of new faculty. The responsibility for running a doctoral program in Counseling Psychology would have been too great for one faculty member. The program coordinator, who was the only remaining faculty member in Counseling Psychology, was said to eventually agree that the program would be better discontinued than struggling along. (He declined to be interviewed for this study.) This admission allowed the dean to move forward. A college administrator said:

The program coordinator got so hopeless that they were not going to be able to build a viable Counseling Psychology program—so concerned about accreditation and how to be faithful to the students we had—that at some point he said we just can't go on this way. And when that was said, the dean moved forth pretty quickly saying we are going to get rid of the program.

Closing programs that are of high quality and demand such as the Counseling Psychology program at KSU are unexpected and unlikely on most campuses. Many believed things like this are not suppose to happen. One college administrator said:

It is an absolutely superb program. It is one thing to phase out a program that is weak and falling away. And it is another thing to phase out one that has some stature. . . .

It was one of the best [programs in the college]. It had some of our very best students. The students who left the program were going into superb jobs and they were all hired. . . . It is tough. It just isn't logical. But when you are faced with having to come down in size and you have way too many students for the number of faculty, the worse thing [to do] is to wait too long.

The program was placed on the table because of circumstances and not as a result of some intentional strategy. A university administrator said:

The Counseling Psych. [closure] was a result of fiscal necessity and really a question of priorities. I don't want to say importance, because Counseling Psych. was a very strong one. But it was not a decision that in the best of times would have been made. The ideal would have been for us to continue to offer a full array of programs in the College of Education.

After the sole faculty member conceded, the CAC discussed the situation and gave the dean its support. Because of the continued widespread discussion by the college's faculty, department chairs, and the dean, the decision to close the Counseling Psychology program did not come as a surprise. One college administrator said:

In a general sense everybody knows what is generally going on. The department chair played a major role . . . and the college advisory council had a major role. This was a process that involved faculty all the way along. I mean the word was out. You didn't need to make an announcement, except when it was final, because we discussed it at the department level and at the college level in these councils and of course the students were informed.

One option that they did not pursue was to discontinue both programs. The college could have decided to close both, but many believed that School Psychology was important to the child-centered mission of the college and made important contributions to the Special Education program.

A formal announcement was made to the students in the program by letter and at a special meeting organized by the program coordinator and the chair to discuss the transition for the students.

After the Decision

Students in the affected program were upset about the closure and worried about being able to finish their degrees in an accredited program. They collected signatures on a petition, which they gave to the provost, and they hired a lawyer. They were concerned about receiving degrees from an unaccredited program. Additionally, the students held a strong emotional attachment to their program. One administrator noted students had a "great deal of anger and probably fear." To address student concerns, the college administrators, the chair and the remaining faculty member met with the students numerous times and had a couple of meetings with the students' lawyer to talk about their concerns. The college administration and the remaining faculty member worked with the American Psychological Association (APA) to secure continuing accreditation for the doctoral students until they finished their degrees.

The provost made arrangements with the well-respected Clinical Psychology program to transfer the sole Counseling Psychology faculty member. He reassured Clinical Psychology that their budget would not have to support the transferred faculty member. Part of the transfer agreement included a reduction of the faculty member's duties within this new unit. During his first year he had none of the other assignments a new faculty member typically would have. The intent was to help him become acclimated to a new unit and allow him to help move the remaining Counseling Psychology students through the program, a departmental promise made to that program's students.

Beyond the initial student protest, the decision to close the Ph.D. program in Counseling Psychology met with little resistance. A university administrator explained it this way:

The faculty who would have voted against it and tried to rally against it weren't there, except for one and he thought it was time [to close the program] because we were not going to make the commitment to shore it up. And it passed the department . . . and you have got School Psych people voting on it presumably and they are going to benefit and others see they might benefit so there is the politics of benefiting from program discontinuance, as long as it isn't yours.

The decision was swiftly approved by the CAC, the EPC, the Faculty Senate and the University's Board of Trustees, and finally by the Ohio Board of Regents. One college administrator said the EPC "discussion didn't last more than five or ten minutes." Neither the Faculty Senate nor the union became involved. A Faculty Senate leader said of the two processes to close doctoral programs in Counseling Psychology and Theatre:

I don't remember much discussion. These were presented as decisions that had been made with the approval of the faculty in the relative departments and, if the faculty in the departments are willing to go along with the cuts, then there is not much basis for the Faculty Senate to overturn the decision. Basically, we see ourselves as representing the wishes and the interests of the faculty. . . . If there was a strong objection on the part of the faculty to some sort of reorganization there would be a lot of discussion in the Faculty Senate. . . . If the faculty themselves are prepared to go along with the decision . . . there is not really much that happens.

WHY THEY BELIEVED THE PROCESS WORKED

Those involved with the process to close the doctoral program in Counseling Psychology believed the process worked because the decision was a logical step, faculty viewed the outcome as beneficial, the leaders followed a legitimate process, it affected a small number of faculty and alumni, students were given assistance in graduating from an accredited program, there existed a climate of cutbacks, and the process included a high amount of discussion within the college.

A Logical Step

Although painful, everyone interviewed thought the decision to close Counseling Psychology made sense because the college simply did not have the resources and had to make a decision on what to continue and what to abandon. People understood the crunch of the state cutbacks and the limits imposed by the early retirement program. They understood that the college simply could not replace departed faculty and without new faculty, the college could not support all of its programs.

Many Perceived the Outcomes as Beneficial

The closures, rather than be a negative, were viewed by many as beneficial. School Psychology saw new money to replace faculty who had left, and the many other units understood that financial shortfalls would not have to be made off of their own backs. The financial flexibility created by the closures gave the dean some leverage for reinvesting in college priorities. The provost said:

The dean and the faculty have got to believe that they will have some opportunity to invest savings themselves. It is not a matter of cut, cut, cut, but it is a matter of yes there may be some reductions . . . but also we will have an opportunity. We will get some benefit out of it. . . . I think there has to be incentives for making the tough choice at the unit level even if it is not their idea . . . if you really want this to work.

The remaining Counseling Psychology faculty member recognized that he simply could not run a one man doctoral program adequately. The dean and the provost worked to intentionally create a good opportunity for the remaining faculty member. They did not want to put him into a "deadwood setting," but rather "into a vibrant setting," according to one College of Education administrator. The dean later noted that the out-placed professor enjoyed continued career advancement and satisfaction in his new department.

Affected a Small Number of Unconnected Faculty

The decision did not have a negative effect on many faculty. Only one faculty member in Counseling Psychology was affected and he was transferred to a stronger unit in another college. The process minimally affected most of the campus. One college administrator reflecting on the closures in both Theatre and Counseling Psychology said:

These were relatively bloodless changes. . . . No faculty member lost a job. Only one in Counseling Psych was transferred. But it was apparent that most faculty would view, at a minimum, that he lost nothing by it. And I think there would be many who would think that he actually gained by it, because the Department of Psychology is one of the premier departments and sets of programs at the university.

The single faculty member, even if he wanted to, could not easily rally other faculty to support him, especially others who were benefiting from the change. An education administrator noted:

Part of it was we did not have a faculty that was championing the cause, so therefore they were not gaining support from other faculty members for their effort. . . . If you had 4 or 5 faculty members whose jobs were on the line that makes for a lot more tension, dissent, [and] anxiety on the part of the faculty.

Neither was the remaining faculty member well connected with other faculty or with the Faculty Senate. He most likely could not gain support for his cause. One College of Education administrator commented: "Nobody cared enough to fight for it. It was very isolated and unto itself. . . . If you are a stand alone and you are small—50 students and a faculty—doesn't make a very formidable force for preservation."

The Process Was Legitimate

The campus operating assumption was as long as those affected by it accepted the decision and the processes used to reach the decision followed agreed-upon procedures, the decision would not attract senate or union attention. One senator said:

It is really very rare for that kind of decision [one that is overwhelming supported by the faculty] to be overturned in my experience. Questions get asked, but unless there is a solid core of faculty who are willing to fight publicly to preserve the program, it tends to go the way of "old flesh."

The union did not become involved because the processes included faculty participation in key decisions. Possibly more importantly, it did not produce any grievances. A union leader said:

I don't think it became a significant issue for us. . . . There was proper consultation and what we were concerned about was that the proper governance agencies, like the faculty senate in particular and other appropriate committees [were involved]. I mean the local faculty and the college advisory council were properly consulted and were agreeable to those things.

Attended to the Needs of People

Students were allowed to complete their degrees and even given additional support and attention that otherwise would not have been offered. The college showed "the utmost commitment to ensuring that the students were treated right. We put them right at the top," said one college administrator. Through the ensuing dialogue, faculty and students believed they were involved in the process and informed about what was happening. One administrator noted:

You really need to attend to the people who are affected by the closing. I think that was probably the key as to why this was not more traumatic than it was. Somehow, you need to take care of your faculty and somehow you need to help students. . . . I think it was our attention to people that probably reduced the opposition on campus and the pain that people experienced, and they experienced a tremendous amount of pain.

External Pressure

The Ohio Board of Regents was pressuring public institutions to re-think their graduate program offering, which helped faculty realize that retrenchments were real and that they might be faced with some more difficult and externally motivated cuts in the near future. One college administrator said, "We were under a mandate to make absolute budget reductions, and so the need and the [pressure from the] surrounding environment was understood."

Additional elements such as the duplication of programs at other local institutions, and the lack of vocal alumni may have played a facilitative role. Counseling Psychology alumni were either ambivalent about the closures or did not exist in sufficient numbers to influence the process. Most alumni left the area upon graduation and those remaining did not protest the decision.

Constant Discussion within the College

Finally, many believed the frequency and abundance of discussion about the problems and potential options available to the college facilitated the process. The dean ensured that the conversation was inclusive, ongoing, and extensive. She believed that the best decisions were made when a high number of people with different interests and perspectives are involved throughout the decision-making process.

Similarities to Closing the Ph.D. in Theatre

Although the focus of this case is on closing the Counseling Psychology doctoral program, similar patterns emerged from the Theatre discontinuance process. First, the change made sense to the majority of departmental faculty and they saw an immediate benefit to closing the Ph.D. program (and creating an MFA). Second, the closure negatively affected only a small number of Ph.D. faculty, two as compared to ten MFA faculty. Third, the two Ph.D. faculty did not form opposing coalitions inside or out of the unit. Finally, the doctoral program produced a small number of alumni who were not vocal about the closures. One departmental faculty member said, "closing it made little more than a ripple."

EFFECTS AND RESULTS

Most people involved in the process of closing the Counseling Psychology program, however painful, thought it was ultimately beneficial for the college (and even for the transferred faculty member). The faculty and administrators interviewed tended to share the same perspectives on the results of this process on the College of Education and on the institution. There were no discernible differences between any sub-groups.

Anticipated Results and Effects

The primary reason for discontinuing the Counseling Psychology doctoral program was to reallocate scarce resources and fill vacant faculty positions in units that were gutted. The positive intended effect was that the college was able to shore up, some of its programs. For example, it used some of the reallocated money to fill School Psychology vacancies.

Positive Unintended Consequences

An unexpected positive outcome was that the Counselor Education program blossomed, as it was no longer a second-class citizen within the department. One academic administrator said:

Our Counselor Ed. program has gotten stronger. It has gotten more resources. It was ranked in the top 20 in *U.S. News & World Report*. . . . And I think it has happened because we used to have tension [with Counseling Psychology that is now gone]. . . . That program has been able to become more cohesive and develop a stronger identity as a program. And I think it has happened because its competitive sister or brother is not there anymore.

A second unintended positive outcome was a higher graduation rate for Counseling Psychology students, because of the extensive outreach the department provided to its displaced students. A college administrator said:

I think we would have had more ABDs had we just continued the program. . . . We have supported it because of a concern for these students that, gosh they are really out there without a support group, how can we best provide support to them? We have actually probably carried some students that, were we not in that circumstance, we might have distanced ourselves from. We would not have communicated with them as much. We would . . . not have extended ourselves as much to them.

Negative Unintended Consequences

On the other hand, the college felt some negative effects from the closure. Faculty from other programs had to pick up the slack left by the remaining Counseling Psychology vacancies, creating a drain on their own programs. This effect was that their finite time was spent with Counseling Psychology students and not spending their time with and energy on their own programs' students.

The process of discontinuing programs also was emotionally difficult for faculty. Faculty understood the commitment and investment by their col-league in the closed program. They also were aware of the program's strength and high quality and to have to close a strong unit because of the lack of resources and competing college priorities was difficult. Said a college ad-ministrator: "It is hard for campuses to give up Ph.D. programs. It gives them a great sense of pride. It is hard for faculty, too. . . . These are not fun things to do."

Cutting programs once, even when it is not intentional but rather created by circumstances, is adequate warning to faculty that it can happen again and causes anxiety. One college administrator said: "Every program knows that they too may go. In the sense once you eliminate a program, it shows that you are just not threatening to maintain quality standards, you mean it."

POSTSCRIPT: NO MORE CLOSURES AT KSU

By 1996, KSU had closed two Ph.D. programs—Theatre and Counseling Psychology. At the conclusion of the second closure the institution stopped its internally driven efforts to realign programs and reallocate funds. The closure of Counseling Psychology occurred at the same time the Ohio Board of Regents undertook its formal review of graduate programs in nine areas. The intent of the Regents' review was to reduce duplication in the state across these disciplines. The Regents process caused the campus to stop its own internally driven efforts and focus on the nine programs specified by the Re-gents. The Regents' review actually halted the momentum of KSU's internal review and reallocation, which had already resulted in two closures. The pro-vost said:

This [Regents review] was over an 18-month process. It took all of our energy away from further evaluating maybe some weak links within our own university. There were a couple of other [programs] we thought we would like to look at . . . but it stopped us in our tracks.

In the end, the Regents' process, which had some of the same intent as KSU's own process, might have actually *prevented* the institution from reducing its graduate program array and further reallocating some of its constrained budget. The energy the campus would have spent on reviewing its own programs went toward the forced outside review and the imposed review made any program cuts distasteful. In fact, in some instances, the campus shifted its efforts to protect doctoral programs it thought strong from the Regents review.

EXPLORING THE KSU CASE

The circumstances, rather than an intentional goal set strategically by campus leaders, led to the closing of Counseling Psychology. KSU simply did not have the resources to rebuild a program gutted by deaths, early retirement, and tenure denials. What happened at KSU arose from a situation different from the other three cases and had a rather unlike process (really no intentional process) making the analysis somewhat different.

At KSU, although there was not much of a process so to speak, the four frames helps make sense of what happened and why the process unfolded as it did. The frames most helpful in understanding what occurred at KSU were the political and human resources frames.

Political Frame

The political frame at KSU is helpful in understanding how and why Counseling Psychology was closed (as well as Theatre). What was instructive is not what the leaders did within the political frame, such as building coalitions or keeping opposing coalitions from forming, but what did not occur.

Within the ranks of the College of Education no opposing coalitions formed. This most likely happened for a number of reasons: (1) some of the faculty from other programs within the department and the college saw the closing beneficial to their own circumstances, especially the faculty in School Psychology who were given the reallocated money; (2) the negative results of the closure were extremely circumscribed, affecting only one faculty member who was not released, but transferred into a strong department; and (3) the closed program did not have champions among college administrators, as the program was not strongly aligned with the college's child-centered mission, or did the remaining faculty member have supporters among the faculty because he perpetuated a disciplinary snobbery.

Beyond the college, others within the university did not form opposing coalitions. The key decision-making groups, such as the EPC and the faculty union, viewed the process as procedurally sound. The union did not become involved because there was no violation of the faculty contract and no grievance filed, and the senate did not become involved beyond approving the recommendation because a majority of faculty within the department favored the action. One union leader said:

From the point of view of the AAUP, this was carried through in a legitimate way. There was proper consultation . . . the local faculty and the college advisory council were properly consulted and were agreeable.

Additionally, no external professional organizations or societies rallied to the cause, unlike the case of Mathematics at Rochester. The American Psychological Association (APA) was concerned with program accreditation and quality assurance, not with reversing the termination decision. Students and former students did not form a strong enough opposition to derail the closing. Alumni were few in number and most, upon completion of their degrees, became disconnected from their program. Current students, although they did attempt to prevent the decision by hiring a lawyer and collecting signatures, were unable to generate adequate support or build a strong enough alliance to reverse the decision.

The closure of the doctoral Theater program had similar characteristics. The MFA faculty saw an immediate benefit. The Ph.D. faculty did not generate adequate support for their program. The cause did not have a college champion, as the program was a scholarly program in a performance and professionally focused college, and neither the senate nor the union chose to become involved.

Human Resources Frame

The dominant characteristic of the human resources perspective is attention to the needs, experiences, and feelings of the people involved with or affected by the discontinuance. At KSU, three elements can be explained through this frame. First, the dean, the chair, and the provost were concerned that the remaining faculty member be placed in a positive situation after the program termination decision. As part of the move, the provost negotiated an agreement with his new department that the Counseling Psychology faculty member would have reduced responsibilities in his new unit so he could become acclimated and help students get through the pipeline. The provost also guaranteed the new department that he would provide the necessary financial support for this new person.

Second, in addition to attending to the needs of the remaining faculty member, leaders cared about what happened to the students in the program. College leaders as well as the sole faculty member worked extensively with students to smooth their transition. They secured continuing program accreditation so students would graduate from a professionally recognized program; they worked with students to help them finish their programs and find chairs in other programs for dissertations; they listened to student concerns; and they went to great lengths to demonstrate that they cared about the students.

Finally, the dean and other college administrators created an environment that allowed people to be involved in the process. They provided ample opportunities for faculty to be part of the conversation, to understand the challenge facing the college, and to explore options. The dean understood that faculty were good problem solvers and sought their input and advice to help reach the most beneficial decision given the stringent constraints within which they had to work.

Structural Frame

The structural frame highlights the roles of different college and campus decision-making bodies involved in the process and their roles as dictated by formal and informal campus policy. For the decision to become final, it had to be accepted by the CAC, by the EPC, and the senate, in addition to the campus Board of Trustees and the statewide Board of Regents. In addition, the faculty union could also have become involved if someone filed a procedural grievance. These bodies acted as a checks and balance system to ensure faculty rights and involvement, a legitimate process, and an appropriate decision given the circumstances.

In the KSU case, it is of interest to note the lack of involvement by the union and senate, rather than their involvement. These governance groups did little except sign-off on the decisions. Although presented with opportunities, they did not play a central role because the process to identify Counseling Psychology for termination was legitimate from their perspectives as faculty were adequately consulted, the affected faculty agreed to the final decision, and the process did not violate any collective bargaining agreements. The same was true in Theatre.

Symbolic Frame

The symbolic perspective provides an additional explanation to the actions of college administrators. First, the administrative leaders helped frame the conversation to focus on the benefits of reallocated resources. Closures are a difficult undertaking, but they believed the process could be made smoother by articulating the benefits to those who influence the decision.

Second, academic leaders sent strong messages to the faculty within the department and the institution when they facilitated the move of the remaining faculty member into what was called a "vibrant" department. Rather than suggest that the Counseling Psychology faculty member remain in his old department (although no longer in his program), the dean and the provost worked to have him transferred to one of the most respected units on campus. The symbolic message was that the institution was concerned for this individual and wanted to ensure that he would end up in a place that would be beneficial. At the same time, by removing him from his old department, they created an important psychological distance between those who made the closure decision and would benefit from it and the individual who was negatively affected.

CHAPTER 6

Leading, Governing, and Deciding: Key Elements in Program Elimination

The preceding chapters tell the stories of four research universities that closed academic programs. The four chapters began to answer two questions: How have institutions gone about the process of cutting academic programs? And what were the effects of the program discontinuance process on the institution? Although leaders at each institution charted their own course, looking across the cases can be insightful for a better understanding of the process of program closure. This chapter continues the investigation comparing and contrasting the four processes with a closer examination of (1) the contextual issues related to program discontinuance; (2) the influence of leadership, shared governance, and external forces on program discontinuance; (3) the effects and results of the process on the institutions; and (4) the differences between closing academic programs while leaving intact the departmental unit and closing both programs and dismantling the departments that house them.

CONTEXTUAL ISSUES

These four cases strongly suggest that context—the situation and environment in which institutions find themselves, and possibly create—has a profound influence on the closure process. Each of the institutions in this study had felt the pain and frustration of living in environments of financial duress and instability. The University of Maryland at College Park (UMCP), Oregon State University (OSU), and Kent State University (KSU) had faced a series of cutbacks in state appropriations. The University of Rochester (UR), although not state supported, also had a series of financially difficult years as it struggled with balancing undergraduate and graduate enrollments and managing its endowment. A history of financial downturns that created extended lean times led many on all of the campuses to be well aware of the problems facing the institution and attributed their difficult situation to uncontrollable external forces. This understanding and appreciation of the situation prevented those responsible for crafting and leading the process as being seen as the so-called bad guy who called for program reduction.

Second, because of the long-term financial difficulties, institutions engaged in other cost-savings strategies prior to engaging in program reduction. None of the four institutions attempted to close programs as a first step. Their other retrenchment strategies consisted of hiring freezes, mid-term budget adjustments, and the halting of travel and purchasing equipment, among others. These were actions that were painful for the institution, and because the financial troubles were continuous, all institutional stakeholders appreciated the long-term nature of the problems. Institutions began to discontinue programs only after they had attempted other measures to save money and that occurred on the heels of a catalytic event, such as a second wave of reductions in state allocations (UMCP, OSU, KSU) or leadership succession (UR).

On a related point, these institutions closed programs while, at the same time, they were trying to save money through other ways. Program termination did not occur in isolation but was part of a larger financial restructuring strategy at all four institutions. These other steps included not filling vacant positions, reducing administrative costs, and reorganizing administrative units.

These contextual elements provided a framework for program discontinuance. They clearly and indisputably reinforced the belief that something radical had to be done. A chair at UR captured this feeling when he said: "too many people knew we had a real problem and avoidance wasn't an option . . . too many people were ready for the change because of what I refer to as the 'dark years.'" The confluence of these elements appears to be a common and important factor across the four institutions in this study. The financial pressures occurred over a lengthy time and came in steady waves. The institutions already had attempted and exhausted methods other than program discontinuance and the efforts occurred after some type of shock jolted them into action. Program discontinuance was simply part of a larger effort to cope with well-understood, drastic resource constraints.

LEADERSHIP

Leadership, shared governance, and external forces were three elements that were conceptual anchors for this investigation. This section explores the role of leadership across the four cases to focus the investigation. The next two sections give similar treatment to shared governance and external forces.

For this study, I adopted a definition of leadership that focused on those individuals expected to exhibit leadership (Birnbaum, 1992). Leadership is purported throughout much of the literature to be a central element in effecting intentional organizational change. Leaders are thought to do something, or a range of things, to bring about the desired change. The intent of exploring leadership in this study was to focus on the perceptions of key actors and what they did and did not do. In the four cases the important actors who held leadership positions were senior administrators, such as the president, provost, or dean, and formal faculty government leaders, such as the chair of the faculty senate or the faculty comprising key committees. Other noteworthy leaders, such as the chairs of the affected departments, played less central roles, and they were interesting for what they did not or could not do instead of for what they did. Although not entirely consistent across all four cases, the following were readily identifiable patterns.

Administrative Leaders

Administrative leaders involved in the process tended to be the senior administrators such as the president, the provost, and, frequently, the deans. Although the termination processes varied, these leaders tended to play some consistent roles. For instance, they either developed the process as part of their efforts to address their current dilemma or were involved in developing a process at an earlier point that they then followed, such as at OSU. Administrative leaders were the primary architects of the discontinuance processes. All of the leaders who took responsibility for running the closure process enjoyed a high level of widespread trust and had the faith of the campus to take the needed actions. The implications of this good will were that key campus constituencies did not scrutinize their actions for hidden agendas or second-guess their intentions. Most of the administrative leaders tended to be long-term institutional citizens who were well recognized as being above board with a deep commitment to the well being of the institution. Only at UR was the president a newcomer; however, he surrounded himself with other respected campus leaders, a dean, and a provost, who had been at the institution for a significant time.

The actions of these administrative leaders can be organized into four chronological stages. First, leaders launched the initiative; second, they kept it on track; third, they participated in identifying programs for termination; and fourth, they facilitated the transition following the announcements.

Launched the Initiative

One of the most important roles for administrators early in the process was framing the challenges facing the institution or, in the case of KSU, the college. They were the conduits to the environment and interpreted how external events would affect the institution. For example, at UMCP, OSU, and KSU, administrative leaders articulated the implications of the state budget reductions and made the connections between the financial problems and the need for closures. At UR they summarized the long-term financial decline and identified root cause of the difficulties.

At all four campuses, administrative leaders spent significant amounts of time and energy talking with a variety of campus constituents about the problems and potential solutions. Leaders at these four institutions created a campus ethos that called for action; however, they framed the reasons differently— because they had no choice at KSU, for survival at OSU, or for campus enhancement at UR and UMCP. At UMCP and UR the leaders evoked symbols and used terms such as "enhancement" and "renaissance" to tie the program closures to larger institutional goals, helping to create a commitment to the idea of program discontinuance. In contrast, leaders at KSU and OSU framed the challenge as a problem for which there was no easy out.

The way leaders framed the challenge—as opportunity or threat—determined to a large extent campus responses, enabling them to harness institutional emotions to sustain momentum. For example, the process at OSU had repeated referrals to cutting muscle and bone, while the process at UMCP was continually tied to enhancement, and UR linked it to academic rebirth and excellence.

Kept the Efforts on Track

Administrative leaders designed legitimate processes to close programs and then made sure that the campus adhered to those processes. The processes used to develop the termination procedure varied somewhat across the four institutions. At OSU, the process was pre-determined as leaders followed an agreed-upon campus policy. At UMCP and UR, administrative leaders designed processes from scratch but built them upon a foundation of past experience. For example, at both institutions the leaders realized that faculty had to be involved, but the notion of involvement varied. At UMCP, legitimacy centered on faculty being true partners throughout the process and having the final say in a senate vote. At UR, faculty did not expect the final say, but they had to be involved in providing information, shaping the process, determining which types of data were collected and from where, and were able to comment on leaders' interpretation of it. KSU stands out as different because discontinuing Counseling Psychology was not something that the campus set out to accomplish, the role of leaders was not one of planning, designing and implementing, but was one that included building supportive coalitions and focusing attention on the problems and potential solutions.

Leaders at all four institutions developed processes that would enable them to close programs. Leaders created processes that would generate some results and not become derailed along the way, even if it meant not attempting to close programs that would generate the largest savings. This approach helped to increase the probability of accomplishing their objectives.

As part of crafting and adhering to legitimate processes, administrative leaders facilitated campus (UMCP and UR) or college (KSU) discussions about different aspects of the closure process. Because leaders recognized that multiple stakeholders had to be involved, they developed means to facilitate conversations across various interest groups and create a common understanding and appreciation that that would allow the closures to move forward. They created supportive coalitions with various campus stakeholders. At UMCP, leaders sponsored open hearings and interviewed a wide range of people; they visited departments and went to many meetings. At UR, leaders facilitated important conversations through individual interviews and with the Council of Department Chairs. At OSU, although confidential, conversations occurred between the Faculty Consultative Group and president and provost. Conversations at KSU were held informally but frequently with faculty throughout the college.

In addition to facilitating conversations among various groups, administrative leaders at UMCP and UR used a variety of tactics to create alliances with potentially competing interest groups so that they would not derail the process. A common strategy across these four universities was to create opportunities for various stakeholders to contribute meaningfully to the process. For example, at UMCP, leaders asked the Senate Executive Committee to develop the criteria and principles for the process to follow and to be integral players. Administrative leaders involved faculty leadership in collecting data through the summer sub-committees and in developing recommendations through participation on the Academic Planning Advisory Committee (APAC). UMCP leaders also asked influential faculty leaders to be responsible for key elements of the process. For example, they recruited specific faculty to sit on APAC summer sub-committees and on the Programs, Curricular and Courses Committee (PCC) of the senate. At UR, administrative leaders involved the Council of Department Chairs (CDC) in helping them develop the processes used and in identifying measures of quality and productivity. Administrative leaders at UR also formed a supportive coalition with the Board of Trustees.

Neither KSU nor OSU took steps to intentionally build supportive coalitions. Instead, the leaders at those institutions turned their energy to prevent opposing groups from creating alliances, a strategy also used by the leadership at UMCP and UR. All four groups of institutional leaders worked extremely hard at creating what one informant from UR called a "defensible" process. To make their processes defensible, leaders recognized the importance of foreclosing potential points around which opponents might rally. For example, so that the process would not become derailed over a procedural issue that violated campus norms of involvement, the campus leaders made sure there were legitimate opportunities for faculty involvement. Administrative leaders also made tenure a non-issue by finding tenured faculty new academic homes. Even at OSU, where some faculty in the College of Education were laid off, the university later re-hired all who wanted to return.

As other examples of leaders foreclosing potential rallying points, UMCP leaders placed faculty from each of the targeted units on the sub-committees investigating potential implications, and they turned over all of APAC's information to the PCC so that nothing was hidden. They also created an appeals process so that people could make their case against the closures. Leaders ensured opportunities for dissenting voices. As one person said, "they may not have liked the decision, but no one could say they didn't have their say." At UR, administrative leaders closed off opportunities for potential appeals to the trustees by getting the board to commit to the idea of closures and the Renaissance Plan, that way opponents could not gain the support of the board to short-circuit the process. UR leaders also intentionally distributed the closures equally across the various disciplinary groups of the College. No particular field, such as the humanities, took a disproportional hit.

Identified Programs

Administrative leaders at all four institutions played an active role in identifying programs for closure. Although the specifics of how they did this varied depending upon the previously established pattern of campus decision making. At UMCP leaders were participants in the first two sets of recommendations, while at OSU and at UR they made the final decisions. At no campus did administrative leaders divorce themselves from the process or let it proceed in a laissez-faire manner.

The administrative leaders at these four institutions additionally worked to make politically defensible decisions, which meant that any opposition could not find needed leverage points to overturn the decisions. The closed programs at all four campuses tended to have low numbers of faculty, students, and alumni. The units did not have champions on or off campus willing to take up their cause. Departmental leadership tended to be novice or ineffective; their alumni small or dispersed; and their faculty disconnected from campus power circles. Each program did not have adequate political muster to sustain itself. Those against the closures could not rally supportive coalitions that had the power to derail the process. The negative example was the Mathematics program at UR. Their administrative leaders did not foreclose rallying points around which opponents coalesced, and the opposition was able to overturn the decision to close the Mathematics doctoral program.

Facilitated the Transition

The final responsibility common to administrative leaders was that they developed mechanisms to facilitate transition after the termination announcements. At OSU, administrative leaders met individually with each person in the affected programs. They helped faculty and staff understand what was happening and why. They worked with faculty to restructure curricula to compensate for newly created holes. They hired affiliate faculty and provided needed money to expedite student matriculation through the closed programs. Central administrators provided counseling services and employment assistance, giving some junior faculty travel money and assisting with developing their curriculum vitas to make them more marketable. The president also held breakfast meetings with individuals from the targeted programs to prepare people for the upcoming transition.

KSU administrators worked out a deal to transfer the remaining faculty member to a new department, made sure he was moving into a well-respected program, and negotiated reduced responsibilities. College leaders also worked with the accrediting body to ensure that students would graduate with accredited degrees. Finally, they found dissertation chairs for students remaining in the program and gave them support and guidance so that they would complete their degrees.

Although leaders at UMCP and UR did not undertake as extensive steps following the closures as the leaders at OSU and KSU, they still ensured students in the discontinued programs reasonable time to finish their degrees and they did not dismiss tenured faculty. Leaders at all four institutions were concerned about the students in the terminated programs and devised procedures to facilitate their graduation. Doctoral students at UR were also offered assistance with transferring to other institutions, such as the payment of application fees and letters of recommendation. That said, UR administrators did not attend very much to the needs of the faculty in the closed programs, because their original intention was that faculty in those units would chose to leave the institution, thereby reducing the number of faculty.

Faculty Leaders

Faculty played extremely important roles in all of the termination processes. However, what they did and how many were involved in key roles varied across the four universities. For example, at UMCP, faculty played active roles in designing the process, making decisions, investigating implications, and providing a system of checks and balances. They, much like faculty at UR, provided information and helped design criteria to make decisions. On the other hand, a limited number of faculty played leadership roles at OSU, and their primary role was limited to providing advice and helping administrators understand potential implications. Faculty leaders at the four institutions became involved because either they held formal faculty governance positions, or they were widely recognized campus opinion leaders. At all four institutions, faculty leaders provided information and advice and served as a system of checks and balances. At UMCP and at OSU, they additionally helped design the processes used to close programs.

Provided Information and Advice

At each of the four institutions, a key faculty leadership role was to provide information about particular programs and advice to administrative leaders about the implications for the institution's well being—two activities central to identifying programs for elimination. They did this through the summer hearings at UMCP and the individual interviews at UR, through informal conversations at KSU and UR, and via formal governance structures at UMCP, OSU and UR. UMCP and UR also tapped informal leaders through their creation of kitchen cabinets composed of faculty leaders.

Created a System of Checks and Balances

Faculty leaders at all four institutions were central to systems of checks and balances. They explored and articulated the implications of proposed changes, and, in most instances, persuaded administrators to make mid-course adjustments when the proposed closure would have negative institutional results. At UMCP, the checks and balances occurred via the faculty-led summer subcommittees that resulted in three units being removed from the list of recommendations. At OSU, the Faculty Consultative Group (FCG) fulfilled that role. At UR, through the individual interviews, faculty helped administrators catch potential mistakes. At KSU, through the college-level College Academic Council (CAC) and the university-level Educational Policies Council (EPC) and senate, faculty fulfilled this function.

Involved in Designing Processes

At UMCP, faculty leaders were instrumental in developing the process to close academic programs. UMCP's faculty worked in conjunction with administrative leaders and independently to ensure that the process was open and legitimate. For example, leaders on the senate and PCC intentionally structured the voting process so that opponents could not complain about voting on all of the recommendations as a block or about taking the easy votes first and saving the controversial ones for last. They also wrote the PCC report in such as way as to emphasize fairness—the PCC report included arguments both for and against each recommendation. At OSU previous faculty senate leaders played an important role in developing the institution's discontinuance procedures. Although the deans did the initial draft of the process, the faculty senate made modifications and accepted the final version before sending it to the president for final approval.

Affected Unit Leaders

This third group of leaders, those responsible for leading programs that eventually were terminated, may be more notable not for what they did, but for what they did not do. First, the heads of the affected units at all four institutions were unable to or did not form coalitions to support their cause. A notable exception was Mathematics at UR. For example, at UMCP, leaders of some closed departments, such as Recreation, tried to generate the support and involvement of state legislators. However, none of their efforts to develop political support off campus were successful. At KSU, there was only one program faculty member, and he had conceded that closure was imminent so he did not attempt to find allies to save his program.

Second, many of the units that eventually closed were led by novice, interim, or weak leaders, which was widely recognized and pointed out by campus leaders at UMCP, OSU and UR. Some heads were criticized because of their inability to provide leadership at a critical junction. Others, because they were inexperienced, did not understand the gravity of the events occurring and did not mobilize their department or rally adequate support for their plight. Still other leaders, either newly appointed or interim, inherited dysfunctional programs or replaced weak leaders of programs that were already under the gun so that they could not do much to save their marked programs. It is difficult to tell if this pattern was true at KSU given the particular circumstances of that closure.

The exception to this trend was the leadership of the Mathematics department at UR, as departmental leaders were able to prevent the closure of their doctoral program. They played the political game effectively, building supportive coalitions both on and off campus. On campus, they brokered deals with the Physics department, and off campus, they were able to mobilize support from powerful and influential groups, including their professional society (AMS) and high profile scientists such as Nobel Prize winners. They generated negative attention for the campus through major news outlets, such as the Sunday edition of the *New York Times* and *The Chronicle of Higher Education* at a time when the institution was looking to ratchet up its academic prestige and recruit more talented students. Finally, the faculty leaders in math were able to negotiate with university administrators and find a middle ground. In exchange for keeping their Ph.D. program and a few of the taken-away faculty lines, they created more linkages with other units and refocused time and attention to undergraduate teaching. They proposed revenue-neutral modifications that met both their and the institution's needs.

Leadership and Program Termination

The individuals in leadership positions in this study adopted one of two positions. They either worked to bring about program terminations or they worked to prevent programs from being closed. To discontinue programs, leaders were responsible for four primary tasks. They launched the initiative, kept it on track, participated in identifying programs for termination, and facilitated the transition following the announcements. To accomplish these tasks, leaders engaged in a variety of tactics. They helped people make sense of what was occurring and stress its importance by interpreting the environment to make the closures seem inevitable. They also worked hard to gain an institutional commitment to close programs by describing crisis and opportunity. They formed political coalitions, kept opposing alliances from forming, and brokered deals with various interest groups. They took care of the affected students and faculty, and they adhered to institutional norms and rules for making decisions and getting things done.

The task of other groups of leaders, those opposing the closures, was to prevent them from occurring. To do this, they had to form supportive coalitions by calling attention to their plight, framing the impact in terms convincing to potential supporters, and creating linkages with powerful interest groups. Only those leaders who were able to exert enough pressure through forming coalitions either on or off campus were able to force the first group of leaders into negotiations (UR) or remove them from the list of targeted programs (UMCP).

In sum, the leadership associated with closing academic programs is highly political. It requires building coalitions to gain support, but also actively keeping opposing coalitions from forming. That said, it is also highly symbolic, requiring leaders to articulate key issues and manage symbols to stress its importance to the institution in terms of enhancement or survival, gain support, and keep the process moving.

SHARED GOVERNANCE

The second anchor of this study is shared governance, the means through which faculty, administrators, and other campus constituents come together to make institutional decisions. Shared governance both has been celebrated and condemned for its role in institutional decision making (Association of Governing Boards of Colleges and Universities, 1996; Blau, 1994; Rosovsky, 1990). Because decisions to close academic programs were suspected to fall in the overlap area of the responsibilities of many groups, it was important to explore what elements of shared governance influenced the decision-making process. The questions concerning shared governance in this study included: who was involved; what types of decisions were made by faculty, by administrators, and collectively; and to what extent was the process shared? This discussion explores the players involved, their responsibilities and obligations with a particular focus on administrative and faculty roles, and the extent to which governance was shared.

The Players Involved

Although the number of people involved in the governance decisions associated with program termination varied by institution, some common roles are apparent. In all of the cases, central administrators initiated and led the process: at UMCP, the provost was the primary leader; at OSU, it was the president; at UR, the dean and provost led the process, with the president playing a strong and visible role; and at KSU, the dean was the primary leader. In addition to administrators, faculty were involved both through formal governance avenues and outside of them. At UMCP, faculty were involved formally through APAC, PCC, and the senate. APAC invited an additional 120 faculty to participate in their summer sub-committees. Informally faculty were involved through the two sets of open hearings sponsored by APAC and as informants in the multiple data collection processes, such as APAC, the summer sub-committees and PCC. At OSU, faculty involvement was limited to FCG of the senate and, depending upon the college, with helping the deans craft initial recommendations. The confidentiality clause and the short time frame at OSU may have curtailed faculty involvement. At UR, faculty involvement principally occurred through the CDC and the individual faculty interviews. However, administrative leaders invited faculty to become involved at various stages by commenting on documents via e-mail and responding to inquiries such as the 12 questions asked in the interviews. Faculty also were kept abreast and discussed the closure process in the Faculty Senate and the Faculty Council. Finally, the dean invited a select group of faculty leaders to comment on the Renaissance Plan prior to its unveiling. At KSU, faculty were involved through conversations leading up to the decision to close Counseling Psychology. They were also involved in discussions in the CAC. Faculty, beyond the college, approved the decision in both EPC and the senate, two formal governance bodies.

The third group involved was the board of trustees. At all campuses except UR, they played peripheral roles, approving the decisions coming from the institution. At UR, the board played a more active role and approved the ideas put forth in the Renaissance Plan and made the required funding available. They attended a retreat prior to the announcement and provided asked for input and support. Additionally, the board chair gave the institution $10 million for implementation.

Responsibilities and Obligations

This section focuses on the responsibilities and obligations of the two primary groups of actors—administrators and faculty. At UMCP administrators decided to undertake program termination, and they chose to use APAC as the first decision-making body. The provost and the associate provost were the primary leaders, designing the process, determining how to involve key stakeholders, and shepherding it through the institution. They became partners with faculty in making key decisions; however, administrators wrote the two primary reports—*Preserving Enhancement* and *Hard Choices*—the second of which was forwarded to the senate for response.

At OSU, administrators played a much more independent role than at UMCP. Prior to Ballot Measure Five, a committee of deans drafted the procedures that the campus later followed. As the closures began, the president and provost held budget hearings with the deans to craft the initial proposal, and they were the ones who made the final decision. The president made the announcement to the campus, and central administrators and certain deans developed mechanisms to help people with the transition following the closures.

Administrators at UR crafted and led the process. They sold the process to the faculty, conducted the individual interviews, interpreted the data they collected (although they did ask for chair comments on the data), garnered board support, and, in the end, made and announced the final decisions. Also, they intentionally avoided an appeals process, as a definitive decision was their goal because they were worried that open hearings would derail the process.

At KSU, the dean and the department chair framed the challenge to the college. They facilitated conversations within the department and college so as to understand the factors driving the decision. They met with the remaining faculty member and, in the end, facilitated his move to a new department.

The roles of faculty varied by process used and the length of time allotted. At UMCP faculty were active partners with administrators and frequently the leaders of the process. They were asked by the provost to develop criteria and principles for the process to follow. The process began through a joint faculty-administrative standing body (APAC), which was instrumental in designing the process and developing the first two sets of recommendations. Faculty were additionally involved through the summer sub-committees in which 120 faculty investigated the implications of recommended closures. Faculty commented during APAC's open hearings, were involved in PCC's investigation (running and participating in their open hearings), and were responsible for taking the final vote in the College Park Senate.

The role of faculty at OSU was consultative. Rather than making the actual decisions, like the faculty at UMCP, faculty at OSU provided advice to administrative leaders. They helped the administration think through implications and encouraged them to remove some programs on the list. In the end, some faculty felt frustrated because confidentiality limited their roles; one said she felt that her "hands were tied."

Faculty at Rochester, although not the key decision-makers, were highly involved in the process. Through the CDC, faculty who were sitting elected department chairs provided needed information, helped the administration think through issues of quality and productivity and helped shape the process. Informal faculty leaders were the first to see the Renaissance Plan, helping to polish it and test reaction. Individual faculty (one third) were involved in the individual interviews and had other opportunities to participate, of which only a few took advantage.

At KSU, two sets of faculty were involved: those faculty within and outside the College of Education. Within the college, faculty were involved in the discussions surrounding the inevitable closure. Outside the college, faculty were involved through the formal decision-making processes to approve closures, the EPC, and the senate. They also might have become involved through the union if a grievance had been filed.

The *Sharing* of Governance

Common wisdom suggests that shared governance is all about involvement. However, the experiences of these four universities suggest that involvement, as a concept, varies across institutions. Although the amount and types of involvement of the various groups varied by the process used, all of these institutions had an adequate amount of sharing in the decision-making process. At none of the institutions did faculty complain that they had not been involved enough or in legitimate roles. Even though the processes were different and the decision-making roles and responsibilities of faculty varied significantly, as did the roles of administrators, all of the processes met a satisfying threshold of collaboration as determined by the history, norms, and expectations of the campus. For example, at UMCP, faculty and administrators made most decisions jointly through APAC or faculty made decisions independently through PCC or the senate, while at OSU, decisions were made sequentially—administrators passed their recommendations to FCG, who returned their modifications to administrators for the final decision. It is unlikely that either of these processes would be acceptable if attempted at one of the other institutions, but at their home, they were acceptable because they were expected.

The sharing of governance can occur collaboratively, where faculty and administrators sit together to make decisions, but it can also occur sequentially where faculty pass along their decisions to administrators or when administrators pass decisions to faculty for approval. These cases show that both processes are acceptable means of governance depending upon campus expectations and norms. These processes also demonstrate that good governance can occur outside traditional formal processes, but at some point, key institutional decisions must be acted upon by formal governance bodies, such as the senate or its subcommittees.

Shared Governance and Program Termination

The decision-making processes used at the four institutions varied greatly creating different roles for formal faculty governance bodies and creating different expectations for the ways faculty and administrators work together. These termination processes occurred in different time frames, from three months at OSU to almost two full academic years at UMCP; they differed in the number of steps involved; and they differed in who made the final decisions, if decisions were made jointly or sequentially, opportunities for appeals, and the number of people involved. Although the processes varied, they nevertheless were in some form a comingling of faculty and administrators working together to solve a campus-wide problem. Shared governance facilitated the discontinuance process in three common ways.

First, shared governance provided the stage from which administrators could gain a commitment to close programs. Through the bodies of shared governance—APAC and senate at UMCP; senate at OSU; CDC, Faculty Senate and Faculty Council and individual interviews at UR; and CAC at KSU—administrators informed and persuaded the campus of the seriousness of the problems it faced. To generate a commitment to close programs through the governance arenas, leaders evoked symbols, such as the enhancement plan at UMCP, and told stories, such as through presentations about the impact of endowment drain and high tuition discounts on the institution at UR. At OSU, the president and provost, by simply requesting the formation of FCG, symbolically stressed the severity of challenge created by Ballot Measure Five. Governance bodies, places where faculty and administrators come together to make decisions, became the platform from which problems were articulated and direction was set.

Second, shared governance brought various interest groups together in legitimate ways to accomplish a high stakes task. Shared governance became the place to create supportive coalitions. These processes occurred for the most part in established governance bodies (APAC and PCC at UMCP; FCG at OSU; CDC at UR; and CAC and EPC at KSU) that had campus legitimacy, rather than in newly created and never tried, ad hoc structures. Administrators and faculty could come together in places where difficult conversations like these were expected by the campus to occur. Outside a legitimate and time-tested arena, the efforts to close programs may have fallen under suspicion. Closing a program, department, or college is no light matter and shared governance allowed the processes to occur in the public domain (even if the conversations were confidential, such as at OSU) and in legitimate ways.

Third, shared governance provided a mechanism to shape outcomes and, possibly more important, to correct potential errors. Administrators recognized that they did not have all the information required to make the best decisions for the university. Thus, they involved faculty, who have different perspectives and experiences to help them understand the implications of closing certain programs. To ensure that they identified appropriate programs, each institution developed its own self-correcting mechanism via shared governance. Administrators asked faculty groups (summer sub-committees, FCG, CDC and individual faculty, and EPC and senate) to help them understand the effects of closures and prevent missteps. Shared governance created a valuable system of checks and balances. At UMCP, OSU and UR, programs were removed because of insights provided by faculty, and faculty at KSU through its EPC and the senate, approved the decision. Because shared governance provided a mutual veto, poor decisions were avoided.

EXTERNAL FORCES

External forces push institutions to undertake program discontinuance (Falk & Miller, 1993; Gumport, 1993; Volkwein, 1984). However, they also exert influence in shaping decision outcomes. In this study external forces were thought of as the effects created by actors who were not campus administrators, faculty, or students. External groups that had the potential to shape the process and its outcomes include system executives, state legislators, alumni, boards of trustees, and professional organizations to name a few. External forces played three roles in the discontinuance processes at the four institutions in this study: they provided the impetus for the closures; they affected the process; and they influenced the outcomes.

Impetus for Closures

Financial pressures brought about by changes in the external environment at all four institutions provided the impetus for closures. At UMCP, the recall of $24 million by the state legislature following on the heels of an earlier comparable reduction pushed the institution to undertake program closure. The legislature additionally created the sense of enhancement when it identified the campus as its state flagship in its higher education reorganization process a few years earlier.

The citizens of Oregon voting for Ballot Measure Five, which changed the property taxation structure and thus state-generated revenue, provided the stimulus for discontinuance at OSU. Without Measure Five the institution would not have found itself in such dire financial straits. A second reason OSU undertook program elimination was to demonstrate to the citizens of the state and legislature that drastic reductions in state funding would cause harm to public higher education and reduce the services and programs it delivered. The cuts were to show, as one person said, "scalps on the wall."

The board of trustees at UR, in response to long-term financial pressures (including overspending of a poorly performing endowment), hired a new president with the explicit intention of financially restructuring the institution, which in turn led to program closures.

Reductions in state allocations also brought about program closures at KSU. The second reduction in four years (an 8% and a 3%), coupled with an internally derived early retirement program, forced the College of Education to close Counseling Psychology. A second external force, the Ohio Board of Regents, created a chilly climate for graduate education, which facilitated the closure of that graduate program.

Facilitating Closures

In addition to providing the impetus for closures, external forces at three of the four institutions facilitated the closure process. At OSU, the chancellor of the system created a three-month time frame to make recommendations that shaped the process by limiting the amount of campus involvement. The short time frame meant that the campus could not create a long and open process to discuss options but rather had to respond quickly. Finally, it was his plan and budget that the legislature acted upon officially closing the programs at OSU.

The leaders at UR used external forces to facilitate their process. For example, to help frame the issue and gain support for closing programs, they pointed to the experiences of other peer institutions experiencing financial trouble such as UCLA and Yale. They also turned to Yale as an example of how not to proceed, such as deciding not to send up any trial balloons prior to announcing the closures. The administrative triumvirate sought and gained board support, which was needed both to politically implement the decisions and provide needed financial resources. The board had the power to prevent the closures from occurring, but did not do so because it agreed to support the administration. Finally, the board chair helped the process along, both instrumentally and symbolically, through his sizable financial gift.

At KSU, external forces were important in selecting Counseling Psychology over School Psychology for closure as another local institution offered a duplicative Counseling Psychology program. Secondly, the fact that high numbers of Counseling Psychology alumni (an external force) left the area, as compared to School Psychology who stayed working in local schools, may have contributed to the program's closure. Finally, another criteria that kept School Psychology and closed Counseling Psychology was the nature of the outreach of the programs. School Psychology was consistent with the child-centered mission of the college while Counseling Psychology was not.

Impeding Closures

In addition to facilitating closures, some external forces worked to prevent them. At UMCP external forces played intervening roles in the case of the three programs that were originally named but taken off the elimination list. Nuclear Engineering was removed because another institution within the state system provided continuing operating funds. Hearing and Speech was removed because it provided an important service to the region through its clinic that APAC believed it was too important (and possibly politically explosive) to lose. Finally, one of the reasons the College of Library and Information Sciences was removed was because off-campus supporters demonstrated the significant role the college played in the state. External forces provided political clout that made closing those programs extremely difficult.

At OSU, external forces constrained which programs could be terminated so the closures would not adversely affect other institutions. The president and the provost coordinated their recommendations with those at Oregon's other public institutions so the state would not lose all of the same programs. Range Management was a program suggested for closure by its college; however, the president said he would not recommend its closure because of the anticipated negative impact on Eastern Oregon University. The well-being of other public institutions shaped what occurred at OSU. The final involvement of external influences in preventing a closure occurred in the second biennium when Veterinary Medicine was proposed for discontinuance. This college was suggested for termination by the state system (an external force) because of its high per-student costs. Internal and external supporters joined forces to create a formidable coalition. They mobilized ranchers and animal lovers and owners across the state and were not only able to save the program but were able to secure a more stable source of income that was not dependent upon state tax dollars.

At UR, external forces played a factor in reinstating the Ph.D. Mathematics program. The external forces at work here were the scholarly associations and influential individuals with whom the Mathematics faculty could form political coalitions. Mathematics formed partnerships with external groups to build support and gain publicity, which prevented the closure from becoming a reality.

External Forces and Program Termination

Program closure, while an important institutional decision is influenced in many ways by forces outside the campus. To facilitate the process, external forces provided important symbols for campus leaders to leverage. For example, UR used external forces like the financial distress at aspirational peer institutions and the gift by the board chair to gain a commitment to close programs. UMCP used the enhancement plan created to comply with a state re-structuring of the higher education system to focus attention and provide a North Star to guide them through difficult conversations. External forces supplied leaders with a rationale for closing some programs (e.g., program duplication such as at KSU where another institution offered the same degree) and important tools (at UR where an external gift of $10 million surely helped).

External factors also helped prevent closures from occurring. For example, various external forces put political pressure on leaders at OSU, UMCP, and UR to stop certain program closures. The preventive-role external forces were among some of the more common reasons why programs were removed from lists of potential targets.

EFFECTS AND RESULTS

One of this study's research questions focused on the effects and results of program discontinuance on institutions. This section compares three types of impacts that occurred across the four universities: (1) the expected results and effects, (2) positive unintended consequences, and (3) the negative unintended consequences.

Expected Results and Effects

The expected results and effects were those sought by campus leaders through program discontinuance, which, for the most part, centered on financial issues, although each sought to alleviate a slightly different problem. At UMCP, leaders sought to terminate programs because a sizable portion of their current state budget was recalled. At OSU, the campus had to prepare to live within the means of a reduced forthcoming budget. At UR, the administration sought to restructure the organization's finances for the longer-term. At KSU, the purpose was to reallocate existing finances with a reduced budget.

According to those interviewed, each of the four institutions accomplished what it set out to do. UMCP saved $6.3 million for reallocation or reversal to the state, but of the money, only $2.8 million was available immediately, what the campus called "near-term discretionary funds." OSU was able to live within its next year's budget. UR saved money by reducing its faculty from 340 to 310. It began to work toward lessening the discount rate, and the Renaissance Plan did begin to increase SAT scores, an indicator accepted on campus that the quality of their students was increasing and a step the administration felt was necessary to lowering the discount rate. KSU, once the College of Education transferred the remaining Counseling Psychology faculty member to another college, was able to re-appropriate that program's budget across the department.

Even though informants at all four institutions believed their processes met their goals and saved money, none set concrete financial targets at the beginning of their processes. In practice, the evaluation of success was subjective. It is interesting that neither UMCP nor OSU set concrete financial goals, particularly given that the two institutions were facing stiff budget reductions and program elimination was touted as a solution. Although the Division of Academic Affairs at UMCP had to cut $10 million from its budget, it did not target portions of this money to closures and the rest from other cost-saving steps. At OSU, no discussion of target savings existed beyond the expected $13.4 million noted by the president during the announcement, nor was there discussion of the final savings at the conclusion of the process. This suggests that although program closures are purported to be money saving strategies, the data is inconclusive about its effectiveness. Campus leaders do not want to or can not determine the actual savings. A dean at UMCP summed up this dilemma when he said:

Now the idea that you would immediately save resources is part of the fiction. If you are not firing faculty, who are tenured, the resource savings are not significant. . . . One of the things that is difficult to see is what the real [financial] results of any of this are, because it is such a complex, interactive system, . . . it would be very, very difficult for you to trace [the money and] to be able to say look at all the money we saved here or look at all the money we saved there. . . . You are saving money, but you have no idea where it went in the end.

Only UMCP evaluated the success of its efforts. At the completion of the process, the Associate Provost wrote a report describing the money saved and reallocated, where it had come from, and how the campus met its goals. Although UR did track the number of faculty lines reduced and the increase in student quality, they, like OSU and KSU, did not publicly document the money saved from closing academic programs.

Beyond financial savings, two of the institutions had a second intended purpose for closing programs. UMCP sought to create a stronger, more focused campus that was described in its enhancement plan. Although both faculty and administrators admitted that it was difficult to substantiate a direct link between the closures and enhancement, most believed that the process contributed to the institution's perceived continued rise. OSU's articulated goal was to send a strong message to the voters in the State of Oregon and to the legislature that reductions in funding, such as those brought on by Measure Five, were harmful to public higher education. Although difficult to find evidence, administrators and faculty believed the campus was successful in this goal because after the first biennium, beyond pressure to close Veterinary Medicine, the institution was not pressured to engage in program closures, and they were able to find savings through other means.

The findings suggest that all of these institutions accomplished what they set out to do and that success is difficult to determine because program and savings targets were never explicit. The success of these processes, as defined by the participants, instead was retrospectively constructed. Campus leaders chose to focus attention on some elements while ignoring others, they determined criteria for success after the process had concluded, and they based part of their evaluation on hard to track money and other parts on ambiguous concepts such as enhancement and making a political statement.

Positive Unintended Consequences

Accompanying each of the processes were unintended consequences, both positive and negative. Three institutions—OSU, UR, and KSU—noted that one of the positive unintended consequences of the process was that many departments undertook self-assessments that resulted in a set of academic improvements. For example, at OSU the College of Agriculture engaged in an extensive examination that led to departmental reorganization and to the development of new interdisciplinary academic programs. At KSU, the Counselor Education program, long in the shadow of Counseling Psychology, blossomed once that program was discontinued with a renewed sense of purpose and self-confidence. At UR, administrators and faculty pointed to the revitalization in the undergraduate mathematics program, although two people skeptically referred to the improvements as revitalization with a "two-by-four." People at KSU and UR also noted an increased attention on students. At KSU, some believed that a higher number of students in Counseling Psychology completed their programs because of the extra attention and structure given them. At UR a renewed interest in undergraduate teaching grew because of the new higher caliber undergraduates, and, for those whose doctoral programs were closed, the lack of other students.

People at UR and OSU additionally said they benefited from new interest in and commitment to inter-disciplinary programs. Because of constricted funds, faculty looked across departmental lines to fund new innovations as no single unit had the needed finances. At UR, interdisciplinary programs were the only place for some faculty to continue to work with graduate students. Thus these programs took on increased importance.

Those at UMCP noted another positive unintended outcome. Many, specifically the faculty, said that, because of the process, they grew confident of their shared governance processes. The residual feelings from a well executed process left many with a strong sense of accomplishment and confidence. However, those same informants then noted that the campus for the most part had been unable to capitalize on its success and missed ripe opportunities to take on other difficult challenges facing the university, which could have been because key leaders were tired and many felt beat-up.

Negative Unintended Consequences

Along with the positive unintended consequences come the negative. Institutional informants noted the presence of many more negative secondary effects than positive ones.

Three of the institutions were deluged with waves of negative publicity because of the closures that lead OSU, UMCP, and UR to be perceived by their publics as unstable institutions. Potential students and their families were worried that more closures might follow and that the closures themselves were brought on by poor institutional management. This sour public image played itself out in enrollment patterns. Both UMCP and OSU saw a decline in the number of applicants. People were gun-shy about enrolling for fear of additional program closures and students feared not being able to get the needed classes to graduate. UR saw a slight dip in certain program's doctoral enrollments.

OSU also noted a backlash from the closed programs' alumni who no longer wanted to support the institution. Some also said that stopping the production of journalism graduates hurt the institution, because the media became less focused on the university as less of its alumni were working in the field. Fewer journalists turned to OSU, their alma mater, for expert sources. Finally, some suggested that the institution lost opportunities for potential enrollment growth. Because of the closures, OSU could not take advantage of a recent demand in the state for teachers.

The discontinuance process also took a psychological toll on all of the campuses. All four institutions noted that the process generated tremendous amounts of stress and anxiety among faculty and administrators. Faculty in the programs that were discontinued had a sense of worthlessness and as one person put it, felt like "a second-class citizen." OSU noted the termination process was all-consuming and took tremendous amounts of time and energy, which in turn, hurt productivity. Many of the faculty at OSU also became risk-averse and less innovative. They did not want to do anything that might bring unwanted attention to them or to their departments. At UR, many of the quality faculty left, a probability acknowledged early in the process by campus leaders. Although the Renaissance Plan called for a reduction in faculty, at least in the targeted programs, some of the younger, more productive faculty left for new opportunities regardless of program. At KSU, because of the high number of students finishing degrees in the discontinued Counseling Psychology program, faculty in other departments faced a high overload chairing dissertations. This had a cascading effect on their own programs as students felt neglected and did not have the opportunities to work with their own faculty.

The Effects of Program Termination

Understanding the effects and results of program discontinuance at these four institutions is a complicated picture composed of many layers. First, UMCP, OSU, UR and KSU said they met their financial goals through program closures. On one hand, the findings suggest that program closures can be a useful strategy to cope with financial difficulties. On the other hand, one would be remiss to suggest program discontinuance is always an effective strategy. The four institutions in this study could not articulate exact savings from the closures, they coupled program discontinuance with other cost saving measures, and some post-closure residuals were financially costly (such as drops in enrollments).

Second, along with the closures came a host of unintended consequences, most of which were negative. All four campuses noted high levels of stress on campus and faculty feeling demoralized, although it was difficult to separate the stress associated with financial distress from that related to the actual closures. Three of the four institutions also noted negative public images. Although they knew that the closures would be difficult, none anticipated the rash of bad publicity accomplishing the closures and its negative implications for the campus. Also, two of the four campuses saw unanticipated reductions in enrollments (UR was intended). OSU, almost ten years later, began to approach pre-discontinuance enrollments.

Finally, although all of the campuses mentioned negative results, the two institutions where leaders framed closures as a step toward improvement (UR and UMCP) believed that the positive results outweighed the negative. The majority of people at UMCP and UR saw the closures as a painful but necessary step towards campus improvement. Leaders reinforced the commitment to improvement and, at least at UMCP, became a key symbol of administrative dedication to improving academic quality. The reverse was true at OSU where the leaders articulated pain and suffering and much of the campus responded by adopting a victim mentality. To the faculty and staff at OSU, the closures were painful and undesirable; it was an answer forced from the outside and not viewed as a constructive period in institutional history. The leaders at KSU framed the issue more neutrally as they saw the closure of Counseling Psychology occurring because of circumstances rather than an intentional act. The interpretation of the process was neither a black day in history nor a necessary step for progress, but a fact of circumstance.

From this study, one can infer that (1) program discontinuance can save some money, although just how much and where is extremely difficult to pinpoint; (2) money might be saved more efficiently through other means as the returns on effort are low and the costs accompanying program discontinuance are substantial; (3) although program closures have a high cost, such as drops in enrollments, poor public image, high levels of on-campus stress, and the necessary investment of time, they may be necessary steps for campus enhancement and improvement. Their payoff is long-term and their consequences may have more of a symbolic than financial impact.

DIFFERENCES BY TYPE OF DISCONTINUANCE

Program termination is actually a set of two related activities. When institutions close academic programs they may have (1) terminated degree programs while keeping intact the units housing the programs (e.g., closing a doctoral program in anthropology while keeping the anthropology department); or (2) terminated both degree programs and the units housing the programs. Entering this study, it was unclear if these two phenomenon would result from two different processes or from similar processes. Briefly exploring a line of inquiry created by this distinction might be important to understanding the type of choices made when discontinuing programs: Why did institutions choose one type of action over another? To what extent are the two types of discontinuance processes similar and different? Are the distinctions important?

Institutions that had engaged in the two different processes were intentionally selected for this study. UMCP and OSU had closed both degrees and the units housing them, and UR and KSU closed programs but kept their departments intact. Although originally suspected to be distinct processes with potentially different impact, the experiences of institutions in this study suggest they are not. In fact, UMCP and OSU engaged in both types of program termination, although they mostly closed the departments that housed the discontinued programs (unit closure).

Early thinking was that the distinction between the two types of discontinuance processes was related to intentional decisions made as part of the process, that institutional leaders would intentionally make choices to discontinue programs and keep units together or terminate both units and programs. The experiences of the four institutions do not support that assumption. The two institutions that closed programs and kept the units housing them did so, not because of an intentional decision, but because of structural factors in the institutions.

Although Rochester's leaders could have closed units as well as programs, they chose not to do so because of the small size of the institution. Administrative leaders said the low number of departments precluded closing whole units as losing even one department at a small school (27 departments and an undergraduate enrollment of approximately 4,000 students) would have a significant impact on the breadth of undergraduate programs they offered. Thus, closing one unit would have a much larger impact on the range of programs offered as compared to an institution the size of UMCP (with approximately 70 academic departments and an undergraduate enrollment of approximately 28,000). To generate a comparative impact UMCP would have to close almost two and a half times as many programs. Institutional size and complexity forced the path not the choice of leaders.

The College of Education at KSU has an atypical structure that led it to engage in program closure and not unit closure. The college was organized so that rather than a department for each discipline (such as Teacher Education, Counseling Psychology, and Educational Leadership), the college was arranged into three large departments composed of multiple programs. To close a department in this college's structure would have meant terminating one-third of its activities. Thus, closing a program in the College of Education was more closely akin to closing a department at most other universities, although the nomenclature was different.

Based upon the above analysis and comparison across cases, this research offers little to suggest that the strategies used differ along types of closures. The differences in processes that did surface across the four cases rather reflect variances in institutional cultures, histories, operating assumptions, organizational structures, and patterns of decision making.

CONCLUSION

This chapter explored the commonalties across the four cases. It highlighted patterns in the context, leadership, shared governance, external forces, and results and effects that are meaningful at a macro level. This synthesis focused on process and results. However, it did not uncover the factors that led institutions to select one set of programs over another. For this we turn to the next chapter. When the rubber hits the road, by what criteria do leaders identify particular programs for closure?

CHAPTER 7

Making the Choices: Criteria Identifying Programs for Elimination

To this point, the book has explored the processes at four research universities to close academic programs, synthesized those processes to say that context matters, that leaders play important roles though framing the closures, designing the processes, and facilitating the transitions. It has noted that shared governance is an essential factor in facilitating (not preventing) these types of hard institutional decisions and that closures have both intended and unintended positive and negative consequences, particularly the findings that tracking the money saved is difficult and these decisions generate additional unwanted problems. The one point yet to be explored is the factors influencing the identification of certain academic programs for termination. When the rubber hits the road, what criteria guide closure decision making?

Common wisdom suggests that cost, quality, and centrality should be the criteria that drive closures. However, the experiences of institutions in this effort suggest that institutional decisions do not adhere to a strictly rational process whereby institutional leaders look to maximize one of these returns, or a combination of them. Rather, as one chair from Rochester suggested, leaders look to close the ones they could get away with. So what criteria *do* guide the decision-making process?[1]

DECISION-MAKING PROCESSES

The most common portrayal of organizational decision-making processes is that leaders identify alternatives, explore their consequences, and make choices based upon a set of rules that differentiate among consequences so that some options are more desirable than others (March, 1994; Pennings,

1986; Pfeffer, 1982). The label organizational scholars use to describe this framework is limited rational choice, where decisions are made in order to bring about best results (March, 1997). Limited rational choice suggests there is a relationship between information, criteria, and outcomes. The decision-making process is limited because not all alternatives can possibly be considered. "Instead of calculating the best possible action, they search for an action that is 'good enough.'" (March, 1994, pp. 8–9). Decision makers look to a constrained list of options that meet some level of acceptability (Simon, 1986) while not perusing an exhaustive list, as they have extreme difficulty anticipating every possible outcome and are unlikely to consider all alternative information even if it was available. People tend to uncover an acceptable outcome before exhausting all possibilities. These constraints, in turn, simplify the decision-making process (March, 1994; March, & Simon, 1992; Perrow, 1986). For example, in the case of program closure, it is likely that not all programs are under consideration for termination.

The intended (but not always realized) purpose of program discontinuance is to strategically reshape an institution by reallocating resources (Levine, 1997; Slaughter, 1995). When it comes to identifying which programs to close, former college president Dickeson (1999) suggests that "programs should be measured with an eye toward their relative value, so that reallocation can be facilitated" (p. 18). The relative values used to prioritize various programs in times of retrenchment tend to focus on maximizing quality among programs and containing costs, while considering centrality to the institution's mission (Gumport, 1993; Slaughter, 1993, 1995).

Dickeson (1999) suggests the following ten criteria in his advice to academic leaders on setting academic priorities: (1) history, development, and expectations of the program; (2) external demand for the program; (3) internal demand for the program; (4) quality of program inputs and processes; (5) quality of program outcomes; (6) size, scope, and productivity of the program; (7) revenue and other resources generated by the program; (8) costs and other expenses associated with the program; (9) impact, justification, and overall essentiality of the program; and (10) opportunity analysis of the program (p. 54). The decision rules he suggests are economic (demand, revenue, and costs), quality, and centrality.

Yet, the decision rules for identifying programs for closure are most likely not straightforward and based upon the decision rules of cost, quality, and centrality (Gumport, 1993), because, as the four processes explored in this book demonstrate, politics and symbolism play important roles. Because of the history, expectations, and norms of collegial decision making (Bess, 1988; Birnbaum, 1988), high-stakes decisions such as these require commitment from numerous stakeholders, specifically from the faculty (Birnbaum, 1992; Rosovsky, 1990). Broader retrenchment decisions, as well as program termination decisions, can become extremely political (Hardy, 1990b; Pfeffer & Salancik, 1980) as faculty most likely will be involved in the decision-making process that identifies the departments of their colleagues, and possibly their own units, as targets for closure. Thus, cost, quality, and centrality might make sense as the logical decision rules for identifying programs for closure, but they might not generate the needed faculty commitment necessary to implement the decisions. As Hardy (1990b) notes, "it is one thing for central administrators to decide on the principle of selective cutbacks; it is another to actually carry them out." (p. 316).

Rather than simply seeking to make the best decision, one that maximizes results within reason, decisions might be made that exchange maximizing outcomes for accomplishing something, even if it is not the best thing. The point behind this perspective is that getting something done, even if not the best thing, is better than getting nothing done. This perspective draws a stark contrast between action rationality and decision rationality (Brunsson, 1982). This argument asserts that decisions can be made based upon rational criteria but yield little action, or they can be made irrationally but take into consideration organizational beliefs, motivations, and commitments that lead to action. "Since decision processes aim at action, they should not be designed solely according to such decision-internal criteria as the norms of rationality; they should be adapted to external criteria of action" (Brunsson, 1982, p. 32). These irrational foundations for decisions may not lead to the optimal outcome in an abstract sense, but they abide by other criteria, such as involvement or historical precedent to accomplish the task. The central issue in action rationality is one of efficiency—how can decisions best be carried out—rather than one of effectiveness (Gladstein & Quinn, 1985; Pfeffer & Salancik, 1978).

The action rationality perspective challenges the common wisdom associated with decision rationality. Rather than thoroughly exploring available options, weighing consequences considering alternatives, and choosing the option that optimizes results, action rationality seeks information that supports particular palatable alternatives and analyzes these in terms of a narrow range of desired results that people will support; it is dominated foremost by the desire to implement and to get things done (Brunsson, 1982; Gladstein & Quinn, 1985). The logic of order is different. The process is not about first identifying the best alternatives and then gaining commitment, but of identifying alternatives essential to obtaining support for action.

In program discontinuance, the decision rationality criteria said to be used to make the choice—such as eliminating the weakest programs or the most costly—might not necessarily be the needed (action rationality) criteria to actually terminate programs.

WHICH RATIONALITY?

This chapter seeks to better understand, from an organizational perspective, the question, when leaders have to make actual decisions about which programs to close, what decision rules are invoked? To what extent did the decision rules reflect decision rationality or action rationality? To answer these questions, the stories of the four institutions provide three sets of informative data: (1) the criteria stated by institutional leaders to identify programs for closure, (2) the decision rules used to reinstate programs earlier identified for closure, and (3) the decision rules used to close programs.

The Stated Criteria

Three of the four institutions—UMCP, OSU, and UR—identified criteria publicly as part of their discontinuance processes. KSU did not develop a formal list of criteria. The three sets of criteria are presented in Table 7.1. UMCP developed its criteria specifically for the closure process in a document called *Criteria for Planning*, which was created by the executive committee of the senate at the request of the provost. The criteria were developed in the form of questions to determine the worth of the program. Among these criteria were issues such as mission centrality, program quality, demand, duplication, and cost. The provost said:

We gave the deans two target figures. What would you do if you were to cut 5% of your budget? What would you do if you were to cut 10% of your budget? . . . We couldn't attack the places where most of the money was, and in academic life, most of the money is tied up in academic salaries. I certainly didn't want to be involved in relieving people of their tenure. We tried to make this as economically motivated as possible, but we basically told the deans, and the deans responded, that the weakest programs were going to have to go. And that you wouldn't get much money by closing X or Y was not going to be an excuse. There were a couple of deans who were serious about suggesting that we eliminate tenure. I didn't want to do it. . . . That process itself [identifying 5–10% in cuts] identified some weak units.

At OSU, campus leaders relied upon a previously developed institutional policy, *Guidelines for Program Reduction*. This document was created by a committee of deans and approved by the faculty senate as part of an earlier program discontinuance process. One administrator said:

We began [as the result of earlier budget cuts] to . . . develop guidelines to help us when it came time to identify those programs that would be eliminated. This was chaired by a dean. . . . What they did, without identifying any programs, they said OK, these are the things that are important. And without knowing or listing them in the right order, they were things like centrality to the mission of the institution, size of the program, measure of its degree of success, measure of its contribution to society in addition to higher education, and so on. These are the guidelines that we used as we began to look at cutting programs out of the system.

Among its criteria were issues one might expect such as reputation and quality, program duplication, and cost. OSU's criteria also included issues such

Table 7.1
Stated Criteria by Institution

Stated Criteria	UMCP	OSU	UR
Mission centrality	Is the program central in terms of growth, preservation and communication of knowledge, and inst. mission?	A program that is essential for every university.	The centrality of the discipline and its current or projected importance to the undergraduate population.
Quality	What is the quality and reputation of the program and faculty?	An objective evaluation indicates national or international reputation.	The quality of faculty and graduate students.
Cost	What are the costs of maintaining vs. increasing its level vs. savings resulting from reductions?	Cost is minimal relative to the tuition or income it generates.	The costs of supporting the research/scholarly mission of the program.
Contribution to region		OSU is better equipped than other organizations. A substantial negative impact on education and issues in the state.	
Demand	What is the current and projected importance and demand for the program?		
Legislative mandate		A program that exists because of legislative statute.	
Uniqueness/ duplication	Does the program duplicate work on campus or within the system?	A program that is the only one of its kind within the state.	
Opportunity for distinction	Are there opportunities for comparative advantage because of time, location, or faculty talents?		A consideration of which disciplines are distinctive or could be with a modest investment.
Impact on instruction and scholarship			Role of grad. students in the delivery of undergrad. instruction and in the conduct of faculty research/ scholarship.
Revenue		Elimination would result in substantial loss of revenue.	
Past investment		A program that represents a substantial capital investment.	
Affirmative action/under-represented groups		A program that is staffed by members of groups protected by affirmative action.	
Dependence of programs			Critical linkages that exist (or should exist) between scholarly or instructional programs across departments.

as centrality to the idea of a university, legislative mandate, service to the state, and a program whose elimination would, according to OSU's *Guidelines for Program Redirection*, "have a substantial negative impact on education and societal concerns in the state." Final criteria focused on past investments in programs, negative effects on underrepresented populations, and anticipated revenue loss. The criteria were framed to justify *not* closing a program.

The stated criteria at UR, called "global factors," were developed by the administrative leaders and announced when the dean unveiled the closure decisions. These criteria included issues such as quality, costs, centrality to undergraduate education, and investment for distinctiveness. They also included criteria not identified by the other institutions such as linkages among units, the involvement of graduate students in undergraduate education (the institution sought to close only graduate programs), and faculty scholarship.

All three institutions included cost, quality, and mission centrality in their list of stated criteria. The only other criteria that appeared on multiple lists were program uniqueness or duplication avoidance (UMCP, OSU) and opportunities for program distinction (UMCP, UR).

Two potential and unresolved problems of applying the stated criteria to decision making are important to note. First, none of the three institutions addressed the issue of relative weights among their stated criteria. In its public document explaining the decision-making process, the leaders of the UR process wrote, "the importance of these factors must be combined with an overall sense of what is best and most feasible given the limited resources for the College as a whole" (*Rationale for the Restructuring Plan*, p. 5). The document used by OSU administrators did not indicate relative weights, although it did acknowledge the challenge:

It also should not be assumed that every stated criterion is of equal weight or that a program will be "scored" by the algebraic addition of its positive and negative features. . . . Many of these . . . criteria are partially or substantially subjective in character, and the balancing of these factors will involve value assumptions and policy choices. These balances will be finally struck and policy choices made at the campus level only after opportunity to address them has been afforded all interested persons in accordance with established . . . procedures. (*Guidelines for Program Redirection*, p. 4)

The ambiguity of the guidelines at OSU created some confusion among those not directly involved in making the decisions. Said one faculty member from a closed program:

If anything could have been communicated [better], it would have been what criteria are being used, because the rumor mill kind of ran rampant. I imagine there were some objective criteria . . . but it was very unclear as to what the criteria were and how these programs were tapped based on that criteria. . . . If there was stated criteria for units then to put together their best case. . . . that didn't happen.

UMCP also did not address weighting in any of its documents. That institution's first report, *Preserving Enhancement*, noted that the joint faculty-administration decision-making body "was acutely aware that many of its goals and criteria tugged the process of decision in conflicting directions" (p. 8). These statements, found at all three institutions pre-specifying criteria, imply the use of other decision rules and that action rationality and decision rationality may very well be two different things when it comes to identifying programs for termination.

The second curious element is the point at which the criteria were presented to the campus. OSU had criteria previously established that was part of a formal institutional policy. UMCP developed its criteria as an early step in the discontinuance process. At UR, the process unfolded differently, as leaders announced the criteria at the *end* of the process once the decisions had been made, not at the beginning. The criteria were summarized in the *Rationale for Restructuring*, a document distributed the same day of the announced closures.

Criteria Used to Reinstate Programs

Exploring the criteria campuses used to *reinstate* programs slated for discontinuance provides more insight into the type of decision rules at work. UMCP originally identified programs that it subsequently removed from the list of affected units (nuclear engineering, hearing and speech, and library sciences at UMCP). UR reversed one decision (mathematics). The president at OSU prevented a recommended program closure (range management) from being acted upon.

At UMCP, informants provided the following explanations for removing the three programs: (1) the costs to dismantle the campus' nuclear reactor and the contribution of funds from another institution sustained the nuclear engineering program; (2) the potential negative impact on the community prevented the university from closing the hearing and speech clinic; and (3) a satisfactory level of projected demand and the on- and off-campus support retained the College of Library and Information Science. At UR, strong political opposition from off-campus scholars and academic societies likely influenced this decision, although not admitted readily by senior administrators. Said one mathematics faculty member:

The American Mathematics Society took this very seriously. They regarded it as a very dangerous precedent for the profession. Their view was that if Rochester could eliminate its graduate math program, then the following year maybe half a dozen other schools would follow suit.

Some UR informants said that the curricular changes and cost-neutral counter-offer made by mathematics, which aligned the department more closely with the goals of the institution's retrenchment plan, convinced the administration to reverse its decision. The dean said:

We continued to get pressure from outside people, and we stood firm to that pressure. . . . We had some private meetings . . . with several key faculty from the math department. . . . We were willing on some dimensions to bargain with them, but we couldn't bargain on the financial end of things. . . . The result was that they came up with a proposal, and we came back with a slightly modified proposal because it was not exactly financially neutral, and then we involved the Physics Department in this. They were the only department after the fact that said that [cutting] math might not have been a good idea.

At OSU, closing Range Management would have negatively affected Eastern Oregon University because it was a joint program. The president said:

We have a program in range management, which is not only housed on this campus in Corvallis, but also on the campus of Eastern Oregon University. We made the decision at the president's level that we were not going to do anything that would significantly damage another institution. . . . We tried to look at the integrity of the whole system rather than just our institution.

In sum, institutions evoked a combination of the following decision rules to determine which programs to remove from the list of closures: cost associated with closure, contribution to community, projected demand, negative effect on other institutions, off-campus political pressure, and alignment with institutional goals. Decision rule overlap to reinstate programs included costs and external political pressure at UMCP and UR. Table 7.2 compares the factors considered to reinstate or remove programs from consideration for closure at the three institutions.

Closure Decision Rules

The final set of criteria to explore are those that were seemingly used to identify programs for discontinuance.[2] The OSU procedure forewarns of the possibility that decisions may be reached for reasons other than the stated criteria. That document said:

Given the great diversity of academic programs, the stated criteria will not include all considerations that may be applicable to individual programs. It is understood that such additional considerations are not rendered irrelevant by their omission and may be therefore considered. (p. 3–4, *Guidelines for Program Redirection*)

The criteria used at UMCP to identify programs for closure were a combination of stated and unstated criteria. A stated criterion was mission centrality, but the decision rule used focused on college mission not institutional

Table 7.2
Comparison of Criteria Used to Reinstate Programs by Institution

Criteria to Reinstate	UMCP	OSU	UR
Costs	Too expensive to dismantle nuclear reactor		Cost-neutral arrangements
Contribution to community	Hearing and speech clinic		
Projected demand	Enrollment in LIS		
Negative effect on other institutions		Range Management at Eastern Oregon	
Political pressure	On- and off-campus supporters for LIS		Involvement of American Society for Mathematics; negative publicity in *NY Times* and *Chronicle of Higher Education*
Alignment with goals			Altered the courses for non-math majors; developed tighter linkages with other units

mission, as some of the programs closed were professional programs in non-professional colleges. For example, urban studies and radio, television, and film (professional programs) were in the College of Arts and Humanities. At the same time, none of the programs slated for termination were critical or core programs (central to the institution's mission) that informants believed the university must have, such as English or chemistry. One faculty member from a closed program said:

We were in a college, Arts and Humanities, that obviously is the cornerstone of a university like ours, but we were a professional program. We were conditional; we weren't English; we weren't history; we weren't art. Parenthetically, the other program that got closed [in the college] was another professional program.

Other factors suggest that the closed programs at UMCP were politically vulnerable, revealing other decision rules at work. The units that were closed did not have champions among institutional leaders; they were programs where no one would (or did) come to their aid; and they lacked strong leaders. One faculty member said:

I don't think it was articulated, but . . . those units [closed] all had relatively weak leadership. One unit was so badly divided that they couldn't even speak to each other. . . . The ones that survived had very strong leadership. There was a certain coherence among the faculty. They seemed to know what they wanted to do. They seemed to be able to hold themselves together.

Some of the targeted units at UMCP had new or novice leaders. The chair of a closed program said, "I was new to the job so I thought it was an exercise. I didn't think they would really implement something as drastic as they were suggesting." Other programs were in political shambles with significant and long-term infighting. One dean illustrated the lack of internal consistency and lack of unit leadership in a program eventually closed from his college. He said:

In many cases, the programs shot themselves in the foot. . . . There was a program that demanded an external review and I allowed it to pick the external reviewers. The reviewers came in and said the program you have sucks and what you ought to do is reconfigure it in a different direction, bring in all new people, which is the equivalent of saying shut it down. Now it is very difficult for a faculty to argue on an evaluation that they demanded, with people they chose. That was one of the programs that was closed. It was a very small program.

The criteria used at OSU were similar in many ways to those invoked at UMCP, and decision makers did follow some of their stated criteria. For example, one stated criterion was a negative impact on education in the state, which prevented range management from being closed. Unstated criteria also were used, many of these related to what one informant described as a "window of opportunity." Among the unstated decision rules was the lack of strong unit leadership: two of the programs had new chairs and the College of Education faculty had recently voted "no confidence" in the dean. Other factors were low numbers of students and faculty.

Another reason some units were identified was that they were not central to the college mission. For example Journalism, a professional program in the College of Liberal Arts, was closed. A faculty member from that college said:

Journalism became kind of a perennial target within the College of Liberal Arts primarily because it was a professional area within a liberal arts academic unit. In a sense, it was a fish out of water. It was seen as too professional or quasi-commercial. If something had to be cut, then it probably ought to be that to maintain the purity of the unit.

Another faculty member discussing the closure of another department (his own) said:

[Our department] sits on the peripherals of both the College of Liberal Arts and the College of Science. . . . It was not a big loss to either one of the deans. It was not a core liberal arts [program] or a core science.

Changes within OSU's College of Education also provided a large "window of opportunity," as described by one person. The faculty recently voted no confidence in the dean. The college was in the midst of a transition to a fifth-year professional model that effectively restructured teacher education and lowered the college's student credit-hour generation, lessening the demand for full-time faculty. It was intentionally reducing its faculty size, enrollment, and course offerings when the institution was seeking to reduce academic offerings. According to one administrator in the College of Education:

It wasn't [just] that we had lost the dean, we had closed down our largest student credit hour generating program. . . . It was a college decision but it was very much driven by the dean at the time. In fact, the model that was developed was not really endorsed by the faculty. That was part of the problem the dean had with the faculty. He was mandating something, and they were telling him something else, and he was unwilling to compromise. In fact that probably . . . caused the vote of no confidence in him and led to his demise.

The decision rules used at UR were similar to those at OSU and UMCP. Among the alternative criterion invoked was the units' lack of strong leadership. A chair of a non-targeted department said:

They were departments that were rather poorly led, and they were basically very vulnerable because they had not made a very good case for continuing. They all had problems, absolutely no doubt about that. . . . Something had to be done because the status quo certainly was not the answer.

Many of the department heads were new or the departments were led by people who could not resolve internal squabbles. They did not understand the severity of the problems or that they needed to take action to prevent the termination of their units. A novice chair of a discontinued program said: "even before I was chair, and in my first year as chair, the handwriting in some ways was on the wall for this department. I didn't read it that way immediately; I mean there were a lot of new things for me to read at that point." Many units also had low numbers of faculty and/or numerous faculty vacancies. They also had low numbers of students and tended to be isolated from other programs.

The reinstatement of the mathematics' doctoral program at UR is an informative negative case example where the decision failed because leaders did not adhere to workable decision rules. Mathematics had (1) a sizable faculty, (2) strong leaders who were able to mobilize their faculty and off-campus supporters, and (3) faculty and program graduates who were well-connected to the national scientific community and able to create unwanted negative attention and gain political support. Because UR leaders violated important decision-making rules, they failed to close the department. On paper, the criteria to identify mathematics for closure might have been well founded, but in action, it was fallible.

Although KSU did not identify criteria publicly for program closure prior to its process, a set of decision rules was invoked for determining that one program, Counseling Psychology, would be closed over another, School Psychology. This decision was based upon the following criteria. First, college administrators elected to retain the program more closely aligned with the college's child-focused mission—Counseling Psychology worked with adults in hospitals and clinics, while School Psychology worked with children. A college administrator noted:

The Counseling Psychology people did nothing with schools. They were less central to the mission. Our mission priorities placed community agencies working with schools and families a priority. They did not take that approach, it was very individual [and hospital based].

Second, Counseling Psychology had a lower number of faculty (one) who did not or could not garner support for his cause. The program at one time had more faculty, but one took early retirement, one did not receive tenure, and two others died. Said one college administrator:

It was easier [to discontinue a program with one faculty member] than if there would have been a faculty with five or six left to move out. We had only one person left. You don't battle the same level of dissention as if we went in to close out a program that had been as strong as it had been in quality with about a dozen faculty members. That was why it was such a good time to do it.

Third, the program also did not have a lot of students or have much support on campus. One college administrator commented:

Nobody cared enough to fight for it. It was very isolated and unto itself. . . . If you are a stand alone and you are small, say 50 students and 3 faculty doesn't make a very formidable force for preservation.

Another said:

It was a relatively small program with a limited number of alumni. I think when we sometimes have larger programs with more alumni, they will get quite active in voicing to the provost or the president about the closure and just that outcry from the public and alumni makes it too difficult a situation to eliminate a program.

Fourth, a program similar to Counseling Psychology existed across campus that could house the remaining faculty member, and a near-by institution offered a Counseling Psychology program.

In an unrelated, earlier process, the Theatre doctoral program at KSU was terminated following a similar pattern. The program was characterized by leadership troubles and internal conflict. As one university administrator commented:

The directors [of the program] came and went; however, that is against the background of a school which had a tradition of internal division. . . . In a relatively brief period of time, we had three directors, all of whom were good, all of whom became subject to controversy within the unit. [They] were blamed for everything from the weather to not giving certain elements [of the department] adequate support.

The Theatre doctoral program also had a low number of students (8) and faculty (2). It was a scholarly program in a professional school and thus not central to the college's mission, and it did not have administrative champions. In fact, the provost thought closing the doctoral program might gain the institution some credit and favoritism with a Board of Regents that had recently initiated efforts to reduce the number of doctoral programs in the state.

In sum, the common criteria across the four institutions included lack of strong leadership (UMCP, OSU, UR); little centrality to the mission of the college (not to the institutional mission) (UMCP, OSU, KSU); low numbers of faculty (OSU, UR, and KSU); and low numbers of students (OSU; UR; KSU). Table 7.3 presents the decision rules used across the four institutions.

The Quality Criteria

Although quality, a frequently articulated criterion, did not surface directly as a used decision rule, evidence suggests that it was invoked as a filtering mechanism. Informants at both UMCP and UR said that although the institution used a process to identify programs for closure, a list of possible targets existed in the heads of key decision makers prior to starting the process. One informant from UMCP said,

If you were to do a poll on campus: Name the 10 likely departments that you think will be hit. I would bet that the seven that were closed would have appeared on 80% of the lists of people who named them at all. . . . And I think that is because anyone who sits in their college knows who the strong units are and who the weak units are, and that wasn't a big deal.

The provost said:

Everybody immediately knew once we knew we were not going to go the equal distribution route . . . that decisions had to be made through a [campus-wide] process. Even if with a little bit of thought you might have guessed how the decisions were going to turn out to be. You just could not say that out loud.

Leaders at UR also implied that they knew which programs would most likely be targeted before the process began. The dean said:

Table 7.3
Comparison of Used Termination-Decision Rules by Institution

Suspected Criteria	UMCP	OSU	UR	KSU
Lack of strong unit leadership	New leaders, vacant leadership positions	Vote of no confidence in Education dean; weak leaders	Weak leaders; novice leaders	
Mission centrality in college, not institution	Professional programs in liberal arts colleges	Professional program in liberal arts college		Adult focus in child-centered unit; scholarly program in professional college (Theatre)
No champion	No support from top admin. or college admin.	No support from top admin.		
Small number of faculty/vacant lines		Faculty vacancies; low numbers of faculty in units	Faculty vacancies; low numbers of faculty in units	Only one or two faculty member (Counseling Psychology & Theatre)
Small number of students		Low number of students	Low number of students	Only 8 students (Theatre)
No linkages with other units			Disconnected department	Disconnected faculty member
Other changes occurring		Moving to a 5th year model in teacher-ed.		
Program duplication				Similar program on campus and nearby

We pretty much knew a group of lets say 10 departments within which we were likely to make some cuts. . . . You don't have to be dean very long to have a pretty good sense of the quality. The problem is you can't specify precisely to a department chair how you know that. In other words, I can't give a department chair a piece of paper that says, "You are an A+ department for the following reasons." Because the following reasons consist of things that are rather subjective. Things like, I have looked through all of your annual reports from the faculty and I have a sense that you got five people in your department who are A+ and could go to Harvard, Yale, Princeton, wherever they wanted to go, at any moment. And then you have got this group here that are B+, great. . . . And then you have got this group here who are so-so. . . . I think [that] if I sat down with every department chair and went through every faculty member one by one, we would pretty much agree on that.

A point of limited rationality theory is that decision makers do not consider all alternatives but start with a constrained list (March, 1994), and the quality criterion helped narrow the possibilities, except at KSU, where Counseling Psychology was widely recognized as a quality program. Quality, although not invoked formally or, for that matter, neither defined nor clarified, most likely played a role in identifying potential programs for closure acting as a filter to narrow the range of potential targets, not as a final determinant. As one informant said, those involved "knew where the water leaked."

One way to interpret the knowing of targeted units before the process is to say that the processes were only for political reasons and maneuvering. However, instead of viewing leaders as crafting a process simply for its symbolic sake (Birnbaum, 1988; Bolman & Deal, 1991) or to rationalize the decisions after the fact (Gladstein & Quinn, 1985), the process did identify specific programs for closure. Leaders may have started with an informal list, filtered by quality, but the process helped to determine which programs specifically to close. The process identified those programs that were not central to the mission of their college; were politically vulnerable; did not have champions or large numbers of politically astute faculty, students, or alumni; and had ineffective or novice leaders. Without a process, these elements may not have surfaced, and quality alone would have been an insufficient criterion, missing the larger action-based criteria.

MAKING SENSE OF DECISION RULES

The purpose of this chapter was to give explicit attention to the means through which specific programs were selected for termination. The experiences of the four institutions suggest that the decision rules evoked to close academic programs were the following: (1) Programs that were closed had weak or novice leaders, (2) were small programs with low numbers of students and (3) with low numbers of faculty, and (4) were not central to the mission of the college that housed them (independent of the institutional mission), such as professional programs in liberal arts colleges or liberal arts programs in professional colleges. The other set of decision rules used were those that determined which programs to reinstate that had once been marked for termination. They included: (1) costs: being too expensive to close (dismantling the nuclear reactor at UMCP) or finding cost-neutral alternatives at UR and (2) external political pressure not to remove programs at UR and UMCP. It is interesting to note that off-campus groups prevented change from occurring rather than providing the impetus to change as is so often presumed.

Second, institutional decision makers, for the most part, did not use the criteria they specified. Although institutions said publicly that closures were to be based upon some combination of institutional mission centrality, quality, cost, contribution, demand, mandate, uniqueness, distinction, revenue, and investment (to name most of the criteria identified by three of the institutions), they used only quality and this was used indirectly as an initial screen. The programs closed did have low numbers of students, but rather than being linked to demand, an expected economic variable, size was political, as the small number of pro-program supporters could not generate adequate political clout. Because decision makers did not make choices to maximize their stated criteria of cost, quality, or centrality, the number of programs closed was not as essential as if they had chosen in ways to optimize results. For example, the amount of money they saved no longer had the same importance. In fact as discussed in the previous chapter, none of the institutions in this study tracked the precise savings from closures.

Third, this study does not support much of the common wisdom of deciding among programs to close. Program closure decision rules have little to do with external demand for graduates, anticipated enrollments, or internal demand for courses, which may be criteria that reflect decision rationality. Institutional decision makers do not distinguish among programs based directly on quality of inputs or outcomes, on the revenue or resources generated, on the impact of programs, or on their history (Dickeson, 1999). In this study, programs were closed that did not have strong unit leaders, that lacked champions on campus, that were not central to the missions of their colleges, and that had small numbers of faculty and students (and thus alumni). As one informant said, "they took the ones they could get away with." Action rationality carried the day.

Focusing particularly on quality finds that this often-identified criterion was used to limit the range of choices, not to specify particular programs. It was used first, informally, imprecisely, and independently. It set the limits of limited rationality by constraining the number of alternatives considered and the amount and accuracy of the needed information (March, 1994). Quality thus played a role in setting parameters, but it did not factor into the choice process at the times or in the ways typically expected, such as a comparative indicator coupled with other criteria such as cost and demand.

Fourth, because institutional leaders did not invoke the stated decision rules but used alternatives, the process of determining programs for closure not only identified particular programs it also surfaced workable criteria. Preferences often are determined through action, rather than action determined through preferences (Weick, 1979). As organizational behavior theorists Cohen & March (1986) state, "Human choice behavior is as much a process for discovering goals as for acting on them" (p. 220). In program discontinuance at the four institutions, the choice of certain programs clearly was shaped by the necessity to act. Acting, in this case determining which programs to close and which were close-able, became the important process.

Finally, the findings suggest action rationality over decision rationality to explain program closure. Institutional decision makers, as this chapter demonstrates, invoke a rationality that can get the job accomplished. They do not follow the pattern of decision rationality suggested by limited rationality theory—identify criteria, typically cost, centrality and quality; determine relative weights among the criteria; collect data for comparison; and make decisions based upon the data to maximize economic benefits. Action rationality may not close the most costly programs, the weakest ones, or those least central to the institution, leading to a watering down of results. For program closure in these four cases, action rationality is political. The decision rules invoked identified programs that did not have the political strength to fight back, were small, had weak or novice leaders, and didn't have advocates across campus. Decision makers, to close programs, followed a rationality based upon power, negotiation, and coalition building (Baldridge, 1971; Bolman & Deal, 1991). When the political rules of the game were not followed, such as with mathematics at UR, closures did not occur. Even though action rationality brought about closures, three of the four institutions developed a list of criteria that alluded to decision rationality. One might conclude that the illusion of decision rationality is needed to keep the process moving, but action rationality is needed to accomplish the task.

CONCLUSION

This chapter suggests the majority of decision criteria identified are *not* used to select programs for closure. Rather institutional decision makers use alternative criteria, ones that lead to action. Simply having stated criteria, and possibly a process to develop those criteria, may be more important to the discontinuance process than serving a utilitarian choice purpose. Stated criteria most likely fulfill a symbolic role needed to generate commitment and action (Birnbaum, 1988; Bolman & Deal, 1991; Chaffee, 1983). The stated criteria, as well as the legitimate process by which they are developed, create involvement opportunities for key actors, capture the attention of influential stakeholders, develop an atmosphere of seriousness, and identify members of potential coalitions, both allies and opposition.

The key point is to understand the importance of identifying workable decision rules, those that lead to action. Although leaders at these four campuses did not adhere to their stated criteria, the processes they used uncovered workable criteria that generated progress. Attention to process is essential, not simply to create legitimate and acceptable processes that are politically acceptable, but also to uncover criteria that will lead to intended outcomes.

The next and final chapter brings together the ideas discussed in this chapter and the previous one to explore the implications for campus leaders. It pays particular attention not only to those leaders seeking insight on terminating academic programs but also offers suggestions for leaders seeking to prevent closures. It explores issues of savings, costs, and tenure and offers suggested revisions of AAUP policy. Finally, it concludes with a discussion for possible future research.

NOTES

1. This chapter is adapted with permission from P. D. Eckel (2002), "Decisions rules used in academic program closure: Where the rubber meets the road." *Journal of Higher Education* 73, no. 2, 237–62. Copyright by the Ohio State University Press. All rights reserved.

2. Because the study was retrospective, the researcher was not present during the discussion, thus the following is inferred from the data collected.

CHAPTER 8

Counsel on Program Elimination

This book has provided case illustrations and discussed the costs and savings of program elimination, the role of leadership, the ability of shared governance to make hard decisions, and the use of criteria. The concluding chapter brings together the findings to provide counsel on program elimination. It presents rationale for why decisions must be defensible; discusses the trade-offs regarding savings, tenure, and program elimination; and makes suggestions both for campus leaders seeking to eliminate programs and for those seeking to fight off program closures. Additionally, it suggests empirically based modifications to the Association of American University Professors (AAUP) policies and suggested practices concerning program termination and shared governance.

DEFENSIBLE DECISIONS

The four cases suggest that institutions discontinued programs at times when campus leaders thought "they could get away with it," to quote one informant. As elaborated in an earlier chapter, program closures were not based on cost, quality, or institutional mission. Rather, the closed programs tended to share some common characteristics, which, when taken together, created political vulnerability. For campus leadership, this strategy raises fundamental questions related to the intent of program termination: Is the purpose institutional enhancement? Is it cost-savings? Is it to narrow curricular offerings? Is it to show symbolic notches in their political belt to state legislatures, trustees, and others pressuring institutions to do something drastic?

Most of the institutions in this study engaged in program discontinuance under the banner of cost reduction (although some made public secondary objectives). If one assumes cost reduction is driving other institutions to consider program discontinuance, then institutional leaders should not limit their focus to politically weak units but also try to close some programs that are expensive and/or unproductive, even if politically well connected.

Leaders trying to reduce expenditures face two challenges in program discontinuance—the first is getting the task accomplished, and the second is meeting their objectives, such as saving money. If their expensive programs are politically vulnerable, they may be able to accomplish both. However, there is a good chance that programs that would save the most money are politically influential, such as expensive programs like medicine and engineering (Slaughter, 1995). Leaders either have to decide between the two competing objectives or find a compromise, because the units that are politically vulnerable may not be the ones that save significant dollars.

Based on the experiences of these four institutions, leaders might chose a middle ground—mixing politically vulnerable and costly programs. Because program discontinuance is difficult, if they begin down the termination path, leaders should ensure that some programs are eliminated, even if it does little to generate immediate savings. By ensuring a visible victory, leaders demonstrate that they are serious about closing programs, that the processes they devised work, and that they are able to complete the tasks they attempt. Early progress should help to generate the momentum needed to close expensive programs that will more directly meet their financial goals. Terminating costly programs creates a sense that the closures served a larger purpose, not just to flex administrative muscle. Without demonstrating that the closures led to savings, critics may protest that the closures were malicious and resulted in little institutional benefit. UMPC is a case in point. Campus leaders demonstrated the financial benefit by including both immediate savings and cost avoidance, the money that would have been spent to improve the closed programs.

Prior to embarking on this strategy of closing both politically vulnerable and expensive programs, leaders should consider the implications of a failed attempt. To what extent would a failed attempt create future constraints in leading the institution? Would the battle be their Waterloo? If the risks of not closing the expensive but well-fortified program are thought to be too great, leaders may want to rethink the strategy of program closure if cost saving is the primary objective. If the primary purpose of closing programs is not financial savings (but for political reasons or to reduce the breadth of program offerings), closing politically weak programs alone may meet their objectives.

SAVINGS, COSTS, AND TENURE

Program discontinuance may not be the best strategy for institutions looking to save significant dollars. The experiences of the four institutions demonstrate that a process that is perceived as legitimate is complicated and difficult and may not generate large savings. Unless the wolf at the door is big, bad, and loud (for example, Ballot Measure Five at OSU), program discontinuance takes time. It takes time to build coalitions, make the case that closures are the necessary strategy, devise legitimate processes, bring faculty into the process, test ideas, and identify programs that are close-able. Program closures also generate their own financial and human costs, including distressed, demoralized, and distracted faculty and administrators; enrollment declines; and poor public image. Terminating academic programs becomes a time- and resource-consuming activity for the institution, taking people and energy away from other possibly important activities that might be useful in putting the institution on firm footings.

One of the more significant cost-saving trade-offs is between retaining tenured faculty and reaching financial goals through salary savings. For the most part, all four institutions intentionally decided to retain tenured faculty even if it meant realizing less immediate savings. (Only one institution laid off tenured faculty and it eventually rehired all who wanted to return.) However, not all institutions beyond these four universities that discontinue programs will retain tenured faculty. Many faculty contracts stipulate that faculty can be released upon the dissolution of their academic departments or when the institution is under financial duress. (Administrators at all four institutions in this study believed they were contractually able to release tenured faculty.) Releasing tenured faculty who have significant salaries most likely will generate immediate and larger savings.

Although many institutions can release tenured faculty as part of program termination, it is probably wise to retain tenured faculty. First, retaining faculty demonstrates an important commitment to faculty and to the academic core at a time when critics may perceive the intellectual life of an institution to be under attack. Second, this strategy makes the process achievable. By releasing tenured faculty, administrators introduce a high hurdle into the process that they may not be able to clear. Administrators create a rallying point for those already opposed to the closures and removing tenured faculty invites external forces into the process, such as the AAUP, other professional bodies, and faculty from other institutions. The mathematicians at Rochester are the case in point. Tenure is one of the most coveted agreements in the academy and dismissing it, even on financially justifiable grounds, can only lead to complications, impassioned protests, and prolonged debates. When tenure is on the table, conversations may turn to the values and traditions of the academy and away from the task of closing programs.

Additionally, the discontinuance process does not end with the announcement of the closures as administrators must continue to work with faculty as the business of the institution continues. Releasing tenured faculty may create residual effects that make it difficult, if not impossible, for administrators and faculty to continue to work together. Trust, shared values, and common beliefs that created the foundation that allowed administrators and faculty to be productive may be lost. Retaining tenured faculty requires a financial trade-off, possibly for the short-run only, but the lingering effects of releasing tenured faculty may cause more problems than the solution provided by program closures.

Also related to savings and termination, administrators at the four campuses did little to track savings upon implementation of the closure decisions. Once the process was underway or completed the effectiveness of the closures became a non-issue. No institution felt compelled to determine or report on the amount saved. No one seemed to care, either on- or off-campus, how much money was saved through program discontinuance although the process was initiated as a cost saving measure. The pressure to close programs came from the outside but a corresponding pressure to report on the success of the strategy did not exist. This phenomenon may be an example of higher education organization where inputs and initiation are more important than outcomes (Birnbaum, 1992). The implication is that accountability in higher education, especially when originating from the outside through legislatures or trustees, may be circumscribed and limited as institutions are more accountable for doing *something* and not for doing the *best* thing. The important lesson here might be that campus leaders should not spend significant time and energy on assessing the effectiveness of their actions (actual dollars saved), but on getting something done, declaring victory, and moving on.

Although its effectiveness as a cost saving measure is unknown—and seemingly immaterial—program discontinuance may play an important symbolic role in the larger objective of saving money because it creates an institutional climate that permits other cost saving steps to occur. For example, deans, chairs, and faculty who are having their travel budgets cut and vacant faculty billets taken away may believe they should not complain as academic programs are being closed, a much more drastic action. In circumstances not marked by program terminations, these actions may bring forth complaints, but the presence of program closures may help create new definitions of acceptable actions. Program closures also may serve other worthwhile purposes beyond saving money, such as sending strong messages to political leaders, furthering institutional improvement goals, or serving as symbols of accountability. To that effect, it may be more important for an institution to be *perceived* to be saving money rather than actually doing so.

THE SEARCH FOR INSTITUTIONAL PURPOSE

This research suggests that the process of closing academic programs may be less about saving money than about the search for institutional purposes, identity, and values. Program discontinuance processes may help institutions clarify goals (i.e., become a leading research university teaching outstanding undergraduates), find understanding in the midst of confusing times (i.e., we are a land-grant institution in a state not committed to higher education), or confirm shared institutional beliefs (i.e., becoming a top-tier research university is possible through the enhancement plan). The process is a search for meaning as well as for savings.

Some clues from all four of the processes that suggest this conclusion include the facts that the institutions developed unclear and potentially contradictory criteria or did not develop criteria to identify programs for closure; they ignored the criteria when identifying programs; they failed to develop objective measures of success; and they were unable to determine the actual amount of money saved through the process.

Discontinuing programs based upon the use of complex, contradictory criteria through an unclear framework to reach unspecified objectives may be an inefficient way to select programs for discontinuance, but it is essential to the search for institutional meaning and purpose, which may be particularly important as institutions try to right themselves during difficult financial times. In situations that bring about program elimination "decisions are seen as vehicles for constant meaningful interpretation of fundamentally confusing worlds not as outcomes produced by a comprehensive environment" (March, 1994, p. 179). Rather than helping identify specific programs for closure, identifying criteria and designing a process to close programs brings key constituents together to sort out different understandings, clarify values, and build common perceptions in a turbulent world where the rules of operating are being re-written. Constant negotiation and discussion during the termination process allows key decision makers to test hunches before committing to a specific choice and contributes information that is difficult to obtain directly on topics such as political allies, historic significance, and dominant campus perceptions.

Program elimination processes help sort out institutional goals, confirm institutional beliefs, and find understanding in ambiguous and uncertain situations. The implication is that suggestions to follow approaches typically described as "rational" (March, 1994) to program discontinuance, such as spending precious time identifying data formats to quantify criteria, developing extensive processes to collect information, and analyzing significant amounts of data (Dickeson, 1999), may not fulfill all of the functions as well as other, more ambiguous and messy processes. What may be important in program terminations are messy processes, such as the ones here, that help clarify goals and aspirations, and produce collective sensemaking. They may lead to action and a better understanding of an institution reborn in changed waters.

ADVICE FOR ACADEMIC LEADERS

This research points to a series of practical insights both for campus leaders seeking to close programs and for those individuals who are fighting closures. The final set of implications to practice offered here is suggested modifications to AAUP policies and recommended strategies based upon this research.

For Those Who Want to Discontinue Programs

The experiences of these four institutions suggest a set of lessons for academic leaders (faculty, administrators, deans, or trustees) considering program closure because the institutions were successful in their endeavors. In each case, campus leaders met their goals of closing programs: they saved or re-allocated (some) money; the institution did not erupt in turmoil; and no academic administrators were forced to resign. These most likely will be the outcomes that those who attempt program closures aspire. That said, the reinstatement of the doctoral program in Mathematics at UR adds an informative negative case example.

Not as a First or Only Step

Academic leaders should not engage in program termination as an initial cost saving measure, but only after other steps that reduce expenses have been taken. Program discontinuance is difficult for those involved and those affected. It is time consuming, creates distress, and distracts from the business of the institution. In this study, program termination occurred only after institutional leaders had engaged in across-the-board cuts, implemented hiring and salary freezes, limited travel, and halted non-essential expenditures. Exploring and exhausting other strategies first may be necessary in order for faculty to support and whole-heartedly participate in the drastic measures of closing programs. Through faculty participation, aspirations of what may be possible (saving all programs) become aligned with a reality that some programs must go (Cohen & March, 1986).

After taking other steps, academic leaders should combine the program termination strategy with other cost savings strategies, as by itself, program discontinuance may not generate the needed savings. Findings suggest that any money saved is difficult to track, may not become immediately available, and may not amount to much. Combining strategies may reinforce the seriousness of the financial situation and demonstrate that all areas of the campus are feeling the pain of the financial downturn. This approach also may help suppress opposing alliances, because faculty in other departments will realize that their programs might be targeted if they actively disagree with the current slate of closures.

Make Closures Seem Inevitable

Academic leaders should frame the challenges and proposed solution—program closures—so that key constituencies (e.g., faculty, students, other administrators, trustees) come to believe that it is *the* solution. Leaders are responsible for articulating the challenges and creating beliefs that program discontinuance makes the most sense as a strategy at this time. They should use various strategies to shape beliefs, create a common sense of reality, and set direction. These approaches might include continuous references to the challenges facing the institution in public meetings and speeches (such as at UR and UMCP), editorials and articles in the student and faculty newspapers about the need to take drastic action (such as at OSU and UMCP), or informal conversations with faculty and campus opinion leaders (such as at UR, KSU, UMCP, and OSU). Leaders can use the institutional stage provided by shared governance to call attention to the institution's plight and the best solution. By evoking emergency measures, such as forming the Faculty Consultative Group at OSU or asking the senate at UMCP to develop criteria to guide closures, leaders can define a reality where program closures are perceived as necessary, acceptable, and even beneficial.

Leaders at the institutions in this study started the public conversations discussing which programs and how many to close, not whether or not to close programs. In no part of any public campus discussions was the potential not to close programs offered. Leaders should convincingly translate environmental pressures to so that the closures seem inevitable and the institution will be better off because of them. At these four institutions, a previous round of budget cuts or long-term financial distress helped create persuasive stress.

Frame the Closures as a Requisite Step toward Improvement

The ways in which leaders frame the purposes for closing programs may lead to different futures. The attitude leaders take can strongly influence widely held perceptions on campus (Neumann, 1995). People on the campus might have higher morale if leaders frame program discontinuance as a necessary step toward a better future. Leaders who tie program discontinuance to greater ends such as enhancement (UMCP) or improving academic rigor (UR) may foster a campus climate that intentionally seeks silver linings in the storm clouds generated by closing programs. Leaders who adopt a positive attitude should not be Pollyannas, but acknowledge the pain and difficulty of the situation and then frame the challenges in aspirational terms.

The attitudes of leaders are contagious. Findings suggest that leaders' attitudes have the ability to shape the perceptions of others. Talking about progress, a better future, and institutional improvement may help facilitate the closures more than talking about pain, suffering, and agony. Even if the attitude adopted by leaders does not directly affect how cuts occur, it may make those involved feel better about their institution, their actions and decisions, and even themselves, and it may help address the negative fallout common to program terminations. Leaders may feel the need to adopt a victim perspective to reach other goals (such as sending a political message to legislators), but they should realize the on-campus costs of such an approach.

Leaders who identify closures singularly as painful obstacles may unintentionally create feelings of victimization across campus that are hard to overcome. A campus that understands the challenges only as threats and not as opportunities and that feels constantly bombarded may adopt a siege mentality. Faculty and administrators within such an institution may have difficulty creatively addressing problems, taking risks, and creating a supportive environment.

Develop a Defensible Process

This study suggests that attention to the processes used to discontinue programs is extremely important. Leaders have to be conscious of not just *what* they are doing but *how* they are going about it. Leaders should strive for a defensible process, one that passes intense scrutiny of critics. Because program discontinuance will most likely have opponents, either against the procedure in general or against specific closures, the process must be intentionally designed so they cannot argue that it was unfair, exclusive, faulty, or dishonest. The strategy of program discontinuance is itself contentious, and processes poorly designed become another point of attack. A solid and defensible process is important because violations of norms can easily unravel hard fought battles and well-intended decisions.

At a minimum, the discontinuance process should include conversations with, and the involvement of, key constituencies. The types of involvement might vary, but they must be perceived by those involved, as well as by others with the power to derail change efforts (such as members of the faculty senate or trustees), as meaningful and legitimate. A particularly important process element is opportunities for faculty to influence the process because of commonly accepted norms of shared governance. These opportunities may be either through formal governance avenues or through informal means, but in such a way that satisfies campus expectations.

Tap Knowledgeable Leaders

As the different processes adopted across the four institutions imply, the specifics that create defensible processes will vary and what is perceived as legitimate on one campus may violate many ingrained norms on another. Thus, leaders must either know the campus intimately enough to design the process themselves, or they must involve knowledgeable insiders whom, in the words of one faculty member, "know where the water leaks." In all four cases, the leaders facilitating the processes were long-time institutional leaders with an intimate knowledge of the institution. Only at UR was the president new, but he worked closely with two campus leaders (the provost and the dean) who had long histories at the institution. Long-time leaders may also have a cache of good will that give the process a credibility to move forward.

Build Upon Previously Established Legitimacy

Academic leaders may benefit from utilizing decision-making bodies and processes already viewed as legitimate rather than trying to develop ad hoc committees that have to overcome suspicion or that need to spend their limited time and energy gaining acceptance. Whether or not the appropriate body is the academic senate depends on the historic patterns in decision making on campus. Even when senates were used, academic leaders also tapped other joint faculty-administrative bodies or faculty-only groups that had established legitimacy and a history of decision-making involvement.

By building on established legitimacy, academic leaders may avoid debates over representation, authority, decision-making turf, and inclusion. The history and culture of the institution already has determined those answers. Leaders can then focus their attention and energy on other procedural issues and the difficult tasks ahead.

Develop Supportive Coalitions

Leaders who want to close academic programs must build an alliance strong enough to permit them to enact their decisions. For example, administrative leaders at UMCP, OSU, and UR built coalitions with their campus senates. Administrators at UR also built an alliance with its board.

To build the supportive coalitions, leaders can engage in a variety of strategies. They may articulate the ways in which program closures will benefit members of various sub-groups in meaningful ways or that, if the proposed action is not accepted, the alternatives might generate additional harm. They might delegate important tasks to potential allies, such as administrators at UMCP asking the senate to develop criteria and guiding principles or asking faculty leaders to sit on the APAC sub-committees investigating implications.

Develop Buffered Arenas for Protest

Since a closing process most likely will generate some protest, leaders should prepare for the disruption by building buffered arenas for protest. Buffered arenas allow opponents to make their case and provide them an outlet to focus their attention and expend their energy in a manner that satisfies their needs but cannot derail the outcomes. These are arenas that generate a lot of light but little heat. For example, UMCP used open hearings at which people opposed to the closures could speak, but they were making their case to already convinced members of APAC or PCC who would only be swayed by overwhelming evidence. Protests on the floor of the Faculty Senate at UR had little impact, because it is not the vehicle that shapes institutional actions as compared to the Council of Department Chairs. Protesters expended significant time and energy collecting data, crafting their speeches, and drumming up supporters but made little headway. Because opponents were preparing for a fight in the buffered arena, they were not engaging in guerrilla tactics elsewhere that might have done real damage.

Use Public Deadlines

In all four instances, leaders set, or were given, meaningful and real public deadlines for the completion of the whole process and for individual components of the process. Public deadlines created a sense of accountability and pressed various decision-making bodies to act. For example, leaders at OSU and UMCP set deadlines for the initial reports from the deans. UMCP's leaders created a timeline for the work of the APAC summer sub-committees. They also set deadlines for getting the report *Hard Choices* to the senate and for the senate to report back to the president with its final recommendations. OSU was given a deadline by the chancellor that helped mobilize campus administrators and faculty sitting on FCG.

Public deadlines created a sense of inevitability as well as a sense of urgency and accountability. By setting deadlines for themselves and for the various decision-making bodies involved, leaders reinforced the gravity of the tasks at hand. Not acting was not an option.

Test Receptivity

By testing how the campus might react to closure recommendations, leaders can make adjustments to the list of proposed programs or devise a strategy to present them with the least potential disruption. If leaders send up trial balloons they might avoid an unanticipated eruption, such as what happened during the earlier attempt to close programs at UR a few years previously.

This testing might be done in the open, such as the release of a preliminary report and subsequent sub-committee investigations at UMCP, or behind closed doors such as the individual interviews with faculty leaders at UR, or the confidential discussions with the FCG at OSU. The process for testing the recommendations should match campus expectations. At UR, leaders decided to question faculty opinion leaders in private and not publicly test their ideas. At UMCP, the opposite was true. Faculty expected opportunities to comment publicly, which they received through the open hearings and the debate on the senate floor.

Testing recommendations also provides a way to build support for the decisions. Allowing key campus opinion leaders early access to the recommendations may help gain their backing, thus widening the circle of allies.

Expect Negative Fallout

Program discontinuance is a situation that not only resolves a set of problems but has the potential to create others. The institutions in this study found themselves facing a host of unexpected problems caused by successful program discontinuance. For example, all of the processes generated negative public perceptions of institutional management and a sense of instability. In some cases, these perceptions directly translated into enrollment drops. Additionally, enrollment loss may be a serious consequence if the institution is tuition-dependent as fewer students may bring deeper financial troubles than those the closures were intended to fix. Alumni, especially those graduates from the closed programs, also may feel betrayed. They may curtail their financial gifts, speak poorly about the institution to prospective students or other donors, or stop other types of beneficial involvement (e.g., drop membership in the alumni association, not volunteer for alumni activities) in a period of financial hard times. Leaders seeking to close programs should anticipate and prepare for a host of negative outcomes.

The responsibilities of those who instigate and lead the closures should not end with the announcement of program closures. Once programs are identified for termination, leaders should facilitate the transition following the announcement and attend to the needs of affected people. The efforts institutional leaders extend helping people through the closures transition will pay off in the future. For if the process leaves the campus bitter and divided or the remaining faculty disenfranchised, the ability of administrators to lead successfully will be compromised.

Leaders should respond to the needs of students, faculty, and staff. Closing units is likely to generate anger in those who remain on campus after their units are closed. The closures additionally may be traumatic for faculty and staff in other units as they may adopt a survivor mentality that can impede their productivity and contributions to the campus.

The negative after-effects can linger for some time and leaders must intentionally work to heal the campus. Simply finding new jobs or academic homes for the displaced may not be enough. Leaders need to design programs to help with the transition, such as forums for people to express their troubles and grief and counseling or career services.

For Those Who Want to Prevent Closures

Understanding the processes through which institutions terminate academic programs not only is helpful for those who intend to close programs but also for those who want to prevent closures. The experiences of the four institutions highlight some weak points in the process and suggest specific strategies to prevent closures. The following recommendations may be useful for those who want to save units from termination.

The first four recommendations are suggestions that might work best prior to the identification of programs to terminate and the last three are for once programs have been named. Because attention is finite and unit leaders frequently do not pick up clues (as one person said, she "did not see the writing on the wall"), some strategies realistically might be invoked only once programs are identified for closure. Defenses are rallied in respect to a threat rather than continually stockpiled.

Become Connected

Units targeted for closure tended to be isolated units that were disconnected from other programs on campus and had little contact with their alumni and other off-campus supporters and the community. A unit that is integral to the activities of other programs, such as offering a significant amount of general education courses or courses required by other majors, shares resources with other units and programs, is a good campus citizen, or provides important diversity to the institution (if that is an agreed-upon objective) is more difficult to consider closing than programs whose activities are not deeply ingrained into the institution. An important strategy is to make connections with others on campus and off.

Highlight Contributions to Campus and Beyond

On a related point, program leaders might prevent their units from being slated for closure by calling attention to specific contributions of the program to the institution and community. In this study, units that publicized the important contributions they made both on and off campus were less likely to be closed than units that did not. Frequently, contributions went unrecognized by campus leaders, thus an important strategy was explicitly informing key decision makers about the work accomplished by the unit. For instance, at UMCP two programs were no longer considered potential targets once campus leaders learned of their contributions to the immediate community—Hearing and Speech because of its clinic serving the region and Nuclear Engineering because of its contribution to another state institution.

Call Attention to Negative Impact

In addition to highlighting contributions, department leaders can also demonstrate that a closure will have negative implications for the institution or community. Rarely do campus leaders want to make a decision that intentionally has a negative consequence somewhere else, either off campus or in another unit. Thus, a strategy to educate campus leaders about the potential damage if a particular program is discontinued might be effective. For example, the president of OSU removed Range Management from the list of potential program closures because of the possible negative effect it might have on another institution.

Those opposing the closures can also enlist the help of others by educating them about potential negative effects. The Mathematics Department at UR was very successful in pleading its case to other mathematicians and researchers. Others, outside the institution, picked up the call saying that if Rochester closed its Mathematics doctoral program, a domino effect might occur, endangering the field. This message rallied the scientific community and well-known scholars to come to the Mathematics Department's aid and put very visible pressure on the institution at a time when UR was trying to recruit more academically talented undergraduates.

Build Coalitions with Others Both On- and Off-Campus

Another effective strategy is to build supportive coalitions. Supportive coalitions are important when no single interest group has the ability to achieve results, since networks consolidate enough power and influence to prevent an unwanted decision. Creating alliances among units wishing to avoid discontinuance creates a stronger front against those interested in closing units.

Coalitions can be built among groups either on- or off-campus. For instance, many departments may form a coalition able to prevent the closure of a specific unit within their college or units across colleges may join together to oppose closing a unit. Additionally, many of the departments in this study were able to prevent termination because they formed strong alliances with off-campus groups. These groups were able to exert adequate pressure to convince institutional leaders to look elsewhere for savings.

Exploit Potential Hot Buttons

Departmental leaders can create supportive coalitions by highlighting potential hot buttons, either process or product issues, around which supporters might coalesce. People can become agitated if they disagree with the decisions being made. For instance, an opposition might form if the programs slated for termination predominately serve women or under-represented minorities. At UR, external groups rallied for Mathematics because of the proposed replacement of research faculty with contract teaching faculty, a sore point in the scholarly mathematics community.

Those opposing the closures also might call attention to procedural violations. Leaders in targeted programs might look for procedural breaches around which an opposing force might coalesce. Some potential examples include the ways in which faculty were involved (or not involved) in key decision making, how information was collected and the way it was used, the lack of an opportunity for appeals, the ways in which decision makers were selected, or how the criteria to judge programs was identified.

Use Atypical Means of Protest

Institutions tend to have acceptable arenas for dissent that have little impact, such as the faculty senate, in some instances (Birnbaum, 1991). To retain a program marked as a potential target, protests should occur outside of these arenas, in places that cause unexpected, rather than expected, disruptions. Mathematics at UR was successful at doing this. By going off campus and gaining the support of Nobel Prize winners and mathematics scholars and by making a commotion in the national media such as the *Chronicle of Higher Education* and the *New York Times,* the department created pressure in areas and of an intensity the campus leadership was not expecting. It was their work off campus that drew the attention of the administrators, not the fiery, but anticipated, rhetoric on the Faculty Council floor.

Negotiate for a Resource-Neutral Alternative

Program closures tend to be proposed as solutions to financial problems. Leaders of programs that are targeted might be able to negotiate resource-neutral alternatives with administrators. By appealing in fiscal terms, they might be able to broker a deal that avoids unit closure. This option might be more realistic if the target program's faculty are not going to be terminated.

Because administrators and faculty have been participating in the process, their perspectives of what is possible may have been altered (Cohen & March, 1986). Proposed alternatives that at one time seemed implausible, may have become more realistic and acceptable.

Argue Discontinuance Might Not Save Money

Finally, those in targeted units might present an analysis of data that discontinuing programs does not save significant amounts of money. The findings of this study suggest that institutional leaders do not know the effectiveness of program termination as a strategy to save money. At best, it may yield little savings and at worst, may be costly because of tuition loss due to enrollment drop and reduced campus productivity because of distractions.

REFINING DISCONTINUANCE POLICY

The AAUP (2001) proposes four guidelines for discontinuing academic programs: (1) that "there be early, careful and meaningful faculty involvement in decisions related to the reduction of instructional and research programs;" (2) that upon the decision to reduce programs, "it should then be the primary responsibility of the faculty to determine where within the program reductions should be made," and that "before any such determinations become final, those whose life's work stands to be adversely affected should have the right to be heard;" (3) "particular reductions should follow considerable advice from the concerned departments, or other units of academic concentration, on the short-term and long-term viability of reduced programs;" and (4) that the rights of tenured faculty be protected and that faculty should be "given every opportunity . . . to readapt with a department or elsewhere with the institution" (p. 193).

Three of the AAUP's recommended actions are consistent with the experiences of the four institutions in this study: Faculty should be involved early on and in meaningful ways; faculty should provide considerable advice on the long- and short-term effects of the closures; and tenure should be protected. Without these three elements the processes at the four institutions might not have been successes. Faculty easily could have formed opposing coalitions around key procedural points halting the process if they were not involved in meaningful ways early on in the process, if they (or their representatives via governance) did not have opportunities to explore the implications and provide advice, or if tenured faculty had been terminated. Additionally, because faculty gave considerable advice as recommended by AAUP, administrators at OSU, UR, and UMCP revised some of their original recommendations. The outcomes may have been damaging to the institution had faculty not articulated potential negative unintended consequences.

The only AAUP recommendation not present in these four processes was faculty having the primary responsibility for determining which closures occur. At none of the four institutions did faculty play this role. Administrators made most of the decisions. Only at UMCP were faculty partners in crafting the recommendations, and only there did faculty make the final recommendations through the senate. Nonetheless, at UR, OSU and KSU, faculty played meaningful roles by providing information and counsel and helping to explore the potential implications of closures.

The findings also suggest new recommendations for AAUP policy and procedures that should improve the shared governance process and set realistic expectations for faculty and administrators. First, the AAUP might recommend that program closures occur in conjunction with other steps to save money, because alone or as first steps, they may be less likely to succeed. Second, it might specify using faculty governance groups to explore the potential implications of proposed closures, which might be done through open deliberations (such as at UMCP) or in confidence (such as at OSU or UR). Third, the AAUP might include language in its document that specifies that the processes used to close programs most likely will vary across institutions because of differences in institutional cultures and norms in decision making. A process that might be acceptable to faculty at one campus where they play consultative roles (OSU) might not be acceptable at another where faculty play major decision making roles (UMCP). Fourth, the AAUP should recognize the important roles administrators play and the direction they provide in program discontinuance. In none of these four cases did faculty carry out the process alone. Finally, the AAUP might note that retaining tenured faculty even when programs are to be closed is important to keeping the conversations focused and keeping the process on track, but keeping tenured faculty from those programs may lead to trade-offs in terms of significant savings.

Beyond the specific AAUP discontinuance guidelines, the findings of this study suggest that AAUP should adopt a broader concept of shared governance. First, this study suggests that the concept of shared governance in practice includes faculty-administrator collaboration that occurs both inside and outside the formal governance structure; it varies by institution as one size clearly does not fit all; it may include decisions where parties act sequentially (e.g., OSU where administrators passed decisions to a faculty group, who in turn passed their decisions back to administrators) and jointly (e.g., UMCP where both faculty and administrators sit on APAC); and it is based upon institutionally defined norms, not on a schema adopted from the outside. Finally, and possibly most importantly, shared governance that is successful (a structure and process that allows many constituencies to make agreeable decisions) is dependent upon expectations that the various parties find acceptable.

SUGGESTIONS FOR FUTURE RESEARCH

Although this study addresses how program discontinuance occurs, the impact of the process on institutions and the roles of leadership, shared governance, and external forces raise further questions. First, because this study was limited to four cases, the common themes should be explored at other types of institutions to see if similarities and differences exist in process and results.

Second, the elements identified here should be further contrasted against the experiences of institutions that attempted but failed to close programs. Although there are probably many more reasons why a change fails than why it succeeds, comparisons may help distinguish the importance of some elements over others.

A third line of inquiry might focus more deeply on the roles and structures of shared governance. Although this study found that shared governance mechanisms can and do facilitate the hard decisions of program closure, critics hold deep-seated assumptions that shared governance is slow and unresponsive (Association of Governing Boards of Universities and Colleges, 1996; Benjamin, Carroll, Jacobi, Krop, & Shires, 1993). It would be interesting to compare the processes and results explored here—which frequently took many months to complete—and the process and results with administratively-driven and quick processes. Does one type of process, administrative or shared, lead to different types or magnitudes of results and effects? What happens when faculty are not involved but expect to be in processes that dictate academic strategy? Related research might explore differences in processes when the closures are externally mandated such as by a governing board or a state legislature. To what extent are processes, timelines, and results similar or different between internally and externally determined closures? What roles do faculty governing bodies play in externally mandated processes? What do administrative leaders do in these situations?

Fourth, the findings suggest that institutions met their budgetary goals but not necessarily through program discontinuance. This raises questions concerning exactly how institutions save money? What actions do they take and are there consistent patterns of cost-saving measures across institutions? On a related matter, in what ways does program discontinuance create an environment that allows these actions to move forward? An additional line of questioning for future research concerning finances centers on why institutional leaders did not thoroughly account for the money saved (or spent) and what role external accountability and outside impetus plays? Why was there no press from external bodies, such as trustees or legislators, to understand the efficiency of program closures?

Finally, it would be interesting to explore the impact of program discontinuance more deeply. For example, one might investigate the long-term effects of program discontinuance on the campus. This research might explore issues such as cost efficiency, campus morale, and financial well being. Differences in process might lead to more or less productivity over the long run across the institution, within departments that were targeted but not removed, or within units where displaced faculty were relocated. Additional inquiries might focus on similar questions at an individual level. These two sets of queries might help uncover some of the deeper and long-lasting costs and benefits of program discontinuance. The interviews with people as long as five years after the events suggest that the process of closing programs leaves lasting marks on faculty and administrators and that the costs and benefits of program discontinuance are not visible immediately or solely on the fiscal bottom line.

CONCLUSION

Program discontinuance has the potential to be disruptive and painful for a campus. At the same time, it can be framed in such a way so that key institutional stakeholders, including faculty and students, regard it as an important step toward institutional enhancement. It tends to be undertaken during periods of financial duress as a cost-savings strategy, yet if done solely for financial reasons, it may be ineffective. This study provided an empirically based exploration of both the processes used to terminate academic programs and the effect of closures on campus. It highlighted the ways in which shared governance can make hard decisions and challenged the ideas purported by the AAUP concerning governance and program termination. It noted the role and impact of leadership and challenged common notions that external forces constantly push institutions to change by identifying instances when they pressure institutions to remain the same.

The intent of this book was to dig deeply into the process of program termination, to understand the nuances and its effects from the inside. The hope was that from the detailed experiences of four institutions, others will find insight and guidance to undertake wisely this difficult, but potentially more-relevant strategy. The context in which American higher education works has changed. Most institutions can neither afford to be all things to all people, nor can they continue offering the same array of academic programs, even with attempts to be more entrepreneurial. They must offer innovative programs and revise curricula that match society's needs, make new choices to do new things, and, with more difficulty, stop old activities because the environment changed. The stakes are increasing and institutions can ill afford to make costly strategic and financial mistakes.

Program closure may not be the saving strategy for all institutions. As the experiences detailed in this book show, the processes can be long and time-consuming, they can be disruptive while under way, and once complete, and in the end, they may not lead towards large savings. That said, many higher education commentators suggest that an increasing number of colleges and universities will have to undertake this process to tighten offerings and to respond to new demands. This study helps institutional leaders decide if program closures are the appropriate strategy for their institution and, second, points out key elements for the journey. The four cases illustrate that neither a single path does not exist, nor can anyone offer a successful seven-step solution. Nevertheless, with proper forethought and reflective and intentional leadership, the course for program closures can be charted successfully.

Appendix: Case Study Methodology for Studying Institutional Change Processes

This appendix describes the research design and methodology used to understand the process of how institutions discontinued academic programs and more generally how case study method can be used to study organizational change processes. Qualitative researcher Pettigrew (1995) suggested that the practicalities of the case study research method are "best characterized by the phrase 'planned opportunism'" (p. 101). This section outlines the processes engaged in the quest to create that "planned opportunism" needed to investigate the program discontinuance process, including (1) the research questions, (2) the research design and rationale, (3) the methods used to carry out the study, (4) the data analysis procedures, and (5) discussions of methodological rigor and limitations of the study.

RESEARCH QUESTIONS

In order to investigate the processes through which institutions discontinued academic programs, this study asked three research questions:

1. How did institutions go about the process of cutting academic programs?
   (a) What elements of leadership influenced the program discontinuance process?
   (b) What elements of shared governance influenced the program discontinuance process?
   (c) What external forces influenced the program discontinuance process?
2. What were the effects of the program discontinuance process on the institution?
3. Are there common themes that were present among the institutional processes used and the elements involved in discontinuing academic programs? What lessons can be drawn from the four cases about the program discontinuance process?

The first question was the grand tour question; it investigated the processes through which programs were discontinued. The primary focus of the study was to capture the ways in which institutions terminated academic programs with specific attention to shared governance, leadership, and external forces. Although these three elements are most likely not the only ones involved, the literature suggests a potential key role for each.

The second question shifted from process to impact or effect. Although the outcomes were similar across institutions in the study, the effects of the process on institutional constituents may differ. This study was just as likely to uncover similar processes of termination that lead to similar outcomes but have different effects, as it was to identify processes that lead to similar outcomes and have similar effects, or dissimilar processes that generate dissimilar effects. Most likely, the effects will shape individual perceptions as well as influence what can be said about program discontinuance processes at the conclusion of the study; thus, they warranted targeted investigation. Additionally, the impact might be perceived differently depending upon sub-group membership or differ from what actually occurred, which would be important to note. For example, faculty may report one set of effects while senior administrators report a different set, or select faculty may perceive a negative public image, when in fact the institution gained unprecedented support from the state legislature.

The final research question looks to identify patterns across the four cases from which lessons might be extracted. At the heart of this study is the desire to draw conclusions that might help inform others about terminating programs.

RESEARCH DESIGN AND RATIONALE

This section outlines the design of the study and explains the methodological choices made. It gives a justification for selecting the case study method with specific attention to multiple case study design, unit of analysis, and site selection.

The Case Study

The phenomena under study almost always "dictates to some extent the terms of its own dissection and exploration" (Leonard-Barton, 1995, p. 40). Case studies are useful because they allow researchers to collect information from a variety of informants and materials across the organization (Leonard-Barton, 1995), helping to form a complicated picture which allows for diverse and often competing explanations of the phenomenon for a deeper understanding (Stake, 1995). Understanding organizational change is a complicated, contextual, and confounding process that calls for a method that accounts for such elements (Pettigrew, 1995). The case study method is effective for studying processes because case studies capture detailed descriptions of dynamic phenomenon (Patton, 1990; Stoeker, 1991).

Patton (1990) outlined the advantage of the case study method to investigate questions such as the ones proposed in this study:

Case studies . . . become particularly useful when one needs to understand some special people, particular problem or unique situation in great depth, and where one can identify cases rich in information—rich in the sense that a great deal can be learned from a few exemplars of the phenomenon in question. (p. 54)

Case studies are used in order to understand "how and why" research questions (Yin, 1994), and to develop in-depth understandings when description and explanation are required, rather than predictions based upon cause and effect (Merriam, 1988). The propensity of case study research is to capture how the people involved in the processes saw things (Stake, 1995) and to understand complex processes that are hard to quantify and control (Merriam, 1988) because the phenomenon was "both historical and idiosyncratic, and statistical analysis was unable to capture either of those" (Stoeker, 1991, p. 94).

Case study methods are most appropriate when three conditions are present: (a) the research questions being addressed are "how" or "why" questions; (b) little control exists over events; and (c) the focus is on a contemporary, real-life phenomenon in which context is important (Yin, 1994). This study met all three requirements.

The Multisite Case Study

Multisite or comparative case studies are a version of the case study method that includes more than one case. This method attempts both to understand the intricacies of each case and to identify general elements which can be compared and contrasted across cases allowing conclusions to be drawn (McPhee, 1995; Merriam, 1988; Miles & Huberman, 1994). "Multi-site qualitative studies address the same research question in a number of settings using similar data collection and analysis procedures in each setting. They consciously seek to permit cross-site comparison without necessarily sacrificing within-site understanding" (Herriott & Firestone, 1983, p. 14). The comparability of multisite case studies allowed generalizations to be drawn from those occurrences common to all of the institutions in the study and for inconsistencies to be identified as well.

Comparison and generalizability across cases or data points in qualitative research differ from that in quantitative research. Rather than generalizability based upon replication and representativeness, as in quantitative research, case studies engender generalizability in the form of "fundamental understanding of the structure, process, and driving forces rather than a superficial establishment of correlation or cause-effect relationship" (Norman, 1970, p. 53, as cited in Gummersson, 1991). To establish comparability and generalizability in case studies, the researcher must, to the extent possible, use transferable and non-idiosyncratic lenses to analyze the case and describe the phenomenon using common terminology. "Translatability assumes that research methods, analytic categories and characteristics of phenomenon and groups are identified so explicitly that comparisons can be conducted confidently and used meaningfully across groups and disciplines" (LeCompte & Preissle, 1993, p. 47).

Unit of Analysis

Case study methods investigate a bounded unit such as an event, a person, a group, an organization, or a process called the unit of analysis (Miles & Huberman, 1994; Merriam, 1988; Patton, 1990). The unit of analysis defines what the case is and what the case is not; it sets the parameters, informs the researcher what to include and what not to, and where to search for information (Pettigrew, 1995; Stoeker, 1991; Yin, 1994). In the multisite case study method, the unit of analysis is constant across the investigated sites, which was the process used to terminate academic programs at each specific institution.

Research in which the unit of analysis is a process addresses questions of how, as compared to content research that focuses on questions of what (who and why are studied in each format but with different foci and implications) (Huff & Reger, 1987). Process research is important for understanding the dynamics of organizational life and for developing theories of organizational change (Van de Ven & Huber, 1995).

RESEARCH METHODS

This section outlines the specific elements of the research. It describes the procedures used to select the institutions in the study as well as the informants at each institution. It additionally discusses the processes followed to collect data through interviews and written materials.

Site Selection and Access

Site selection requires that the researcher delineate the relevant cases. Sites can be selected because they are typical, comprehensive, extreme, unique, critical, comparable, or accessible (LeCompte & Preissle, 1993; Patton, 1990). This study used a combination of selection criteria. It selected institutions based upon institutional characteristics, maximum variance, and accessibility.

First, as this study was one of program discontinuance, each institution must have discontinued at least one academic program within six years. That time frame was selected to increase the likelihood that those involved with the process were still employed on campus or might be easily contacted and that the event might still be fairly fresh in the minds of potential informants.

Second, the decision to discontinue a program must have been implemented and the program not reinstated. Examples exist of institutions making a decision to close programs which caused such uproar that the decisions were reversed (Steigler, 1994). Implementation-based criteria were selected to define program discontinuation, because, often in events such as these, the decision to terminate and the actual implementation of the decision are loosely connected; decisions may be made but not automatically and sequentially acted upon (Baldridge, 1983; Gladstein & Quinn, 1985; Huff & Reger, 1987). Criteria included no longer accepting new students, the removal of the program from the university catalogue, and, where applicable, the termination or reassignment of program faculty and administrators.

Third, only universities classified as Research I or II Universities (Carnegie Foundation for the Advancement of Teaching, 1994) were identified because the processes to respond to financial constraints may vary by type of institution (El-Khawas, 1994).

Fourth, to explore the nature of program discontinuance and address questions concerning similarities and differences in unit closure and degree closure, four institutions were identified, two which had engaged in one of the two types of closures. Although the distinctions were not hard-and-fast, it was possible to categorize and select institutions based upon their dissolution of (a) both unit and degree or (b) degree only.

Finally, institutions were selected because they were believed to be accessible (Patton, 1990). Access is a valid selection criteria in studies in which the pool of potential sites is shallow, thus limiting the use of other selection criteria.

To identify potential institutions that had discontinued academic programs, I conducted an electronic search of *The Chronicle of Higher Education*; reviewed past issues of *Academe*, the AAUP's magazine; *Trusteeship*, AGB's magazine; searched Department of Education data bases (i.e., IPEDS); and contacted the National Association of State Universities and Land Grant Colleges (NASULGC), the American Association of State Colleges and Universities (AASCU), and the American Association of Universities (AAU). I searched the publications because closures would most likely be reported in one of those three publications, and I contacted the three associations because they were thought to collect data such as program discontinuance on member institutions.

Program discontinuance may be a much-touted process, but one that is apparently infrequently completed on campus. I was surprised to find only a small number of research and doctoral universities meeting selection criteria. Because of the small pool of potential institutions and the high need for access to a constrained number, factors such as institutional size or the types of institutional control (e.g., public versus private, and system versus non-system) could not be included as selection criteria. I was unable to limit the number or the types of disciplines which were discontinued because institutions frequently eliminate a cluster of programs through one centralized process in which it is difficult to differentiate among processes used to terminate specific programs, and because institutions may modify both the number of programs and the specific programs to be eliminated as their processes unfold (Falk & Miller, 1993; Gumport, 1993).

The institutions were then sub-divided into two groups by the type of program discontinuance in which they engaged. Two institutions that had terminated units and two institutions that had terminated degrees were then identified, institutions to which I could obtain access. A contact person at each institution was telephoned to confirm that the media and association reports were accurate (the Department of Education data did not yield any institutions). The phone calls confirmed that academic programs were terminated, that the process occurred within the last six years, and that the programs had not been reinstated.

Once institutions were identified and confirmed, the chief academic officer (CAO) at each institution received a letter explaining the study, asking for permission to include the institution in the study, and requesting a phone conversation. The purpose of the phone call was to further discuss the study and offer institution anonymity, address any questions the CAO might have, ask for assistance distributing a letter of introduction to those potentially involved requesting their cooperation, and request related written documents. Four universities agreed to participate in this study: University of Maryland at College Park (UMCP), Oregon State University, the University of Rochester, and Kent State University. Although offered anonymity, none of the institutions desired it. Upon their approval they are identified.

Selecting Informants

In this study the informants were the primary source of information as the "researcher's account of the studied scene should be built on the information provided by the most knowledgeable (and candid) members of the scene." (Van Maanen, 1979, p. 545).

The first round of key informants were identified from referrals made by the primary informant, who was centrally involved with and highly informed about the process used and someone able to provide referrals (Merriam, 1988). During the initial phone call to the CAO, he or she was asked to identify the person who chaired the program discontinuation process or someone who was highly involved who might be willing to act as the primary informant. This person was contacted and asked to participate in the interviews and to provide a list of names of other people involved in the program termination decision or affected by the decision.

The primary informant was asked to consider three types of people who might become informants: (a) individuals involved in making the decision including administrators and faculty, such as those key central administrators or members of involved governance committees, and if applicable, others such as staff or students; (b) those involved from outside the institution such as board members, alumni, or community members; and (c) those faculty and administrators in the closed units who were still on campus. The office of the CAO was then contacted to obtain the addresses, e-mail addresses, and phone numbers of potential informants.

Letters were sent to potential informants informing them of the study and asking them to participate. I followed up the letters with phone calls. Between 12 and 15 interviews were scheduled for each institution, a realistic number of interviews that could be conducted over the course of a three-day site visit. Attempts were made to ensure that the pool of informants included faculty and administrators as well as others from outside the institution, and included those involved in the termination process as well as affected by the decisions who still worked on campus.

When additional informants were needed beyond those identified by the primary informant, the second set of informants was identified through snowball or network sampling, a process through which the original set of informants was asked to identify others who might provide additional information (LeCompte & Preissle, 1993; Patton, 1990). A generic list of potential informants (e.g. faculty senate chair, associate provost, chief financial officer, deans) was drafted prior to the phone calls to the CAO and primary informant to act as a confirmation tool. Individuals holding positions not mentioned were brought up so as to potentially jog informants' memory and to ensure that the range of potential informants was suggested.

Collecting Data

When studying institutional change through a case study approach, data should be collected that is process oriented, comparative, historical, and contextual so that themes and patterns might be identified (Pettigrew, 1995). Data collection should not just be a reporting of facts and events, but rather should get at the meanings organizational members make from and assign to those facts and events (Van Maanen, 1979). Getting to a level of linkages and connections was significant because "meaning depends on which content gets joined with which content, by what connection. Content is embedded in cues, frames, and connections." These are the raw materials of sensemaking (Weick, 1995, p. 132) and of explanation.

As this study was retrospective, the researcher was not present during the change efforts. Thus a major challenge of this research was to collect comparable, retrospective data on events and processes that occurred (Glick, Huber, Miller, Doty, & Sutcliff, 1995). The potential of any study to provide a useful, valid description and generalization depends on the analyst's ability to first collect and then reduce data to "a manageable form without distortion or loss of meaningful detail" (Herriott & Firestone, 1983, p. 18). Additionally, the researcher should strive to give adequate attention to "alternative accounts rather than accord one privileged status" (Pettigrew, 1995, p. 99). To do so, this research incorporated information from a variety of sources including written documents and interviews of a range of people on each campus, including faculty and administrators involved in the process and faculty whose programs were closed. During data analysis, notes were made highlighting both convergent and divergent stories.

Data was collected during site visits at each of the four institutions. The collected data included the interviews with informants, institutional documents, school newspaper accounts, speeches, and other written material related to the discontinuation process. So that generalizations across cases could be made, care was taken to ensure that similar data was collected at each institution.

Interviews

Interviews were important data sources because in studying organizational change qualitatively "researchers are in the perspective business" (Pettigrew, 1995, p. 107). They must seek out and listen to different stories that help create a picture of what occurred, how it occurred, why, and with what impact. Interviews are important sources of direct quotations, the building blocks of qualitative research. As Patton (1990) noted:

Direct quotations are a basic source of raw data in qualitative inquiry, revealing respondents' depth of emotion, the ways they have organized their world, their thoughts about what is happening, their experiences and their basic perceptions. The task for the qualitative researcher is to provide a framework within which people can respond in a way that represents accurately and thoroughly their points of view about the world, or that part of the world about which they are talking. (p. 24)

The purpose of the interviews was to extract a story of the key events describing how each institution discontinued its academic programs. Stories are central to draw out what occurred for the following reasons:

First, stories aid comprehension because they integrate that which is known about an event with that which is conjectural. Second, stories suggest a causal order for events that originally are perceived as unrelated and akin to a list. Third, stories enable people to talk about absent things and to connect them with present things in the interest of meaning. Four, stories are mnemonics that enable people to reconstruct earlier complex events. (Weick, 1995, p. 129)

To elicit information from respondents, I used focused interview protocols, which are a set of structured, open-ended questions that follow a predetermined pattern with the intention of eliciting comments on specific topics (Yin, 1994) and capturing the perspectives of those involved in the processes without predetermining key points or elements (Patton, 1990). The interview protocols included introductory questions and a series of follow-up targeted questions. The purpose of the introductory questions was to elicit a grand tour of the process and describe how the program was discontinued (Spradley, 1979, p. 87). Following the response to the grand tour questions, the researcher asked targeted questions focusing on leadership, governance, and external influences and the perceived impact of the process on the institution.

Interviews were conducted with participants over the course of a three-day site visit. Interviews, for the most part, were conducted in the offices of the informants and were tape-recorded. Individuals who were key players but who had left the institution or who had scheduling conflicts were interviewed by phone. Two interviews were conducted this way. These interviews were also tape recorded and documented by notes taken by the researcher.

The interviews lasted between 30 minutes and two-and-one-half hours, with the average time being one hour. At the start of the interviews, the researcher explained the purpose and design of the research as well as issues of confidentiality. In this study, generic titles were used (i.e., faculty leader, senior administrator) and each informant was reassured that no names would be used. Senior administrators were asked to be identified by title, to which all agreed. All informants were given the option of not having the interview tape-recorded or of stopping the tape for any portions of the discussion. Only one person requested only one part of the interview not be taped, whereby I took copious notes.

Follow-up interviews were conducted with select informants once all of the interviews had been collected and an initial read of the interview logs had been completed. The follow-up interviews were conducted by telephone in order to clarify certain comments and explore key propositions (Merriam, 1988; Spradley, 1979) that they made in their first interview. Notes taken by the researcher documented these interviews.

Written Data

In addition to interviews conducted by the researcher, additional data were obtained from written sources discussing the program discontinuance process. Written materials are important sources of information in qualitative case studies because they provide additional information and chronicle processes and activities (Merriam, 1988). Written materials can be used to either help formulate questions or confirm researcher hypotheses or hunches (Patton, 1990).

I reviewed meeting minutes, institutional reports, speeches, other relevant campus documents and on- and off-campus newspaper accounts. The documents were primarily obtained from the informants and collected at each institution. Newspaper accounts were identified through electronic searches and at meetings with campus archivists. Background documents were additionally collected to provided information about the institution, such as its mission and strategic plan. When informants were contacted and agreed to participate in the interviews they were asked if they had any relevant documents or if they knew about documents that might be helpful and how they might be obtained.

DATA ANALYSIS

Data analysis is at the heart of qualitative case studies. It is the process through which the data collected begins to take shape, form a story, outline patterns and trends, and make sense (Merriam, 1988; Miles & Huberman, 1994). In case study research, the final product begins to unfold and emerge from the patterns found in the cases under study with limited advance knowledge about what the important dimensions will be (Patton, 1990). Case studies attempt to go beyond the cataloging of the facts to find the meanings attached to those facts by the organizational participants, as Pettigrew (1995) noted:

What is critical is not just events, but the underlying logics that give events meaning and significance. Understanding these underlying logics in the process of change is the goal, and this requires data on events, interpretations of patterns in those events, when they occur in socially meaningful time cycles, and the logics that may explain how and why these patterns occur in particular chronological sequences. (p. 100)

Two sets of materials were analyzed for this study—interview transcriptions and written materials. From the collected data case reports or case data bases were drafted which included all of the potentially relevant material collected from the site visit (Yin, 1994). Developing case reports included a four-step process: first, creating a working outline immediately following the campus visit based on information from the interviews; second, reading each of the interview logs noted where items and statements fit into the original outline, expanded the outline, or differed from it; third, upon re-reading each interview log, placing text into the outline or making modifications to the outline based upon the presented evidence, and followed the same procedure for each log; and finally, going through a similar process for all of the other collected materials. This process led to the drafting of each case report or case database.

Out of the case reports, each case study was crafted telling the story of the discontinuance process. Following the crafting of the cases, two three-step data analysis processes were used. The first process was for within-case analysis and the second for cross-case comparison. First, the four frames were used to pattern code within each case, a process to link bits of data into "a smaller number of sets, themes or constructs" (p. 64). Second, memos were created, a process of writing up ideas and notions of the patterned codes which "go beyond just reporting data, . . . tying together pieces of data into a recognizable cluster, often to show that those data are instances of general concept" (p. 73). Third, I developed a set of propositions for each case using the vocabulary of the four frames.

The second three-step process was carried out for cross-case analysis. Each case and the with-in case frame analysis was read and pattern coded searching for information concerning leadership, shared governance, and external forces. The codes arose from the research. A second memo process looked for connections among codes for the three areas across cases. Third, a series of propositions within and among the cases attempted to explain how program discontinuance occurred and the elements of leadership, shared governance, and external forces that influenced the process (Miles & Huberman, 1994).

Organizing Frames

As a heuristic device to help identify the patterns in the stories told and paint a complete picture of the discontinuance process, the four Bolman and Deal (1991) frameworks (structural, political, human resources, and symbolic frames) were incorporated. Following examples set by Allison (1986), Birnbaum (1990, 1991), Olsen (1979), and Strava (1979), this study identified alternative explanations to more comprehensively describe the process of discontinuing academic programs through the use of multiple lenses. The use of alternative models helps create diversified descriptions that explain what occurred (Bolman & Deal, 1991; Pennings, 1986; Van de Ven & Poole, 1995). The common organizing framework also facilitated cross-site comparisons (LeCompte & Preissle, 1993).

RIGOR AND LIMITATIONS

The research questions lead to findings best described in terms of patterns and themes rather than confirmed hypotheses and explanations that were tested against common sense and plausibility, not against predictive theories, both of which support the use of case study methods (Daft, 1980, as cited in Weick, 1995; Pettigrew, 1995). This section discusses the ways this study ensured a sufficient level of rigor and notes its limitations.

Methodological Rigor

Yin (1994) identified the following three principles as central for establishing an ample level of methodological rigor in case study research: (1) the use of multiple sources of evidence; (2) the construction of a data base of information or case report specifically for the case study; and (3) the development of a logical chain of evidence describing the rationale and the processes used that connects the findings to the collected data. This study adhered to those three principles through the following mechanisms. It satisfied the requirement of multiple sources of evidence in two ways. First, the interview data was collected from a range of informants involved with the process; second, in addition to using multiple informants, this study also obtained information from written material, an alternative source of evidence. Multiple sources of evidence help the researcher develop "converging lines of inquiry" (Yin, 1994, p. 92), increasing the accuracy of the study and making it more convincing to the reader.

Second, a case database was constructed. The information collected through the interview logs and from the written materials comprised the database or case reports. The study's database is a distinct pool of data separate from the final report. The database was the source from which the researcher drew his analysis. The purpose of creating a separate data repository is that it allows other investigators the ability to review the evidence directly and not be limited to the final analysis of the researcher (Yin, 1994).

Finally, a chain of evidence was developed. The researcher created a chain of evidence that described the process through which analyses were made following the three-step process detailed by Miles and Huberman (1994): pattern coding, memoing, and drafting propositions. The chain of evidence allows readers to link the analysis to specific instances in the case data base and to the research questions, allowing an external observer to "trace the steps in any direction (from conclusions back to initial research questions or from questions to conclusions)" (Yin, 1994. p. 98).

Additional safeguards to ensure trustworthiness and credibility of the findings (Lincoln & Guba. 1985) were taken. For example, I engaged in peer debriefing, a process of conversing at periodic intervals with non-involved professionals to keep the inquirer honest in drafting propositions, explore methodological next steps, and help make sense of the data by talking through it (Lincoln & Guba, 1985). The debriefings were done once a month with peer researchers involved in writing their dissertations. Finally, at least one key informant from each of the institutions read each case and offered suggestions. In two of the cases the individual responsible for leading the process read and commented on the case. In the third instance, the institution's president at the time of the closures read the case, and in the final case, two participants from different stages of the process commented on the draft case.

Limitations

Any study is bound to have limitations; it is what makes the study manageable (LeCompte & Preissle, 1993). The most significant limitation of a retrospective study is the difficulty of crafting an explanation from reconstructed events (Leonard-Barton, 1995) as the data is based upon informant recall that is highly subjective (Pettigrew, 1995; Weick, 1995). This difficulty is caused by several participant biases and misperceptions. For example, most respondents recount the history of events beginning at the point at which they became aware of or entered the scenario, such that they might not be familiar with the early elements of the institution's efforts or the "pre-history" which strongly dictates how the change unfolded (Kanter, 1983).

Early events and actors also tend to disappear into the background as later events and people come forward (Kanter, 1983). People tend to hold more prominently in their minds events which occurred more recently than in the distant past. They judge the value of events, not based upon their impact or a cause-and-effect pattern, but by chronological proximity. Glick, Huber, Miller, Doty, & Sutcliff (1995) described this phenomena and its impact on data collection:

> Informants may selectively neglect some events that are important, or focus on trends that are actually unimportant but are temporarily conspicuous to the informant. If too many truly important events are omitted, the theoretical explanations will be inaccurate and will lack descriptive relevance. If non-important events are included, they may be falsely accepted as important possible antecedents of other changes. (p. 139)

Retrospectively, equally plausible alternatives also tend to disappear into obvious choices, and confusions and meandering paths become clear-sighted strategies (Kanter, 1983). Rarely do people attribute good results to poor analyses or incorrect actions, view good actions as having no impact, or find poor results coming from good actions or accurate perceptions (Starbuck & Milliken, 1988). Retrospectively, things tend to make sense almost too well, as individuals make connections looking back in ways which link events that were incomprehensible while in progress (Weick, 1995).

Informants may additionally provide information that is incorrect or revisionist (Leonard-Barton, 1995; Van Maanen, 1979) to hide controversial practices or decisions, or not reveal personal defects, mistakes, or taboo activities. Informants may also unwittingly provide false information because they either were misled or given poor information by others, or because they were unaware of certain aspects of their own activities (Van Maanen, 1979).

Another limitation from informant bias comes not from the interviews but from the documents. The documents used were not produced for research purposes. They should not be taken as literal recordings of events (Yin, 1994), because they were produced to inform, persuade, bias, or create commitment to action. They were not representative of the complete process but captured only a biased portion of it (Merriam, 1988).

But not all of the limitations come from the informants. In qualitative methods, the researcher is the data collection instrument, opening the door for potential researcher bias (Merriam, 1988; Spradley, 1979). Much of the sense made from the data collected in case studies is based upon the "culture of the researcher, not the researched" (Van Maanen, 1979, p. 541). It is the worldviews of the researcher that help inform what he or she sees and interprets.

Another limitation is that of completeness of the phenomenon studied. "Is it all here?" is a frequent question of case studies as researchers attempt to capture highly complex, ambiguous, and uncertain processes in their rich contexts.

Qualitative researchers lay claim to portrayals that tell more or less, the whole story of the research. Simultaneously, they know they never get it all; they know they only get pieces, views and aspects of what they seek to describe. Most qualitative researchers cope with the impossibility of completism, by making trade-offs. (LeCompte & Preissle, 1993, p. 317)

In this study, it is most likely completely not all here because data collection is a selective process (Miles & Huberman, 1994) limited by constraints including time and money. Nevertheless, I am confident that the information collected reveals significant and salient information concerning the processes of how institutions discontinued academic programs.

Finally, the scarcity of program discontinuance created two limitations. First, program discontinuance is not an every-campus phenomenon. Because most campuses have not succeeded with cutting programs, I selected institutions from a pool identified from *The Chronicle of Higher Education, Academe,* and *Trusteeship.* This may suggest that the institutions investigated were those newsworthy enough in some way to make the higher education press, thus they may not be representative of the processes used at institutions which did not make headlines. Second, because of the rarity of successful program discontinuance, access became an overriding selection criteria. I was unable to hold constant elements such as institutional control, the number or size of departments, or the coupling of the process which led to terminated departments with other cutback processes such as administrative restructuring; other terminations; or the merging of majors, departments, or colleges.

References

Adelman, C. (2000). *A parallel postsecondary universe: The certification system in information technology*. Washington, DC: Office of Educational Research and Improvement (ED).

Aldrich, H. E. (1979). *Organizations & environments*. Englewood Cliffs, NJ: Prentice Hall.

Allison, G. T. (1986). Conceptual models and the Cuban missile crisis. In J. M. Pennings (Ed.) Decision making: An organization behavioral approach, 2d ed., 311–40. New York: Markus Wiener.

American Association of University Professors. (2001). *Policy documents & reports* (9th ed.). Washington, DC: AAUP.

Association of Governing Boards of Universities and Colleges. (1996). *Renewing the academic presidency: Stronger leadership for tougher times*. Washington, DC: Association of Governing Boards.

Baldridge, J. V. (1971). *Power and conflict in the university: Research in the sociology of complex organizations*. New York: John Wiley & Sons.

Baldridge, J. V. (1983). Rules for a Machiavellian change agent: Transforming the entrenched professional organization. In J. V. Baldridge & T. Deal (Eds.), *The dynamics of organizational change in education*. Berkeley, CA: McCutchan Publishing.

Behn, R. D. (1988). The fundamentals of cutback management. In K. S. Cameron, R. I. Sutton, & D. A. Whetten (Eds.), *Readings in organizational decline: Frameworks, research and prescriptions* (pp. 347–356). Cambridge, MA: Ballinger.

Benjamin, R., Carroll, S., Jacobi, M., Krop, C., & Shires, M. (1993). *The redesign of governance in higher education*. Santa Monica: RAND.

Bensimon, E. M. (1992). The meaning of "good presidential leadership": A frame analysis. In M. W. Peterson, E. E. Chaffee, T. H. White (Eds.) *Organization and governance in higher education* (4th ed., pp. 389–398). Needham Heights, MA: Ginn Press.

Bess, J. L. (1988). *Collegiality and bureaucracy in the modern university: The influence of information and power on decision-making structures.* New York: Teachers College Press.

Birnbaum, R. (1988). *How colleges work: The cybernetics of academic organization and leadership.* San Francisco: Jossey-Bass.

Birnbaum, R. (1990, November). *Negotiating in an anarchy: Faculty collective bargaining and organizational cognition.* Paper presented at the annual meeting of the Association for the Study of Higher Education, Portland, OR.

Birnbaum, R. (1991). The latent organizational functions of the academic senate: Why senates do not work but will not go away. In M. W. Peterson, E. E. Chaffee, & T. H. White (Eds.), *Organization and governance in higher education* (4th ed., pp. 195–207). Needham Heights, MA: Ginn Press.

Birnbaum, R. (1992). *How academic leadership works: Understanding success and failure in the college presidency.* San Francisco: Jossey-Bass.

Blau, P. M. (1994). *The organization of academic work* (2nd ed.). New Brunswick: Transaction.

Bolman, L. G., & Deal, T. E. (1991). *Reframing organizations: Artistry, choice and leadership.* San Francisco: Jossey-Bass.

Boulding, D. (1975). The management of decline. *Change, 7*(5), 8–9, 64.

Breneman, D. W. (1993). *Higher education: On a collision course with new realities.* (AGB Occasional Paper No. 22.) Washington, DC: Association of Governing Boards.

Breneman, D. W. (1997). *Alternatives to tenure for the next generation of academics. New Pathways: Faculty careers and employment for the 21st century. A project of the American Association for Higher Education.* Washington, DC: AAHE.

Breneman, D. W. (2002, June 14). For colleges, this is not just another recession. *The Chronicle of Higher Education,* p. B7.

Brunsson, N. (1982). The irrationality of action and action rationality: Decisions, ideologies and organizational actions. *Journal of Management Studies, 19,* 29–44.

Callan, P. M. (2002, February). *Coping with recession: Public policy, economic downturns and higher education* (National Center for Public Policy and Higher Education Report NO. 02–2) Washington, DC: National Center for Public Policy and Higher Education.

Cameron, K. S. (1983). Strategic responses to conditions of decline: Higher education and the private sector. *Journal of Higher Education, 54*(4), 359–380.

Cameron, K. S., & Tschirhart, M. (1992). Postindustrial environments and organizational effectiveness in colleges and universities. *Journal of Higher Education, 63*(1), 87–108.

Cameron, K. S., Whetten, D. A., & Kim, M. (1987). Organizational dysfunctions of decline. *Academy of Management Journal, 30,* 126–138.

Cameron, K. S., Whetten, D. A., Kim, M., & Chaffee, E. E. (1987). The aftermath of decline. *Review of Higher Education, 10*(3), 215–234.

Carnegie Foundation for the Advancement of Teaching. (1994). *A classification of institutions of higher education.* Princeton, NJ: The Carnegie Foundation for the Advancement of Teaching.

Chaffee, E. E. (1983). *Rational decision making in higher education.* Boulder, CO: National Center for Higher Education Management Systems.

Chaffee, E. E. (1984). Successful strategic management in small private colleges. *Journal of Higher Education, 55*, 212–241.

Chait, R. (1998). Illusions of a leadership vacuum. *Change: The Magazine of Higher Learning*, 30(1), 38–41.

Clark, B. (1995). Complexity and differentiation: The deepening problem of university integration. In D. D. Dill & B. Sporn (Eds.), *Emerging patterns of social demand and university reform: Through a glass darkly* (pp. 159–170). Tarrytown, NY: IAU Press.

Clark, B. R. (1998). *Creating entrepreneurial universities: Organizational pathways of transformation.* New York: IAU Press.

Cohen M. D., & March, J. G. (1986). *Leadership and ambiguity* (2nd ed.). Boston: Harvard Business School Press.

Cole, J. R. (1994). Balancing acts: Dilemmas of choice facing research universities. In J. R. Cole, E. G. Barber, & S. R. Graubard (Eds.), *The research university in a time of discontent* (pp. 1–36). Baltimore: The Johns Hopkins University Press.

Dickeson, R. (1999). *Prioritizing academic programs: A comprehensive agenda for colleges and universities.* San Francisco: Jossey-Bass.

Dill, D. D., & Sporn, B. (1995a). University 2001: What will the university of the twenty-first century look like? In D. D. Dill & B. Sporn (Eds.), *Emerging patterns of social demand and university reform: Through a glass darkly* (pp. 212–236). Tarrytown, NY: IAU Press.

Dill, D. D., & Sporn, B. (1995b). Implications of a postindustrial environment for the university: An introduction. In D. D. Dill & B. Sporn (Eds.), *Emerging patterns of social demand and university reform: Through a glass darkly* (pp. 1–19). Tarrytown, NY: IAU Press.

Dougherty, E. A. (1979, April). *What is the most effective way to handle program discontinuance? Case studies from 10 campuses.* Paper presented at the National Conference of the American Association of Higher Education, Washington, DC.

Drucker, P. F. (1994, September-October). The theory of the business. *Harvard Business Review, 72*(5), 95–104.

Duderstadt, J. J. (2000). *University for the 21st century.* Ann Arbor: University of Michigan Press.

Eckel, P. D., & Kezar, A. (2002). *Taking the reins: Transforming Higher Education.* Washington, DC: ACE/Oryx Press.

El-Khawas, E. (1994). *Restructuring initiatives in public higher education: Institutional response to financial constraints.* (Research Briefs, Report No. 5, Vol. 8). Washington, DC: American Council on Education.

Fairweather, J. S. (1988). *Entrepreneurship and higher education* (ASHE-ERIC Higher Education Report No. 6). Washington, DC: George Washington University.

Falk, D. S., & Miller, G. R. (1993, Fall). How do you cut $45 million from your institution's budget? Use processes and ask your faculty. *Educational Record, 74*(4), 32–38.

Fisher, J. L. (1994, Summer). Reflections on transformational leadership. *Educational Record, 55*, 60–65.

Florijn, M. W. (1996). *Report on budget retrenchment at University of Maryland College Park.* Unpublished manuscript, University of Twente, Enschede, Netherlands.

Gioia, D. A., & Thomas, J. B. (1996). Identity, image and issue interpretation: Sense-making during strategic change in academia. *Administrative Science Quarterly*, *41*, 370–403.

Gladstein, D., & Quinn, J. B. (1985). Making decisions and producing action: The two faces of strategy. In J. M. Pennings (Ed.), *Organizational strategy and change* (pp. 198–216). San Francisco, Jossey-Bass.

Glick, W. H., Huber, G. P., Miller, C. C., Doty, D. H., & Sutcliff, K. M. (1995). Studying changes in organizational design and effectiveness: Retrospective event histories and periodic assessments. In G. P. Huber & A. H. Van de Ven (Eds.), *Longitudinal field research methods: Studying processes of organizational change* (pp. 126–154). Thousand Oaks, CA: Sage Publications.

Green, M. F. (1988). Toward a new leadership model. In M. F. Green (Ed.), *Leaders for a new era* (pp. 30–51). Washington, DC: American Council on Education/Macmillan.

Green, M. F. (1996, October). *Wanted: Presidential leaders to reinvent higher education: Visionaries, magicians, saints, and lunatics encouraged to apply*. Paper presented at the meeting of the Pennsylvania Association of Colleges and Universities, PA.

Gummersson, E. (1991). *Qualitative methods in management research*. Newbury Park, CA: Sage Publications.

Gumport, P. J. (1993). The contested terrain of academic program reduction. *Journal of Higher Education*, *64*(3), 283–311.

Gumport, P. J., & Prusser, B. (1997). Restructuring the academic environment. In M. W. Peterson, D. D. Dill, & L. A. Mets (Eds.), *Planning and management for a changing environment: A handbook on redesigning postsecondary institutions* (pp. 452–478). San Francisco: Jossey-Bass.

Gumport, P. J., & Sporn, B. (1999). Institutional adaptation: Demands for management reform and university administration. In J. Smart and W. Tierney (Eds.), *Higher Education: Handbook of Theory and Research: Vol. 14* (pp. 103–145). New York: Agathon Press.

Hardy, C. (1987). Using content, context and process to manage university cutbacks. *The Canadian Journal of Higher Education*, *17*(1), 65–82.

Hardy, C. (1987/1988). Turnaround strategies in universities. *Planning for higher education*, *16*(1), 9–23.

Hardy, C. (1988). Investing in retrenchment: Avoiding the hidden costs. In K. S. Cameron, R. I. Sutton, & D. A. Whetten (Eds.), *Readings in organizational decline: Frameworks, research and prescriptions* (pp. 369–380). Cambridge, MA: Ballinger.

Hardy, C. (1990a). Strategy and context: Retrenchment in Canadian Universities. *Organization Studies*, *11*(2), 207–237.

Hardy, C. (1990b). "Hard" decisions and "tough" choices: The business approach to university decline. *Higher Education*, *20*, 301–321.

Hardy, C. (1993). The cultural politics of retrenchment. *Planning for Higher Education*, *21*(4), 16–20.

Hardy, C. (1995). Managing strategic change: Power, paralysis and perspective. In P. Shrivastava & C. Stubbart (Eds.), *Advances in Strategic Management: Challenges from within the Mainstream* (pp. 3–37). Greenwich, CT: JAI.

Hardy, C., Langley, A., Mintzberg, H., & Rose, J. (1983). Strategy-making in the university setting. *Review of Higher Education*, *6*, 407–433.

Harvey, J., & Immerwahr, J. (1995a). *Goodwill and growing worry: Public perceptions of American higher education.* Washington, DC: American Council on Education.

Harvey, J., & Immerwahr, J. (1995b, Fall). Public perceptions of higher education: On Main Street and in the boardroom. *Educational Record, 76*(4), 51–55.

Heifetz, R. A. (1995). *Leadership without easy answers.* Cambridge, MA: Harvard University Press.

Herriott, R. E., & Firestone, W. A. (1983). Multi-site qualitative policy research: Optimizing description and generalizability. *Educational Researcher, 12,* 14–19.

Hovey, H. A. (1999). *State spending for higher education in the next decade: The battle to sustain current support.* San Jose, CA: National Center for Public Policy and Higher Education; State Policy Research, Inc.

Huff, A. S., & Reger, R. K. (1987). A review of strategic process research. *Journal of Management, 13*(2), 211–236.

Ikenberry, S. O., & Hartle, T. W. (2000). *Taking stock: How Americans judge quality, affordability, and leadership at U.S. colleges and universities.* Washington, DC: American Council on Education.

Jick, T., & Murray, V. V. (1982). The management of hard times: Budget cutbacks in public sector organizations. *Organizational studies, 3*(2), 141–169.

Kanter, R. M. (1983). *The change masters: Innovation and entrepreneurship in the American corporation.* New York: Simon and Schuster.

Keller, G. (1983). *Academic strategy: The management revolution in American higher education.* Baltimore: Johns Hopkins University Press.

Kennedy, D. (1994). Making choices in the research university. In J. R. Cole, E. G. Barber, & S. R. Graubard (Eds.), *The research university in a time of discontent* (pp. 85–114). Baltimore: Johns Hopkins University Press.

Kezar, A., & Eckel, P. D. (2002). The effect of institutional culture on change strategies in higher education: Universal principles or culturally responsive concepts? *The Journal of Higher Education, 73,* 435–460.

Kotter, J. P. (1995, March-April). Leading change: Why transformation efforts fail. *Harvard Business Review, 73*(2), 59–67.

Kuh, G. D., & Whitt, E. J. (1988). *The invisible tapestry: Culture in American colleges and universities* (ASHE-ERIC Higher Education Report No. 1). Washington, DC: ASHE.

LeCompte, M. D., & Preissle, J. (1993). *Ethnography and qualitative design in educational research* (2nd ed.). New York: Academic Press.

Leonard-Barton, D. (1995). A dual methodology for case studies: Synergistic use of a longitudinal single site with replicated multiple sites. In G. P. Huber & A. H. Van de Ven (Eds.), *Longitudinal field research methods: Studying processes of organizational change* (pp. 38–64). Thousand Oaks, CA: Sage Publications.

Levine, A. (1997, January 31). Higher education's net status as a mature industry. *The Chronicle of Higher Education,* A48.

Levine, A. (2000, October 27). The future of colleges: 9 inevitable changes. *The Chronicle of Higher Education,* p. B10.

Levine, C. H. (1978). Organizational decline and cutback management. *Public Administrative Review, 38,* 316–325.

Levine, C. H. (1979). More on cutback management: Hard questions for hard times. *Public Administrative Review, 39,* 179–183.

Levine, C. H., Rubin, I. S., & Wolohojian, G. G. (1981). *The politics of retrenchment.* Beverly Hills, CA: Sage Publications.

Lincoln, Y. S., & Guba, E. G. (1985). *Naturalistic inquiry.* Beverly Hills, CA: Sage Publications.

Manns, C. L., & March, J. G. (1978). Financial adversity, internal competition and curriculum change in the university. *Administrative Science Quarterly, 23,* 541–552.

March, J. G. (1994). *A primer on decision making: How decisions happen.* New York: The Free Press.

March, J. G. (1997). Understanding how decisions happen in organizations. In Z. Shapira (Ed.), *Organizational decision making* (pp. 9–32). New York: Cambridge University Press.

March, J. G., & Simon, H. A. (1992). *Organizations* (2nd ed.). London: Blackwell Business.

Marginson, S., & Considine, M. (2000). *The enterprise university: Power, governance, and reinvention in Australia.* New York: Cambridge University Press.

Massey, W. E. (1994). Can the research university adapt to a changing future? In J. R. Cole, E. G. Barber, & S. R. Graubard (Eds.), *The research university in a time of discontent* (pp. 191–202). Baltimore: Johns Hopkins University Press.

McCannell, S. G. (1991, February 13). Spanier discusses effects of cuts to chamber of commerce. *The Barometer,* p. 3.

McPhee, R. D. (1995). Alternate approaches to integrating longitudinal case studies. In G. P. Huber & A. H. Van de Ven (Eds.), *Longitudinal field research methods: Studying processes of organizational change* (pp. 155–185). Thousand Oaks, CA: Sage Publications.

Melchiori, G. S. (1982a). Smaller and better: The University of Michigan Experience. *Research in Higher Education, 16*(1), 55–69.

Melchiori, G. S. (1982b). *Planning for program discontinuance: From default to design* (AAHE-ERIC Higher Education Report No. 5). Washington, DC: AAHE.

Merriam S. B. (1988). *Case study research in education: A qualitative approach.* San Francisco: Jossey-Bass.

Miles, M. B., & Huberman, A.M. (1994). *Qualitative data analysis* (2nd ed.). Thousand Oaks, CA: Sage Publications.

Mintzberg, H. (1987). Crafting strategy. *Harvard Business Review, 65*(4), 66–75.

Mintzberg, H. (1993). *Structure in fives: Designing effective organizations.* Englewood Cliffs, NJ: Prentice Hall.

Mintzberg, H. (1994). *The rise and fall of strategic planning.* New York: Free Press.

Morino Institute. (2001). *Venture philanthropy: The changing landscape.* Washington, DC: The Morino Institute.

Mortimer, K. P., & Tierney, M. L. (1979). *The three "r's" of the eighties: Reduction, reallocation and retrenchment* (ASHE-ERIC Report No. 4). Washington, DC: The George Washington University and ASHE.

Neumann, A. (1995). On the making of hard times and good times: The social construction of resource stress. *Journal of Higher Education, 66,* 3–31.

Neumann, A., Bensimon, E. M., & Birnbaum, R. (1989). *Making sense of administrative leadership: The "L" word in higher education* (ASHE-ERIC Higher Education Report). Washington, DC: ASHE.

Newman, F., & Courturier, L. (2001). *The new competitive arena: Market forces invade the academy.* The Futures Project. Providence, RI: Brown University.

Newman, F., & Scurry, J. (2001). *Higher education in the digital rapids.* The Futures Project. Providence, RI: Brown University.

Nystrom, P. C., & Starbuck, W. H. (1984, Spring). To avoid organizational crises, unlearn. *Organizational Dynamics, 12*(4), 53–65.

Office of the Vice President for Academic Affairs & Provost. (1991). *Preserving enhancement: A plan for strategic academic reallocation.* University of Maryland at College Park.

Olsen, J. P. (1979). Choice in an organized anarchy. In J. G. March & J. P. Olsen (Eds.), *Ambiguity and choice in organizations* (2nd ed., pp. 82–139). Bergen, Norway: Universiteetsforlaget.

O'Toole, J. (1995). *Leading change: Overcoming the ideology of comfort and the tyranny of custom.* San Francisco: Jossey-Bass.

Parkhe, A. (1993). "Messy" research, methodological predispositions, and theory development in international joint ventures. *Academy of Management Review, 18,* 227–268.

Patton, M. Q. (1990). *Qualitative evaluation and research methods* (2nd ed.). Newbury Park, CA: Sage Publications.

Pennings, J. M. (1986). The nature of strategic decision making. In J. M. Pennings (Ed.), *Decision making: An organizational behavior approach* (2nd ed., pp. 201–243). New York: Markus Wiener.

Perrow, C. (1986). *Complex organizations,* 3d ed., New York: Random House.

Pettigrew, A. M. (1995). Longitudinal field research on change: Theory and practice. In G. P. Huber & A. H. Van de Ven (Eds.), *Longitudinal field research methods: Studying processes of organizational change* (pp. 91–125). Thousand Oaks, CA: Sage Publications.

Pettigrew, A.M., Ferlie, E., & McKee, L. (1992). *Shaping strategic change: Making change in large organizations. The case of the National Health Service.* Newbury Park, CA: Sage Publications.

Pew Higher Education Roundtable. (1997). *Turning Point.* Policy Perspectives. Institute for Research on Higher Education, University of Pennsylvania.

Pfeffer, J. (1982). *Organizations and organization theory.* Boston: Pitman.

Pfeffer, J., & Salancik, G. R. (1978). *The external control of organizations: A resource dependence perspective.* New York: Harper and Row.

Pfeffer, J., & Salancik, G. R. (1980). Organizational decision making as a political process: The case of a university budget. In D. Katz, R. L. Kahn, J. S. Adams (Eds.), *The study of organizations* (pp. 397–413). San Francisco: Jossey-Bass.

Prewitt, K. (1994). America's research universities under public scrutiny. In J. R. Cole, E. G. Barber, & S. R. Graubard (Eds.), *The research university in a time of discontent* (pp. 203–17). Baltimore: Johns Hopkins University Press.

Rosovsky, H. (1990). *The university: An owner's manual.* New York: W. W. Norton.

Rothblatt, S. (1995). An historical perspective on the university's role in social development. In D. D. Dill & B. Sporn (Eds.), *Emerging patterns of social demand and university reform: Through a glass darkly* (pp. 20–52). Tarrytown, NY: IAU Press.

Rubin, I. S. (1979). Retrenchment, loose structure, and adaptability in the university. *Sociology of Education, 52,* 211–222.

Schein, E. H. (1992). *Organizational culture and leadership* (2nd ed.). San Francisco: Jossey-Bass.

Schmidt, P. (1997, June, 6). Engineering complex at Va. Commonwealth U. helps lure Motorola. *The Chronicle of Higher Education*, p. 30A.

Schuster, J. H., Smith, D. G., Corack, K. A., & Yamada, M. M. (1994). *Strategic governance: How to make big decisions better.* Washington, DC: American Council on Education/Oryx Press.

Scott, W. R. (1987). *Organizations: rational, natural and open systems* (2nd ed.). Englewood Cliffs, NJ: Prentice Hall.

Selingo, J. (2002, April 19). States with the biggest deficits take aim at higher education. *The Chronicle of Higher Education*, A24.

Senge, P. M. (1994). *The fifth discipline: The art & practice of the learning organization.* New York: Doubleday.

Simon, H A. (1986). Theories of bounded rationality. In C. B. McGuire & R. Radner (Eds.), *Decision and organization: A volume in honor of Jacob Marshak.* Minneapolis: University of Minnesota Press.

Slaughter, S. (1993). Retrenchment in the 1980s: The politics of prestige and gender. *Journal of Higher Education, 64,* 250–282.

Slaughter, S. (1995). Criteria for restructuring postsecondary education. *Journal for Higher Education Management, 10*(2), 31–44.

Slaughter, S., & Leslie, L. L. (1997). *Academic capitalism: Politics, policies, and the entrepreneurial university.* Baltimore: Johns Hopkins University Press.

Spradley, J. P. (1979). *The ethnographic interview.* Philadelphia: Harcourt Brace Jovanovich.

Stake, R. E. (1995). *The art of case study research.* Thousand Oaks, CA: Sage Publications.

Starbuck, W. H. & Milliken, F. J. (1988). Executive's perceptual p-filters: What they notice and how they make sense. In. D. C. Hambrick (Ed.) *The executive effect: Concepts and methods for studying top managers,* 35–65. Greenwich, CT: JAI Press.

Steigler, S. M. (1994). Competition and the research university. In J. R. Cole, E. G. Barber, & S. R. Graubard (Eds.), *The research university in a time of discontent* (pp. 131–152). Baltimore: Johns Hopkins University Press.

Stoeker, R. (1991). Evaluating and rethinking the case study. *The sociological review, 39,* 88–112.

Strava, P. (1979). Constraints on the politics of public choice. In J. G. March & J. P. Olsen (Eds.), *Ambiguity and choice in organizations* (2d ed., pp. 206–221). Bergen, Norway: Universiteetsforlaget.

Strohm, P. (1981). Faculty responsibilities and rights during retrenchment. In J. R. Mingle (Ed.), *Challenges of Retrenchment* (pp. 134–152). San Francisco: Jossey-Bass.

Temple, R. J. (1986). Weak programs: The place to cut. In B. W. Dziech (Ed.), *Controversies and decisions in hard economic times.* (New directions for Community Colleges, Report No. 53, pp. 65–69). San Francisco: Jossey-Bass.

Van de Ven, A. H., & Huber, G. P. (1995). *Longitudinal field research methods: Studying processes of organizational change.* Thousand Oaks, CA: Sage Publications.

Van de Ven, A. H., & Poole, M. S. (1995). Explaining development and change in organizations. *Academy of Management Review, 20,* 510–540.

Van Maanen, J. (1979). The fact of fiction in organizational ethnography. *Administrative Science Quarterly, 24,* 539–550.

Vignola, L., Jr. (1974). *Strategic divestment.* New York: AMACOM.

Volkwein, J. F. (1984). Responding to financial retrenchment: Lessons from the Albany experience. *Journal for Higher Education, 55*(3), 389–401.

Walker, D. E. (1979). *The effective administrator.* San Francisco: Jossey-Bass.

Weick, K. E. (1979). *The social psychology of organizing* (2nd ed.). New York: McGraw-Hill.

Weick. K. E. (1995). *Sensemaking in organizations.* Thousand Oaks, CA: Sage Publications.

Weitzel, W., & Jonsson, E. (1989). Decline in organizations: A literature integration and extension. *Administrative Science Quarterly, 34,* 91–109.

Whetten, D. A. (1981). Organizational responses to scarcity: Exploring the obstacles to innovation approaches to retrenchment in education. *Educational Administration Quarterly, 17*(3), 80–97.

Williams, D., Olswant, S. G., & Hargett, G. (1986). A matter of degree: Faculty morale as a function of involvement in decisions during times of financial distress. *Review of Higher Education, 9*(3), 287–301.

The Wingspread Group. (1993). *An American imperative: Higher expectations for higher education. An open letter to those concerned about the American future.* Racine, WI: The Johnson Foundation.

Yezer, A. M. (1992). Do procedures that succeed in a growing institution fail in a period of decline? *Journal of Higher Education Management, 7*(2), 15–21.

Yin, R. K. (1994). *Case study research: Design and methods.* Thousand Oaks, CA: Sage Publications.

Zammuto, R. F. (1986). Managing decline in American higher education. In J. C. Smart (Ed.), *Higher education: Handbook of theory and research* (Vol. 2, pp. 43–84). New York: Agathon Press.

Index

About the Author

PETER D. ECKEL is Associate Director for Institutional Initiatives at the American Council on Education. He is also the author of *Taking the Reins: Institutional Transformation in Higher Education.*